The New Literacy

Critical Social Thought

Series editor: Michael W. Apple
Professor of Curriculum and Instruction and Educational Policy
Studies, University of Wisconsin-Madison

Already published

The New Literacy

Redefining Reading and Writing in the Schools

JOHN WILLINSKY

Routledge

New York   London

First published in 1990 by

Routledge
An imprint of Routledge, Chapman and Hall, Inc.
29 West 35 Street
New York, NY 10001

Published in Great Britain by

Routledge
11 New Fetter Lane
London EC4P 4EE

Library of Congress Cataloging in Publication Data
Willinsky, John, 1950-
      The new literacy : redefining reading and writing in the schools /
   John Willinsky.
         p.   cm. — (Critical social thought)
      Includes bibliographical references.
      ISBN 0-415-90054-9   ISBN 0-415-90055-7 (pbk.)
      1. Literacy programs. 2. Language arts. 3. Language acquisition.
   4. Literacy—Social aspects. I. Title. II. Series.
   LC149.W5   1990
   372.6—dc20   89-28928

British Library cataloguing in publication also available

To Paul, David, and Aaron
reason enough

Contents

Series Editor's Introduction

In one of his more compelling statements, the French sociologist Pierre Bourdieu states that "Taste classifies and it classifies the classifier."[1] That is, to call something "good culture" is not simply a neutral description. It sets up a polarity between the classifier and the classified. It signifies a relation of power. *Someone* thinks this is good and it can only be good if someone else's culture is bad.

Nowhere is this more apparent than in schools. What counts as legitimate knowledge in our educational institutions has always had close connections both to those groups who have had economic, political, and cultural power and to conflicts over altering these relations of power.[2] The class, race, and gender stratifying effects of this knowledge and the cultural processes surrounding it are more than a little visible in many nations. While schools do offer important paths to upward mobility for some individuals, it is clear that the manner in which this process works is still related in important ways to the structures of social inequalities in the larger society.

Further, many children—often those from poor, working-class, minority, and other similar communities—find themselves increasingly alienated from the culture involved in the curricula and teaching that organize their lives in classrooms. Yet it is not just these children who are alienated and bored. Recent research documents similar and widespread feelings among more advantaged students as well.[3]

Part of the reason for this is the sense of meaningless that pervades so many classrooms. Even with all of the hard work teachers are clearly doing, so much of the curriculum—especially in those most "basic" areas of reading and writing—seems increasingly unconnected to the real lives of the students. In response to this, a diverse movement has arisen to make reading and writing more personally meaningful and to make the processes of the formation of literacy more powerful. This is what John Willinsky calls the New Literacy.

The activities associated with the New Literacy come at an opportune time, given the growth of mechanistic policies and programs in schools today. As I have argued at greater length elsewhere, the work of teachers has been increasingly subject to the rationalizing logics of management. The results have been the deskilling of teaching with its accompanying loss of control over the activity of classroom life, an overstandardization of curricula and teaching, and the introduction of management ideologies and techniques that may be utterly inappropriate in an education that aims at promoting democracy in more than name only. These logics have a long history and are linked to the gender, race, and class relations of the larger society in very complex ways. Teachers are not, and never have been simply puppets in the face of these pressures, however. They have consistently sought ways to retain some of their hard-won autonomy, especially when there have been attempts to impose programs from above.[4]

Willinsky clearly recognizes these dynamics and sees that the writing and reading programs organized around the New Literacy are one form, and an important one at that, that teacher resistance can take to the overly administered, top-down mandates that are currently holding center stage in education. In his words:

> The New Literacy speaks directly to teachers reasserting control over the work that goes on in the class, even as it attempts to hand a greater part of the locus of meaning over to the student. It represents a taking hold of the curriculum by the teacher at a fundamental level by challenging the meaning of literacy in the classroom as well as the nature of a teacher's work with the students.

Beneath these altered teaching strategies is a larger impetus, one that is aimed not only at challenging the conventional forms of classroom life but at questioning our accepted conceptions of literacy itself. The New Literacy involves increasing the student's control over text and meaning and, hence, changes the relationship of teacher and student. Yet, while important, this is not all. The New Literacy is not seen as an isolated set of skills. Rather, it goes well beyond this to recognize literacy as a *social process,* as a "form of life" that connects community and school, history and biography.

That acting on this recognition is in part a political as well as a pedagogical act is made clearer in those instances where school systems and their attendant bureaucracies are markedly resistant to serious alterations in the standardized models they now employ. Put simply, it is often very hard work to get these more dynamic educational practices on the agenda.

Willinsky notes the difficulties here.

> Programs such as the New Literacy are not simply advocated and implemented in compliant schools; they are more often risked and lived by teachers and their classes. In attempting to bring in the new, teachers often find themselves caught in a struggle to gain a secure spot in the curriculum and the school for these innovations.

The issue of the politics of reading and writing isn't fully encompassed by talking about the risks and difficulties of instituting and defending programs in the New Literacy, however. Even in times of great economic unrest and in crises in meaning and authority relations when societies such as our own show their moments of greatest weakness, such societies continually prove that their ability to reproduce themselves—often at very great cost to the poor and disenfranchised—lies not only in the strength of their armed forces, industries, and governments, "but in the rhythms and textures of culture, consciousness and everyday life."[5] The mechanisms of cultural control may prove to be just as significant as economic and political control. Thus, the relations of inequality that dominate our society are reproduced, and contested, in the "mundane" activities that organize our daily lives. This points to a crucial principle in interpreting what we so easily take for granted in education. We should look at educational activity, even that which seems to be aimed at genuinely reforming everyday practices, as inherently *contradictory*. This is of considerable importance in the story Willinsky wishes to tell.

In our society, activities seemingly simple and fundamental such as reading and writing can be at the very same time "forms of regulation and exploitation and potential modes of resistance, celebration and solidarity."[6] For most people, literacy has a "nonpolitical function." It is there to help form the intellectual character of the person and to provide paths to upward mobility. Yet, historically, reading and writing have had strong links to particular regimes of morality as well. They were there to produce a shared system of beliefs and values, to help create national ideological unity.[7] Reading and writing, when aimed at introducing students to "good literature," could serve as Willinsky puts it "as something of a moral technology of the soul."

This emphasis on literacy as both "moral technology" and economically driven skills is of course not the only way one could and should approach the issue. The authors of a well-known book on the politics of literacy put it this way: "This process of instating the value of writing, speaking and reading [should not be seen] as 'life skills' for our allotted places in the labor market but as a means to power and control over our whole lives."[8] Our aim, then, is not to create "functional literacy," but "powerful literacy," "political literacy." In this way, the acquisition and building of relevant forms of reading and writing can enable the growth of genuine understanding and control that extend well beyond the school.[9] In many ways, it is the struggle between functional literacy and powerful literacy that is represented in the New Literacy. This tension is clearly recognized in Willinsky's treatment of the sometimes competing tendencies in this educational movement.

In his view, the New Literacy is inherently contradictory. There can be no doubt that it is a considerable advance over the reductive and atomized curricular and teaching practices that have been spawned out of the back-to-basics movement and the attempts to link education more closely to the needs of business and industry. Yet, the New Literacy "also shows signs that it has brought itself on stream in educating the young for the new corporate age." Speaking at his ironic best, Willinsky notes that "these programs have an executive class edge." They do represent efforts by teachers and students to create more meaningful and creative reading and writing, but still there is that "edge." As he puts it, "they would, after all, encourage independent and collaborative projects while drawing on peer support networks and conferencing with professionals to enhance the production values of the final literate product. It can all sound and seem very marble and glass, office-tower work."

This is counterbalanced by other tendencies within the pedagogical practices associated with the movement, however. In the building of a "lively home [for an] engaging and critical community [in] the classroom," students and teachers can also be empowered to rethink "the world-in-progress" and their own place in it. Surely, these tendencies are not inconsequential in a society in which the commitment to the common good and our sense of community have withered and privatization and profit are often seen to count more than people's futures and their very lives.

Taking these issues seriously, Willinsky also has some very important things to say about gender and the processes of reading and writing. This is done not only at the level of how one reads and writes, but what one reads and writes as well. To take but one of the more interesting examples, one of the prime practical foci of the New Literacy is to enhance self-directed reading on the part of all students. Yet, what if self-directed reading leads to a "self" we don't like? What if many girls choose only to read adolescent romance novels with their visions of women as only finding fulfillment in romance and their gender, race, and class stereotypes?[10] How do we cope with the politics of pleasure (after all, some girls may *choose* these books) and what might be called the politics of emancipation (aren't we supposed to take them beyond such stereotypes)? These are very real issues, ones that are entailed in many of the practices of the New Literacy in schools, and Willinsky never shies away from dealing with them honestly and insightfully.

The volume does not stop here though. It traces the roots of the various strands associated with the New Literacy back to conceptions of popular literacy and romanticism. At the same time, the author reviews the proposals, and the research used to support them, that a number of advocates of the New Literacy in the United States, Canada, Britain, and elsewhere have put forward for altering the ways reading and writing go on in schools.

One of the attributes that makes *The New Literacy* such a powerful book is the author's insistent focus not only at the level of theory and politics but at the level of what actually happens inside schools. Willinsky takes us inside classrooms and, in the process, enables us to see the strengths—and the weaknesses—of his own and others' work with students. The reader comes away from the book with a feeling of having partly participated in the experiences Willinsky recounts. In some ways this is due to his engaging style that is nicely suited to his very evident knowledge of the historical and current drama of the struggle to redefine what counts as literacy in schools.

The book concludes with the author suggesting not only one, but a number of alternative futures that are possible for the New Literacy. Willinsky rightly challenges the movement to connect its curriculum and teaching practices with a politics of social and cultural empowerment. He quotes from Roger Simon approvingly: "Teaching and learning must be linked to the goal of educating students to take risks, to struggle with ongoing relations of power, to critically appropriate forms of knowledge that exist outside of their immediate experience, and to envisage versions of a world which is 'not yet'—in order to be able to alter the grounds upon which life is lived." New Literacy programs are obviously part of the way there already. By redefining reading and writing in our educational institutions as the active pursuit of meaning and treating such active pursuit as the *right* of every student, new communities of discourse can be created. Our task is to connect these communities and the strengths that students develop within them to the recreation of the communities into which these students will go. *The New Literacy* is an invaluable step in making this possible.

Michael W. Apple
The University of Wisconsin, Madison

Notes

1. Pierre Bourdieu, *Distinction* (Cambridge: Harvard University Press, 1984), p. 6.
2. See Michael W. Apple, *Ideology and Curriculum* (New York: Routledge, revised edition, 1990) and Michael W. Apple, "Social Conflict and Curriculum Accords," *Educational Theory* 38 (Spring 1988), pp. 191–201.
3. Linda McNeil, *Contradictions of Control* (New York: Routledge, 1986).
4. See Michael W. Apple, *Education and Power* (New York: Routledge, ARK Edition, 1985) and Michael W. Apple, *Teachers and Texts: A Political Economy of Class and Gender Relations in Education* (New York: Routledge, 1986).
5. Janet Batsleer, Tony Davies, Rebecca O'Rourke, and Chris Weedon, *Rewriting English* (New York: Methuen, 1985), pp. 9–10.
6. Ibid., p. 5
7. Ibid., pp. 66–67. See also Allan Luke, *Literacy, Textbooks and Ideology* (Philadelphia: Falmer Press, 1988).
8. Batsleer, et al., *Rewriting English,* p. 164.
9. Ibid., p. 165. For an exceptional treatment of "political literacy" in theory and practice, see Colin Lankshear and Moira Lawler, *Literacy, Schooling and Revolution* (Philadelphia: Falmer Press, 1988).
10. See the outstanding analysis of adolescent romance novels in Linda Christian-Smith, *Becoming a Woman Through Romance* (New York: Routledge, in press).

Preface

I was first introduced to the New Literacy in action while teaching in the northern Ontario community of Goulais River. In 1982, Ruth Fletcher, who was teaching down the hall from me, created a comprehensive and engaging literacy program in a grade one and two classroom that I still consider to be an inspiring model of the New Literacy in action. Early in the school year, she made the difficult decision to forsake the basal reading program in favor of library books and to work with blank paper which she handed out each morning instead of prepared worksheets. She was happy to have me sit in and observe her class during my spare moments and to bring my class down to share in her students' energetic and productive engagement with literacy. In return, I offered to help her document the program, to build her case. This book is something of a belated extension of that project. What began for me in Ruth's classroom was followed by opportunities to run my own versions of it in other classes and to discover how it had developed in different forms around the world; I found that it had deep roots in a rocky past and was still struggling against the times to offer teachers an alternative method of teaching students to read and write.

After working with New Literacy programs for awhile I realized that I was drawn to it for the way it reflected a concern for the word that had carried me and a few good friends through high school with paperbacks in hand and notebooks in pocket. The literacy we put together and learned from each other in those formative days was, I now suspect, something of a literacy against schooling. It was a literacy that attempted its own form of rebellion, declaring in its inarticulate, muffled way, that the Dostoevski I read sitting in the hallways and the adolescent angst I wrote in the coffee shop was a protest against the forms of literacy the school was promoting with its set texts and assignment sheets. In my own teaching sometime later, I tried to bring such moments to students in a literacy that ran to filling hallways with broadside newspapers and creating musicals based on the life of Patti Hearst. Although a career can form around such moments, a curriculum cannot. What Ruth Fletcher showed me was that a coherent program in literacy could be shaped around students finding their own way onto the page; she was able to find a place for that personal sense of literacy's importance in the public forum of the classroom. In its own imperfect but attractive way, this was a literacy for "deschooling" or at least a form of reschooling.

Ruth ultimately found it a rewarding experiment in curriculum innovation, and one that, as I complete this book, she now happily carries on in a one-room school on the northern shore of Lake Superior. Yet initially she was more than a little troubled by a sense of having plunged recklessly off the certain path of the recommended reader and workbook. Part of what I learned from Ruth was that programs such as the New Literacy are not simply advocated and implemented in compliant schools; they are more often risked and lived by teachers and their classes. In attempting to bring in the new, teachers often find themselves caught in a struggle to gain a secure spot in the curriculum and the school for these innovations. On the simplest level, the problem is nothing more than overcoming the seduction of prepackaged reading and writing programs which would do it all for the teacher through text, workbook, handout, and so on, with great assurances that it has all been done. However, a more serious problem for teachers wanting to take the leap into the New Literacy is that in many jurisdictions teachers have over the last decade found their professional authority eroded and their curricular choices further determined by school administrators quick to call for test scores.

Finally, the innovative teachers often face another struggle. As Ruth began to experiment with these new programs, it gradually became apparent that her colleagues felt there was something amiss. It seemed no more than a chill in the air as classes passed in the corridor, or a pointed question about her program in the staffroom that seemed a comment on what was being attempted. And, in fact, it wasn't until I saw it happen to other teachers experimenting with this approach in schools where I wasn't teaching that I realized it represented a professional concern. To lead a class off into the New Literacy encourages in students a different form of independence. It moves teacher and student out of traditional patterns of classroom behavior. Even as the teacher must at times have doubts about the wisdom and workability of these new plans, she can be surprised and often hurt to find that these self-doubts are becoming a public, staffroom concern.

Fortunately this matter of isolation is becoming less of an impediment as New Literacy support systems, such as the National Writing Project and the Association of Whole Language Support Groups, spring up. But no less so today do I want to acknowledge the courage of teachers trying to decide on their own what might be best for the class. This sense of going it alone often seems an integral part, if too much so, of the professional experience of the classroom. As the New Literacy speaks foremost to the working consideration of the classroom, it is hardly unfair to ask it to address this aspect of the educator's profession. As it turns out, Ruth also introduced me to the possibilities of collaborative research in our work with her class; this process has become one of the New Literacy's responses to an empowering literacy which would be shared with the classroom.

In working with this innovation in literacy, I came to realize that this discomfort works in both directions. Teachers happy with their teaching can suddenly feel put upon by the excitement in a neighboring classroom or in-service presentation, as these innovators seem to imply by their example that what others are up to with children and books is now less than adequate. Certainly, the New Literacy often has that attention-grabbing element to it as students grow prolific in their productions, performances, and publications. Again if I might turn to my experience, an instance of this reform in another school in my school district developed into a "lighthouse project" that others might be guided by its accomplishments. The set of classrooms run by a pair of dynamic teachers was soon recognized by the school administration as the site for innovations in primary school literacy, especially as it was happening in one of the less promising schools in the older downtown area. The resulting extra attention, support, and most notably, additional facilities and resources which the administration was happy to provide had repercussions among the staff as the school served as a beacon for, among other things, a certain resentment from among teachers who felt that their work, if somewhat less showy, was overlooked and underfunded by comparison. The resentment surfaced in a survey conducted on the new program: "It hasn't been proven that child-centered approach works best, yet it is being pushed upon us. The class at Beacon Street is a model and has been given special privileges." The New Literacy is intended to engender expression and individual voice, to establish a new sense of community and discourse. In at least one sense, it can seem to frustrate these very elements for a certain segment of teachers.

This book tries to remain sensitive to this issue and certainly cannot be accused of singing the unqualified praises of the New Literacy. To help educators curious about or committed to New Literacy programs, it does present its best arguments and finer moments, but it also raises questions about shortcomings, in classroom practices, research findings, and theory, shortcomings that have become apparent through my own work with the New Literacy and through the work of others. The book challenges advocates of New Literacy programs to explore new measures, to prove itself in difficult settings. It is not a guide in the steps of implementing these various practices. Although there is a "how-to" element to what follows, as I describe the variations and innovations that have developed on this theme of a New Literacy, the book remains dedicated to chasing down awkward whys and wherefores, to balancing praise and foreboding, to comparing this encouragement of the child's writing to recent thinking on discourse and subjectivity.

It takes as one of its premises the fact that educators facing the challenge of new programs gladly suffer a certain intellectual curiosity about them. Whether they feel attracted toward these innovative programs or suspicious of their familiar refrain, educators need to recognize that the New Literacy represents a different form of education in reading and writing that has had implications for teacher, student, and researcher; the New Literacy has within it a potential for social change that extends far beyond the classroom as literacy remains a very powerful vehicle in this society. On a more personal level, as well, educators should be able through this discussion to gain some insight into basis of their own responses to this paradigm. It may allow them to situate themselves in relationship to a larger conception of literacy than afforded by exigencies of everyday classroom practices, of imminent bells and the dictates of textbooks found on stockroom shelves.

Ruth Fletcher developed her program out of her own sense of what was needed, out of what she would have for herself and her students in the classroom, even as she was herself ostensibly unaware of the development of this movement on an international scale. It is odd, then, that I have come to treat the New Literacy as a very bookish phenomenon, represented in the published statements of its most eloquent advocates in the United States, Australia, Britain, Canada, and New Zealand. Although I have included, as illustrative material, scenes from Ruth's classroom during that important year, my concern this time is other than this process of simply getting down the wonders and shortfalls. In the courage and vision of this teacher, I felt the potential of a *new literacy* for teacher and student; her work reminded me that the courage of individual teachers is education's best hope.

Since my time in Ruth's classroom, I have continued to employ and develop with my students various elements of what I first learned from Ruth and her students, from Allan, Carl, Jim, Karen, Melanie, Melinda, Robin, Sherry, and Ted. I have also attempted various ways of making the case for the New Literacy, from recording the wonders that students have brought to the page to seeking for a trace of a significant statistical difference in matched samples of grade one students working in and out of the New Literacy. The approach here, however, is to stop for a moment, amid the enthusiasm and support, and grow far more cautious and critical, to find the place of this movement in such diverse and yet not unconnected phenomenon as Wordsworth, Woodstock, and post-structuralism. In this forum I want to raise the questions that tend to be overlooked in the easy flow of classes and workshops on the New Literacy, as I encourage prospective teachers to discover that, if they wish to teach writing, they might put away the textbook and take up the pen and processor themselves. I also want to keep in mind those teachers who have reminded me, at the very heights of my sometimes trying enthusiasm, that the educational road over this century is littered with the broken bottles of miracle cures, the tattered billboards of forgotten innovations.

Acknowledgements

For their helpful readings of this text while it was in progress, Lon Dubinsky, Roy Graham, Dawson Harms, Helen Harper, and Ann Walker have earned my gratitude. My collaboration with Jim Bedard, Ruth Fletcher, Mark Hunniford, Debbie Lee, and Roger Simon has contributed to this book, and I wish to express my appreciation for the opportunity of working with them. I am also indebted to the Spencer Foundation for the time I spent as a National Academy of Education Spencer Fellow and to the Social Sciences and Humanities Research Council of Canada for underwriting some of the research reported in the book. Parts of this book first appeared in *The Alberta Journal of Educational Research, Curriculum Inquiry, Journal of Education, Language Arts,* and *Reading-Canada-Lecture.*

1
Introducing the
New Literacy

Three scenes from the New Literacy

Not ideas about the thing but the thing itself

Wallace Stevens

Scene 1: In a Nova Scotia classroom, Kathleen Hefferman has her students keep journals for their study of kites; eight-year-old Craig begins his first entry with, "one time i was flying a kit with my freind," and Kathleen reflects on this process:

> The journal in our classroom is a dialogue journal between student and teacher, and therefore Craig is aware of his audience—a trusted adult. The relationship between teacher and student has been built up over several months of communicating in the journal. Craig knows that the journal is his place for recounting events, sharing feelings, and asking questions. He knows that the message he has to share is more important to this particular reader than his accurate spelling and punctuation so he writes freely, says what he has to say about his kite experience and considers the piece finished. What the teacher does now in response to the writing, and in response to the child as author, has the potential either to inhibit the child's writing or to encourage, nurture, and extend it (Hefferman, 1982, p. 85).

Scene 2: In an Australian high school, Garth Boomer is observing a sophomore class that has been reading a novel and is now finding a way into the work that can be the source of both personal and group response to it:

Later in the lesson, as requested by Mrs. Bell, they negotiate themselves into friendship or "convenience" groups and each group receives a worksheet which asks them to establish what is meant by "self-awareness," and "in search of inner self" in relation to the novel. It is suggested that they brainstorm personal examples and then report to the class. After this they are to prepare a reading/performance or presentation of a poem which reveals one of these themes, explaining how it relates to the novel. The instruction reads: "Decide how the group will go about this. In what way can the group support each other? How will you present the poems and your reactions? Decide on group and individual tasks" (Boomer, 1985, p. 102).

Scene 3: In a college in the United States, Walker and Elias are working with a writing program that guides students through scheduled conferences between the writing instructor and the writer:

Teacher: I probably might start by having you tell me a little bit about how this went for you while you were writing it and how you felt about it when it was done.

Student: Well, um, I liked my ideas . . . I started writing about something more like we talked about in class and I got off on a little bit different subject, as you can tell, which I was a lot more interested in what we were doing, so I was more excited to write about that, and I had quite a few ideas on the subject. I had trouble fitting it into categories, so I was a little concerned about coherence as a whole.

Teacher: What would you say worked out the best for you in writing the paper? What do you remember as being the best thing about it?

Student: The ideas, probably.

Teacher: Good. I think you're right. That's exactly what the strength of the paper is. What are you least satisfied with? What would you have liked to work on more?

Student: I didn't think my diction, my sentences were good, cuz I had time to work on it, but not enough . . . (Walker & Elias, 1987, p. 276).

Such is this educational phenomenon which I am terming the "New Literacy," if only in three of its many guises. Although it may not seem so at first glance, these classroom programs share a common core of radical assumptions about teacher and student, and about language and literacy. Yet at this point they share these assumptions without knowing it, without being part of a concerted educational movement. There is no overarching body, such as there once was with Progressive Education Association which provided a collective identity for an equally diverse set of innovative programs earlier in this century. For want of this public sense of a common cause, for what might be gained by comparing notes on a shared approach to education, I feel justified in reaching with a free hand across the international educational community to pull together this particular array of programs under a single title. The strength of the connections among them is part of this book's argument, as is the fact that each of these innovations falls within a much larger educational phenomenon than a simple adding up of the different reading and writing strategies would suggest.

My interests in the New Literacy go beyond proposing connections. In the first instance, these programs have something to learn from each other, as they operate at different educational levels and on different aspects of literacy. By assembling the common assumptions about literacy that link them, by digging about in the roots of these assumptions in search of a greater coherence for this larger project that unites them, I hope to clarify the direction they appear to be headed in this collective sense. At its most presumptuous, this book would add to these innovations by making something larger of them, by setting them within a theater of educational and intellectual developments; it would confront this New Literacy with the implications that arise from what is, in essence, a radical and subversive proposal for changing the nature of literacy in the schools, even as it begins with the seeming innocence of keeping a journal about flying a kite. But, as well, the story of the New Literacy remains a personal one for me. As I have sought to understand my own attraction to these different but linked manners of teaching, I hope to help others see what is at stake in this alternative approach to literacy in the schools.

The innovation in these programs is not so much the classroom strategies that they have introduced. Soliciting personal responses to poetry or conducting writing conferences between instructor and writer can amount to little more than a gimmick that enlivens a lesson. More interesting is the conception of literacy that underlies these experiments and explorations in the teaching of students to read and write. I am contending that beneath these teaching strategies is a desire on the part of the educator to restructure the life of the classroom through an approach to literacy which challenges conventions of classroom organization and the typical roles of teacher and student. Which is to say that this *new literacy* is about more than instructional techniques for reading and writing, just as literacy is about more than the ability to score at or above the mean on standardized tests. To begin to think about what this new literacy might be about requires, in the first instance, a different manner of thinking about literacy.

However, before getting under way I must qualify my presumptuous designation of a *New Literacy*. I am not so "new" myself as to imagine that each of the programs described here is not without precedents in earlier, education experiments. Among the earlier claims on new-ness is John Dewey's program of "New Education" (1900) introduced at the University of Chicago Elementary School; in Great Britain, shortly thereafter, the New Education Fellowship became well known for its "taint of pedagogical and political radicalism" (Cremin, 1961, p. 248). More recently, with an assist from Marshall McLuhan, a "new literacy" has been declared for the "reading" of film and other media (Foster, 1979; Gordon, 1971). The point is well taken, and I would graciously acknowledge these two precedents in the use of this book's title. However, the concern among the innovations I am reporting on is with a literacy that resides in its original home with print and the concerns of reading and writing; this speaks to a change in the educational climate over the last decade, in the ways of renewal and redefinition in education. Thus, after thinking a good deal about an appropriate label for this phenomenon, I decided that I could do no better than group these reading and writing programs under the somewhat generic heading of the New Literacy, with the upper case treatment serving as an extra touch of boldness to assist me in making the case for its existence. The use of "new" has its own ironies in our society, no less so in education than in a commercial sense. It retains about it that hopeful quality and offers no further description of what it modifies than the wish to be seen to freshen up or revitalize an older product or concept.

Whether the use of "new" is warranted, however, is a decision upon which we have all learned to withhold judgement. The rub of it is that the "New Literacy" is an hypothesis on my part, not so much in its *originality,* as in the currency of its challenge to the educational scene. Thus, taking into account the fact that the label is borrowed rather than invented, and perhaps only a placeholder until a more lasting coinage occurs, I should caution you against letting drop references to the "New Literacy" at, say, the educational conference equivalent of the proverbial cocktail party—the wine and cheese reception. I suspect that no one outside of this readership will understand what you are talking about. Which is to say, I suppose, that you'll fit in wonderfully at the reception. In the meantime, however, this yet-to-be-certified school of thought has been waiting on someone to step back far enough from the fray that the pattern of connections begins to become apparent among the different segments of it which have emerged over the last twenty years, segments which have gone under such names as Whole Language, the Growth Model and its related developments in Language for Learning and Writing Across the Curriculum, Socio-Psycholinguistic variations with Schema Theory, Reader-Response Theory and Transformational Reading, along with the variations of the Writing Process Movement including the Bay Area Project which has grown into the successful National Writing Project.

My claim is that a "New Literacy" lies latent and unrealized among this host of different experiments in the teaching of reading and writing. My use of this label is meant to form an umbrella under which I can gather and examine an array of innovations in the teaching and researching of reading and writing, innovations that have made inroads in programs from the primary grades to college composition. An umbrella may be a particularly apt metaphor for the process of pulling together these programs, if only because they must weather continuing indifference, if not outright opposition, from the elements of political conservatism that continue to hold sway on the educational front. The times are not entirely conducive to the liberal inclinations of the New Literacy.

In Great Britain, they were opposed repeatedly by the *Black Papers* of the 1970s which took great issue with "this 'sociological' attitude," as an early *Paper* put it, and the apparent rejection of standards: "The progressive emphasis on either endogenous creativity (undisciplined by any inwardness with the language of greatness) or social relevance (applying the human reductiveness characteristic of much of the contemporary) has replaced an earlier concern with quality" (Bantock in Cox & Boyson, 1975). More recently, the *Kingman Report* (Kingman, 1988), which dared a moderate path in rejecting grammar lessons while setting attainment targets in standard English, was cooly received by a considerably less progressive government and press. In the United States, storms of accountability began to break in the 1980s hitting the schools in waves, amid headlines on the declining standards in the schools and a bevy of blue-ribbon committee reports of a nation at risk. In an unusual proclamation of public interest in declarations of the educational decline of the west, E. D. Hirsch's *Cultural Literacy* (1987) and Allan Bloom's *The Closing of the American Mind* (1987) spent a good deal of time on the best-seller lists during the period in which I have been writing this book. Yet in spite of having to make allowances for this turn in the weather, the New Literacy is still on its way to being a major player in the educational marketplace, to pick up on the language of the times, and one that speaks in a relatively new way to the place and standard of literacy in society.

The work of the New Literacy

To begin to gain a sense of what is being revitalized in the case of the New Literacy, it would be helpful to imagine literacy as a way of working the world. This may strike you as an odd and not very promising beginning for literacy, but it will prove helpful in appreciating how it is to be redefined in these innovative classrooms. I use the term "work" to stress the sense in which literacy can be understood as a social practice that takes certain materials and turns them to certain ends in a given setting, an activity that takes up a place in a life, as working on something does. In this scheme of things, as I will reiterate throughout this book, literacy is better understood *not* as an isolated skill, as something one can do on demand, but as a social process in the daily landscape; one works with someone else's writing or writes for another under a roof of one sort or another in building something that will be of use to yourself or others. Although I will go on to make much more of literacy as a psychological and political event in this book, I want to begin with this initial belabored conception of it. This regard for literacy as actively making something of the world is part of the reorientation that is necessary to appreciate the New Literacy project.

The New Literacy is challenging the meaning of literacy and the nature of this work with language; these programs are suggesting above all else that literacy can be worked in another fashion and toward different ends in the classroom. The workshop will come up as more than metaphor in this description of New Literacy programs, and given the raw material of language as a sort of freshly milled lumber, the New

Literacy opts not only for a new set of projects to be cut and jointed from that wood, but employs a new set of tools for working it and runs the shop as a cooperative enterprise. To begin with what will be a bookfull of definitional statements about this project, I would suggest that New Literacy programs are intent on altering the meaning of this classroom work. As can be seen from the three scenes cited in the opening of this chapter, the shift involves increasing the students' control over the text and its meaning. But to shift this meaning of literacy also necessarily alters the relationship between teacher and student. The teacher, as an authority on what needs to be known and done, begins to turn over more of this responsibility to the student and to the meaning that comes from somewhere within the student's work with literacy. In these terms, then, the New Literacy's proposal is to reshape the *work* of the classroom around a different form of reading and writing. The moral, psychological, and social worth of this literacy begins with the students as sources of experience and meaning. To alter the form of literacy in this fashion clearly entails redefining the role and relationship of teacher and student.

One of the major contentions of this book is that the New Literacy is as much about the way educators work with students and texts in a classroom as it is about actually improving instruction in literacy. Although I want to bring before you instances from the research on literacy that support, temper, and undermine the case for the New Literacy, I believe that there is another story underlying the reasons that educators turn to or away from the sorts of programs that fall under my rubric of the New Literacy. Rather than basing its claims on comparative research with other programs, the New Literacy begins with a much simpler, if more profound, question for educators who have grown a little weary of waiting for the definitive research answer to effective education. The New Literacy poses the question in terms of a personal philosophy and the sense made of how people should work together in a classroom: Are these the lessons that I want students to learn about literacy? Is this how I want to spend my days, working in this way with students and with books? These are the questions that raise the doubts about the common fare and initiate the interest in what New Literacy programs have to offer.

Yet it would be misleading to suggest that questions of classroom effectiveness and accountability are spurious for advocates of the New Literacy. The New Literacy consists of programs that have students actively engaged in writing and reading, programs that produce hours

7

of focused discussion, reams of notes and drafts, scores of performances and publications. While attention is given to process in a whole new way, these are processes that are productive, that are effective in eliciting from the student indications that learning is going on in one form or another. Yet it is also fair to say that these indications of process—the talk, drafts, and finished pieces—have not produced a consensus within the educational community that this is a superior way of teaching literacy. As I shall examine in the chapters that follow, the research comparing the New Literacy to other programs has not often decided in its favor, although neither has it conclusively refuted its value. This is why I return to the one point that does seem clear about the New Literacy. In ways that this book will explore, it constitutes a different form of thinking and practice about teaching and literacy. That is to say, the New Literacy is about new institutional goals for the schools, new professional goals for teaching, and new educational goals for literacy. In fact, I wish to make this principle of shifted goals in the work of the classroom a defining characteristic of the New Literacy: *The New Literacy consists of those strategies in the teaching of reading and writing which attempt to shift the control of literacy from the teacher to the student; literacy is promoted in such programs as a social process with language that can from the very beginning extend the students' range of meaning and connection.*

This statement stands against a literacy which is defined as the ability to perform at a certain level on a standardized test and which asks education for preparation and practice in that ability. It is to resist treating literacy simply as a competence that people have or do not have at some arbitrary level. The distinction might be made clearer by drawing on the analogy of riding a bike. Those moving toward New Literacy programs are insisting that the point is not to develop the ability to ride, which leads to sessions of practicing and demonstrating the skill. The advocate of the New Literacy claims that if bikes are worth riding then the learning should begin with the intent of taking you places, if only to the end of the block on that first shaky run. What is important about riding are the places to which you ride and the pleasures gained along the way. In the process of this riding with a purpose, the skill naturally improves. Which is to say, the New Literacy challenges traditional conceptions of learning to read and write when it declares that purpose and intent are foremost concerns with literacy. But more than that, New Literacy programs would shift the locus of intention and purpose to the student as much as possible, rather than letting it reside in the teacher and the curriculum guidebook.

In this frame of mind, "literacy" is nothing in itself. Literacy is understood as the working of language in its written form, in reading a novel of a favorite author or writing a resignation letter, and that work takes place in a setting which contributes to its meaning, whether in a classroom or an office; the nature of that experience of literacy in the classroom is what constitutes an education. This is an aspect of the New Literacy taken from the educational philosophy of John Dewey who held that the classroom is poorly conceived as a preparation for life; it should be treated as the thing itself, or as he put it in his *Pedagogical Creed,* "education which does not occur through forms of life, forms that are worth living for their own sake, is always a poor substitute for the genuine reality, and tends to cramp and deaden" (1988, p. 169).

Even with bolstering from the distinguished Dewey, this distinction between literacy as an ability and a purposeful activity may seem a trivial starting point for what would claim to be new. Yet this difference suggests both structure and substance for the programs of the New Literacy. These programs are meant to change the meaning of work in the traditional classroom full of desks with, perhaps, a line of windows along one side looking out on the school yard; they propose that these classrooms can take on a different sense, if the meaning of literacy shifts to the student, if literacy becomes a way of working the path between home and school, weekend experience and school-day knowledge. Student and teacher, rather than using literacy to set up a separate field of school knowledge, can now insist from the first day of school on making the classroom a workshop for furthering the students' intentions and meanings with a world that extends beyond the reaches of the textbook. But this is to lay out the New Literacy in bold and idealistic terms. Not surprisingly the whole of this connection between life and page has not been achieved by any one program that I am setting with the scope of the New Literacy, nor is this likely to happen except in odd flashes and quiet moments. But in each of the various programs, there is this common urge for a new way of working with language and literacy.

Thus, a second, more telling, means of introducing the New Literacy is to describe the host of new hats that teachers slip on as they enter the classroom: In the literature which has heralded this alternative, teachers are often cast as *coaches* finding new ways to maximize the children's personal best in achieving their own goals in reading and writing. Once the student is up and writing, teachers can switch into patient *editors* helping the students find their own voice; they later act as *agents* promoting the work around the school and community, and *publishers* drawing on the resources of the school to get the word out. The point is that the teacher takes on a new role, in fact, a new array of roles, in mounting these programs. It becomes a process of redefining the nature of teaching. Ira Schor in his "critical thinking" version of the New Literacy goes so far as to speak of a "withering away of the teacher," recalling Marx's withering away of the state in the ideal stages of communism, when all is in harmony (1977, p. 98).

The students, for their part, find themselves accredited as *meaning-makers* beginning in the first grade as they are awarded advanced standing on what they have already taught themselves about symbol and language, from the golden twin arches to the graphics that distinguish cereal boxes. They quickly grow into *authors* in these classes, as they soon find themselves in self-expression; and then they are also junior *scientists* as they are seen to be testing hypothesis after hypothesis about the nature of language and about their own learning processes within literacy. They, too, have the chance to play editor and publisher in the enhancement and promotion of their own and other students' work.

But new roles and scripts require new settings and backdrops; coaches often feel more comfortable teaching in gyms than classrooms, and editors may not feel comfortable teaching at all, preferring to work more directly with a writer on a manuscript in a quiet office or while doing lunch. Although only so much is possible given the architectural standards of school buildings and the quality of cafeteria food, the New Literacy's reorganization of time, space, and, above all, authority in the classroom can still go some distance in altering the nature of the educational experience. Taking these elements boldly in hand and with only a minimum of interior redecoration and a good deal of talk, the New Literacy attempts to turn ordinary classrooms and lecture halls into dynamic writing workshops and research centers, think tanks, and publishing houses.

As I noted above, this reorganization of literacy in the classroom has taken many shapes; it is not the vision of any one educational guru. The New Literacy has come along a winding road out of the Progressive Education movement. It has gladly picked up discarded ideas along the way and used them to refashion a more engaging form of literacy and learning. Yet I realize that a starting point in recent educational history would help in initially locating this project. Certainly the best candidate for realizing the moment of conception is the often celebrated meeting of British and American educators at the Anglo-American Seminar on the Teaching of English at Dartmouth College in 1966. In London that year, teachers had begun to talk about talk in the classroom which was soon to develop into the Language Across the Curriculum movement. The British had something to share at Dartmouth and the sharing gave rise at that historic meeting to what John Dixon (1967) identified as the promise of a Growth Model. Dixon contrasted this model to the two traditional, towering giants of the English program, the Heritage and Skills Models. The Growth Model drew on the work of such figures as James Britton and Douglas Barnes in England; the Americans may have been less sanguine about the meeting, but they had their comparable and inspirational figures in James Moffett and Louise Rosenblatt who were beginning to work a similar pattern of change. To foster the growth of the child through "language and learning," "universes of discourse," and "transformational reading" soon became the call of this incipient New Literacy on both sides of the Atlantic.

In Great Britain, the 1970s brought what Peter Doughty (1974) confidently called a "progressive consensus" in the teaching of English. It had introduced the fundamentals of the New Literacy into the English classes of innovative teachers. "Workshops" were set up; teachers became "entrepreneurs" and "consultants" while students were transformed into "participants" and "researchers" (Doughty, 1974, p. 14): "The progressive in English teaching requires, therefore, the establishment of a new set of social relationships for the classroom, between teacher and pupil and between pupil and pupil" (p. 16). One of the early programs that made this new attitude readily available to English teachers in Great Britain was *Language in Use* (Doughty, Thornton, & Pearce, 1971). In setting English in a new political direction, *Language in Use* deliberately turned from the guiding light of literary criticism to the stark tones of sociolinguistics which was leading an intellectual fight to broaden the democratic mandate of equal opportunity in education. This reorientation meant radically new lessons for the students, lessons about language in the street and home, not just in literature, lessons on language's multiple functions and students' natural competence, against traditional notions of correctness and a single standard. This new tact had emerged out of a highly charged political debate over language and dialect, social class and school success; the point was eventually established that many judgements condemning the quality of students' language carry residual class and racial prejudices.[1]

This new understanding of students and the politics of language under-writes much of the New Literacy's approach to writing although it goes unspoken now for the most part. Margaret Mathieson bluntly identifies it, in her history of English teaching, as a moral and ideological effort to "remedy social injustice" perpetuated against working-class students (1975, p. 159). This concern with social injustice marks the history of the teaching of English, beginning with Matthew Arnold's nineteenth-century promise that poetry would (re)form the soul of the (working-class) pupils which he supervised for many years. Yet it is well to recall that these reformers were no less morally committed than Arnold to rectifying a troubling situation through education; teaching English in that sense has remained an ethical endeavor, making up for the failings of organized religion in Arnold's day and in this case for the shortfalls of the democratic promise to hear the voice of the many.

It remains difficult to assess exactly how many inroads the New Literacy has made in the teaching of English since Dartmouth and that early progressive consensus. At best, I can offer a few rough and assorted measures to give some indication of how well these programs have taken in the schools:

1. The National Writing Project, which began introducing teachers to the writing process model in 1973, had 172 sites operating abroad in America and abroad in 1989 and is continuing to grow.[2]

2. In a feature article on new directions in reading, the *New York Times* reports that "a controversial development that has come to be known as whole language" is "happening" in "countless" schools around America. The article notes that New Zealand, with "one of the highest literacy rates in the world," had been using an approach similar to whole language for 25 years (Salmans, 1988, p. EDUC69).

3. The Australian government has spent over $8 million on implementing Whole Language programs over a five-year period (Luke et al., 1989).

4. In Great Britain, a research team headed by Peter Mortimore has discovered that in the 50 London primary schools in their study, 19 percent of the teachers had dropped the basal reading program in favor of children choosing their own literature to read (Mortimore et al., 1988, p. 86). Douglas and Dorothy Barnes have found that

personal writing, which might serve as a crude indicator of New Literacy influence, made up 21 to 45 percent of the topics that secondary students addressed in their English classes (1984, pp. 80–84).

5. The province of Nova Scotia has mandated Whole Language as the approach to be taken with literacy instruction throughout the school system (Church et al., 1989).

It seems safe to suggest that the New Literacy is a presence on the educational scene. Yet the issue for me is not the rising market share of New Literacy. I remain interested in the aspects of the New Literacy which draw a teacher to these programs and in where New Literacy programs are heading with literacy and learning. The question is also whether the educators advocating and participating in these programs know where they are headed. On one level, this book is intended to inform readers of the challenge and promise posed by the New Literacy. But on another level, it would step into the fray, contributing to its cause by uncovering the venerable roots of its claim on literacy and then, too, challenging it with questions about the latent politics of this new power which advocates of the New Literacy have yet to ask. That is, what I intend with the New Literacy in this book is itself mixed. I would praise it for its accomplishments with students and teachers. It has, at least in my own modestly down-cast eyes, made me a better teacher of reading and writing. But having moved this far into it, I would also press ahead with queries about the limits of its best intentions. As I have already begun to indicate, the New Literacy speaks to a radically different way of schooling, in the first instance, and to a different educational conception of literacy and learning in a larger sense. By taking up the range of its positions in the teaching of writing, reading, and literature in the first part of the book, I would prepare the way for a critical coming to terms with the issues of meaning, self, history, and politics which makes up the second part of the book.

The private and public spirit of a new literacy

In order to appreciate what is at stake in altering a student's relationship to reading and writing, the remainder of this chapter explores the aspects of literacy necessary to establish a new version of it for today's schools. While we carry on as if we understand in a general sense what this thing, *literacy,* is all about, when pressed for a precise definition we appear to be less than certain about it. However, there is good reason for that reluctance, and I'm not so foolish as to leap in with a sound and certain definition of literacy, having already offered notions of it as a form of work with language and a social process of extending meaning and connection. Yet as the New Literacy can be understood as an attempt to redefine or give new meaning to literacy as it is taught and worked in the schools, it seems fair to begin by exploring the histories of meaning that lay nestled in the central term to this project. The story has just enough fascinating twists to it to justify the obvious pedantry of reaching for the *Oxford English Dictionary* and trotting out the word's pedigree. But recall that we are turning to it for a history of the word's changing use and context, as opposed to an authoritative definition.

The first point of interest is that the term "literacy" only found its way into print late in the nineteenth century. The *OED* gives the *New England Journal of Education* of 1883 credit for the first use of "literacy" when it claimed that "Massachusetts is the first state in the Union in literacy in its native population." In this fashion "literacy" entered the language in the early days of public education through one of its professional journals. It would seem fair to say that "literacy" is part of the invention and the promise of public education. On the other hand, the word's negative form, "illiteracy," turns out to be the far older term, with citations in the *OED* dating back to the seventeenth century, referring to an unfamiliarity with letters and reading. Now, it should be noted that the term, "literate," dates back to the fifteenth century, and was used to describe one who can read and write, but, as the *OED* points out, the term was closely related to "literature" and "literary." We might speculate, then, that "literacy" came into the language lacking that element of cultured refinement and stands for a different sort of familiarity with letters. Literacy represented a more common and basic acquaintance with a little reading and less writing, arising from the development of a secular and civically minded system of public schools. Before that move, literacy was associated with elitist, religious, and technical orders that have promoted reading and writing for rather different purposes than today's schools, as Daniel Resnick and Laren Resnick's (1977) work on different periods of literacy beginning with the Protestant Reformation has shown. Their point is very much one of how distinct and recent this expectation is of a universal literacy as necessary for the welfare of the state. But it is also worth noting that this was literacy as a public service, as a schooled population was necessary for order, commerce, and good government. There was another sort of literacy that had already arisen among the people that goes by the name of popular literacy, which had not always been well-received by those in authority; it does, however, have remarkable parallels with the New Literacy, as I will explore in some detail in Chapter 7.

But if literacy has its beginnings in civic efforts to educate the masses in the ways of the modern state, it has also taken on a more personal and a more sociable connotation. Let me pursue what seem to be private and public senses of literacy for a moment as concepts that are helpful in suggesting two directions in which the New Literacy would move the classroom. In trying to get close to the *private* significance of literacy, I tend to recollect moments, almost stolen, that have been spent alone with a book and then, in looking for the *public* side of literacy, I recall nervous times of ceremony and my own shaky text. For example, there was a haven that I vividly remember creating around a book one fall when I was teaching in an old school; each day noon-hour for a month I went to a deserted classroom to be alone with William Faulkner's *Light in August,* the voices of the children outside the window gradually increasing as that day's hour came to an end. Or from the public side of a literacy on display, what comes to mind is my slight, nervous speech to a provincial teachers' association which tried hard to thank the association for caring enough about education to send a teacher back to school, to graduate school, with its generous support; the success of the talk hung for me afterwards on an anonymous handshake and a few words of appreciation from someone in the audience. Literacy, in such instances, seems to entail acts of separation and connection that take their meaning from both the text and context.

In the first instance, reading and writing may seem to afford us private moments and space in which to be alone, as we stand on a crowded bus going crosstown with a paperback that protects us from the unending sameness of the trip. The text absorbs our attention; we use it to amuse and remove ourselves. But literacy is more often a public means of organizing and regulating people. It signifies and enacts a power in the world. This public side of literacy is bound in the texts of the law, government, and workplace. Here, even for the most literate citizen, the realm of meaning often becomes the domain of the professional, as lawyers protect the interests of clients in the reading of the law and write business documents that will be binding. The public voices of corporations and politicians are often the work of professional writers who would save their clients from telling too much. We find our link to this public world spelled out in the columns of the morning newspaper and the scripts of the nightly news. Yet amid cries from some that the image is replacing the text as the dominant form of expression in this society, there is a world of indications that print still acts as an informative and regulating medium of great forcefulness in structuring this society. This professional and public literacy becomes part of the daily web of meaning in which we find ourselves; sometimes we hardly notice it at the periphery of our vision and sometimes in occupies the center of our attention.

Although the New Literacy reaches out from the classroom through its interests in student publication and in learning about writing from professionals, it also has to take in these public lessons about the power of literacy which have traditionally gone missing in the classroom. New Literacy advocates, like many of us, tend to treasure what seems the personal side of literacy, but the larger lesson is that reading and writing exist at every point within reach of public organizations that are easily lost sight of in this romantic sense of the private phenomenon of literacy. That is, the dichotomy between private and public sides is a convenient but shortsighted view of literacy and one which the New Literacy has at least begun to overcome by utilizing the connections between private and public aspects in the classroom. These programs bring more of the personal sense of literacy—as children choose their own books and find answers to their own questions—into the sociable workings of this public place and the children are encouraged to share their favorite books and their findings. In expanding the public realm and reach of this literacy, the New Literacy is embracing the democratic imperative of education which John Dewey identifies when the assertion that "democracy is more than a form of government; it is primarily a mode of associated living, of conjoint communicated experience" (1944, p. 87). The New Literacy would have that form of democracy and would demonstrate the ways of literacy within it within an ever-increasing circle of associated living.

But if this is the direction in which the New Literacy is moving toward, it should also be made clear what it is moving away from on this scale of private and public concerns. The tradition that the New Literacy is opposed to is the one in which schools have treated literacy as a private ability open to public scrutiny: students are asked to read this to themselves and respond to the questions that they might be assigned a mark on a scale of one to a hundred ascertaining precisely how well they can read a description of Iceland or appreciate Shakespeare. The public forcefulness of literacy as a measure of a students' worth is felt by the young reader and writer in their daily classroom lives.[3] Equally so, under this public pressure teachers select programs and search for materials with this double concern for fostering literate students as both private readers and public performers. This educational concern with public assessment is exacerbated by the perennial public outcries over the "literacy crisis" and "declining educational standards." How perennial, you might ask. Harvey Daniels in his book on the crisis, *Famous Last Words: The American Language Crisis Reconsidered* (1983), has been able to trace the cycle of complaints with a few gaps back to a tablet from Sumerian times.

The grounds for rejecting this crisis mentality are worth considering for a moment. A crisis can seem to warrant a suspension of debate, and if these innovative programs are to get a fair hearing, the threats of literacy crisis dominating the current educational climate need to be allayed and placed in perspective. Working from the period of 1880 to the present in American education, Lawrence Stedman and Carl Kaestle (1987) provide a profile of achievement that indicates a steady rise in literacy through increased school attendance. Although they are duly modest about their conclusions, based as they are on a diverse set of sources, these two historians feel that the common and recurrent perception of a crisis in literacy is not warranted by the facts: "The reading achievement for a given age level has been stable throughout most of the twentieth century" (p. 42). Yet they also acknowledge that this does not mean that the perceived problem or crisis is completely groundless. Stedman and Kaestle suspect that the current sense of crisis is based on a mismatch of skills between the demands of the schools and the workplace, which can be translated through functional literacy tests and informal observation into substantial "illiteracy" figures. If the mismatch of school and workplace is one current problem, another problem their work pinpoints is that school attainment has ceased to rise while the dropout rate is increasing. The initial need to get people to school has been met and now, with students leaving early or taking the wrong sorts of lessons away with them, it will clearly be that much more difficult to improve the general state of literacy. Stedman and Kaestle's historical statement of the educational dilemma plays, to my mind, into the hands of the New Literacy. Here are a series of programs that will prepare students for turning literacy to their own ends, whatever situation they find themselves in. The promise of these programs is that measure of

17

flexibility and the possibility of a new level of attainment in terms of quality and engagement.

But there is more to the current crisis than Stedman and Kaestle admit to their analysis. Ira Shor (1986) has gone to some length to demonstrate how the current American literacy crisis has been constructed as part of a "conservative restoration." In his terms, the literacy crisis amounts to a political attack on the schools as social agencies that represented a liberal state of mind in what was becoming a conservative era.[4] The New Literacy represents a faith in the social agency of public education as a forum for mobilizing and empowering the young; it is part of a liberal faith in the plurality of voices that need to be heard. Yet before dismissing the literacy crisis out of hand, I would note that Jonathan Kozol (1985) has adeptly cut through the ideological spectrum in his poignant portrait of illiteracy among what he feels is an underestimated segment of the America poor and unemployed. There is little point in denying that many people suffer illiteracy and that educational provision must be made for those who would seek help with learning to read and write. However, I still believe, in looking at the available information, that the current sense of *crisis* is neither warranted nor productive.[5]

This climate of accountability has taken its toll on the nature of teaching and the work of the classroom. As increased pressure has been placed on school districts for performance, the teaching profession has suffered a loss of autonomy to packaged kits and programmed learning materials which have shifted teachers into the position of managers or technicians. Michael Apple has continued to explore this process of "deskilling" in the classroom, drawing our attention to its implication in the patriarchal domination of administrative structures in schools (1986, pp. 31–53; 1982). As he notes, some teachers have found ways to resist the imposition of teacher-proof programs from above, and New Literacy programs are one form that resistance can take. The New Literacy speaks directly to teachers reasserting control over the work that goes on in the class, even as it attempts to hand a greater part of the locus of meaning over to the student. It represents a taking hold of the curriculum by the teacher at a fundamental level by challenging the meaning of literacy in the classroom as well as the nature of a teacher's work with the students.

Yet within this context of concern and crisis, the New Literacy has shown itself adaptable. It is no accident that these programs have a strong self-promotional campaign built into them as the children publish, produce, and perform their work in a proud demonstration of their literate involvement and achievement. While parents are clearly moved by the test scores that their children bring home, New Literacy advocates believe with reason that these same parents are equally impressed by more direct demonstrations of literacy as the child hands them a carefully researched and richly anecdoted family history or an equally thorough report on community garbage disposal intended for city hall. The New Literacy is banking on the sense of ownership and personal stake in the work to make the difference.

If for many of us, the seeds of the New Literacy were planted during the 1960s reawakening of progressive education, the program has taken shape within this climate of educational restraint and crisis. The New Literacy's transformation of the child-centered experiments of the 1960s has been based on finding a more *productive,* if alternative, structure for the classroom. In light of the crisis mentality, the New Literacy has learned a lesson about what John Goodlad (1983) has identified as the "non-events" of curriculum innovation of that earlier and daring period. With all of its interest in process, the New Literacy is still determined *to produce* writers and readers, but to produce them in a learning environment that eschews the back-to-the-basics response that has dominated the educational crisis mentality. On the other hand, the New Literacy also shows signs that it has brought itself on stream in educating the young for the new corporate age.

At a buzz-word level, these programs have an executive-class edge. They would, after all, encourage independent and collaborative projects while drawing on peer support networks and conferencing with professionals to enhance the production values of the final and literate product. It can all sound and seem very marble and glass, office-tower work. While editorial meetings at the classroom publishing house may not be a training ground for the leveraged buy-out artists, neither is it so removed from hustling projects and prospectuses for tomorrow's Wall Street jungle. The New Literacy seeks for both teacher and student a working environment that fosters a spirit of independence and creative excitement. It can approach at times a mythical cross between the high-pressure dynamics of advertising account work and the warm, collaborative spirit of a 1960s pottery studio. But tempering both these aspects is a domestic element that is found in the furnishings of this new classroom with carpet, floor lamps, and different centers of activity for reading, playing, and making things, all laid out like a renovated home with the walls knocked out. Valerie Walkerdine, who worked in one such progressive setting in the late 1960s, has described how the teacher is moved homeward: "the teacher is no authoritarian father figure, but

19

a bourgeois and nurturant mother" (1986, p. 58). This workplace, in which students are at home among teachers who would assist their individual and collaborative projects, has been aptly characterized by David Cohen as "a distinctively cosmopolitan and upper middle-class style of family life, in which parental discipline is self-consciously relaxed, in which children have plenty of money and free time, and need not work, and in which personal independence is highly valued" (1988, p. 27). In Cohen's view this has limited the implementation of progressive education programs, and I have certainly met teachers who appear to reject New Literacy programs because it just does not seem to them to resemble teaching, that is, the kind of work they see themselves doing in a classroom.

But if the New Literacy offers an upper middle-class hominess with a little corporate panache, it is going to fail an overwhelming majority of the students as any form of preparation for life outside the classroom. The escape from what appears to be a late 1980s callowness lurks in a final lesson from that legacy of the 1960s. Madeleine Grumet (1988) puts her finger on it when she describes how teachers during that period naively proposed a new education in manner doomed to failure: "Oblivious to the far-reaching epistemological and political implications of this approach to schooling, the teachers who had transformed their classrooms into places of active exploration and group process failed to create the political and ideological structures required to sustain and enlarge the movement" (p. 24). In her work on women and teaching, Grumet has taken the first steps in offering politically sensitive structures for reorganizing teaching; Grumet recasts teaching as a form of reproductive labor, a labor connected to the personal lives of teachers and to their collaborative association with others, colleagues and students. For Grumet, teachers have it within their grasp to realize and to some degree recreate the public sphere of the classroom in their own images of education within the democratic state. As schools have failed to make good their promise to all children of an equal education, as color, class and gender continue to exert a structural influence that insures children do not have the same range of opportunities, the New Literacy has to find ways to keep these issues in the forefront of its efforts to increase the level of literate participation and enfranchisement. These are issues that the New Literacy needs to be pressed on and I intend to do my share of pressing in the course of this book.

Part of the New Literacy's argument with the schools is that literacy takes its meaning and force from the circumstances in which it is used and the ends to which it is put. The New Literacy is caught up in the play of power and structure in the classroom, as well as in the society at large; it is also the mediating grace between friends sharing a paperback. This is a latent political and personal challenge to the New Literacy which its programs have found ways of addressing from within the classroom. The meeting of the personal and the political is one of those powerful calls inherited from the 1960s. The challenge remains latent because this meeting is rarely realized in discussions of what the New Literacy is up to in the classroom. New Literacy programs happily embrace that friendly aspect of literacy through a regular sharing of students' stories and other forms of collaboration in the classroom. Yet the advocates of these programs are not always ready to deal with the politics of this realignment of work in the school, as if drawn to the beat of this exciting music while hesitant about what this driving beat may really be all about. These questions of power and politics in literacy need to be faced by advocates of the New Literacy and other interested parties. They need to hear from the likes of Walkerdine and Henry Giroux as educational critics who have not shied from dancing to this beat. Out of her own teaching experience with the child-centered experiments of the 1960s, Walkerdine sounds a blunt cautionary note: "Although some have suggested that progressivism frees working class children from harsh authoritarianism, I would suggest precisely the opposite. Progressivism makes the products of oppression, powerlessness, invisible" (1986, p. 59). Giroux, too, lays literacy out in bold political tones: "To be literate is *not* to be free, it is to be present and active in the struggle for reclaiming one's voice, history, and future" (1988a, p. 65, original emphasis).

This radical element is not something from outside the New Literacy, but lies at its center as it begins with a critique of the way literacy is treated in the classroom. To give greater credence to the reader's response to a text is to acknowledge that the reader is a major contributor to the making of the literary experience. It would have the students invest themselves in their writing and thereby risk fostering a nation of outspoken writers. It clearly portends more than improved language arts classes. But what precisely will this restructuring of the classroom around a new form of literacy produce among people who come to possess it, we might ask? Is it to amount to little more than a flood of letters to the editor of the local newspaper? Or might it mean something more to suddenly have a greater part of the population able and willing to go public with their case and stories, demanding a greater attentiveness to their voices and additional outlets for their new-found voices in the process?

In trying to realize what is at stake in this new form of literacy, I have brought together advocates of the New Literacy with those who have spoken out for students unduly silenced through the politics of gender, color, and social class. With a certain degree of idealism, I am pressing for a New Literacy that is not totally absorbed in overcoming such malaises as writer's block in the English classroom or boredom in the face of reading an assigned novel. There is something more to be done with writing and reading. The New Literacy needs to wrestle with this promise of a new empowerment in literacy. It needs to face up to what might lie in this talk of power and come clean with its best intentions. To begin to realize this potential for addressing the larger issue of literacy in this society, New Literacy programs will have to get involved in the tensions that tear at education, that continue to frustrate the dream of an equitable society. To offer students a greater say on and over the page may be a rhetorical flourish of these new programs, but then someone has to call their bluff. It may be more political than educators sometimes feel comfortable with in thinking about the young, but the challenge raised by the New Literacy is against a tradition which goes far beyond conventional teaching methods. Consider the extent of the assault: from students entering the first grade who are regarded as bringing a degree of literacy and a feel for language that makes an entire publishing industry obsolete to the college level where the literary canon has been cracked and opened to writers who were once considered to be marginal. The New Literacy introduces a radical program of studies along two dimensions, the one unsettling the school and the other disturbing the acquired habits of the student. This to be a literacy which plays *against* institutional authority and a literacy which works *within* the student. The first might be described as a form of "deschooling" that restructures the classroom around the students' rather than the teacher's pursuit of meaning. The second is taken up with the literacy that would transform the student from supplicant to advocate in search of what has not been expressed or found before, a literacy that engages the student and which would encourage a greater engagement with the world.

I use Ivan Illich's (1970) term, "deschooling," which may strike some as dated as bell-bottom jeans, because in his desire to free education from schooling in favor of "learning webs," he arrived at two key items that can be found nestled in the New Literacy: "the inverse of schooling is possible: that we can depend on self-motivated learning instead of employing teachers to bribe or compel the student to find the time and the will to learn, that we can provide the learner with new links to the world instead of continuing to funnel all educational programs through the teacher" (p. 104). The locus of meaning and connection moves to the student in search of the world. Illich is inverting the classroom rather than dis-establishing it, and the New Literacy seems to me to be about such an inversion, with the teacher and the student trading places. The New Literacy represents something more of a reschooling than a deschooling process. It would keep many of the trappings and all of the certification functions, but it is motivated by the same frustration of educational meaningfulness, if more on the side of the individual student and teacher than the issue of a more just school system.[6]

But if the challenge of the New Literacy moves outward to the limits of the educational institution, it also works within the confines of the classroom. The literacy proposed here would help students find their voices, help them find what lies within as they connect with what they have read and as they discover what they have always known through their writing. This directing of literacy's powers within raises questions about the nature of this self that would be nurtured and written by this literate engagement, questions that this book pursues in Chapter 8. As it turns out, the search is not one for the hidden soul of truth that lies within us all, although it is sometimes cast that way. The writer's encounter with the self-same soul has served for two centuries as an emblem of the literary artist's quest and it must now confront another aspect of these times with the rise of a poststructuralist sensibility: Without forsaking the Romantic preference for organic metaphors, the writer now faces becoming an onion, as self-exploratory writing is a peeling back of the layers revealing only other, inner leaves, one after the other, no truer or more certain than those on the surface, but more translucent, slippery, and no less tearful, perhaps, in the peeling.

The New Literacy is set upon sketchy theories of meaning and self which need to meet current thinking about the nature of subjectivity that arises from within language. This postmodern unsettling of the self must be reckoned with in these proposals for a classroom in which students write out of themselves, listening hard for their own voices, and voicing their responses to the works of others. At this point, the New Literacy is happily heading on down the road, on track with literacy, perhaps, slowing down for school zones and always with an eye on the rearview mirror; given the enthusiasm of advocates of these programs, the whole thing seems top-down and driven by the feel of the wind in the hair. I

23

figure that more can be said about what's driving this thing and where it could be headed, if only from the back seat where I sit curled up with maps and guidebooks from here and there.

A true shift in the nature of literacy, on the scale which the New Literacy has brought forward, has ramifications that spill over the edges of the classroom, that go beyond the promise of better motivated students in language arts and English classes. These ramifications need exploring as they might unfold within an education system that has not bestowed its gifts in literacy, and the corresponding credentials, with the degree of equality promised time and again over the course of this century. They need to be explored so that teachers can confidently face difficult choices about the nature of the work and the form of life that they would have in the classroom. The promise of education in a democracy is one of extending opportunities, of participation in processes of development, expression, and power. The New Literacy would seem to have taken a piece of this promise as part of its mandate and needs to be encouraged in running with it.

Notes

1. The sociolinguists who provided the grounding for this work were M. A. K. Halliday (1973) and Basil Bernstein (1971), while the landmark works in the social class and racial elements were Harold Rosen's *Language and Class* (1972), which alerted educators to the continuing class bias of Bernstein's work, and Labov's "The Logic of Nonstandard English" (1973) which also served as a corrective to Bernstein.

2. To give an example of what a site might represent, in the city of Calgary 130 teachers (out of approximately 6,000 in this school district) by 1988 had taken a university course in the methods of the National Writing Project and are participating in the project with their own classes and through in-service with other teachers; approximately 25 new teachers are added to the project each year through these courses. The headquarters of the National Writing Projects is in the Faculty of Education, University of California at Berkeley. In a similar development, there has also recently formed a North American Confederation of Whole Language Support Groups.

3. Sarah Freedman (1987) in an excellent study of assessment and writing in the schools, put her finger on the problem when she concluded that "radical reorganization of classrooms will be needed in order to make *writing* and *learning* more important or even as important as *grading* from the students' point of view" (p. 161). Such is the ambition of the New Literacy programs and its key to competing with grades is the matter of self-engagement and enhancement which it offers students.

24

4.   Henry Giroux (1988a), another critic of the crisis mentality, has pointed out that conservative forces in America have made literacy their issue in a strategy of attacking the schools among other social services. He treats the publicity about the crisis as part of the efforts of "conservative political interests" to secure more workers with functional literacy skills (p. 61). Yet it often seems that the postmodern corporate capitalists are opting for offshore factories and Third World workers with little concern with the education and literacy of these people. Still his point is well taken that literacy has to be reclaimed by liberal and progressive interests as a positive educational issue.

5.   I found on examining the details of a recent Canadian study commissioned by a newspaper chain that set the level of illiteracy in this country at 20 percent that the rate was arbitrarily set and that a good number of designated illiterates were active readers with no complaints about their abilities. National headlines of one-in-five illiteracy levels may well draw some support for adult literacy classes, but it still distorts our understanding of the state of literacy in Canada (Willinsky, in press).

6.   Illich's disdain for the schools is part of a long Romantic tradition which I work with at its source in Chapter 7; David Cohen (1988) describes the American rendition of this aversion as "loving education and hating school" and finds its redeemer in John Dewey's incorporation of a natural education in a formal school (1988, p. 3). As already noted, Dewey's spirit is a presence, if unspoken, in the New Literacy which is also seeking its own resolution to this set of mixed feelings.

2
Writing in the Real

Ariel was glad he had written his poems.
They were of a remembered time
Or of something seen that he liked.

*   *   *

His self and the sun were one
And his poems, although makings of his self,
Were no less makings of the sun.
    Wallace Stevens, "The Planet on the Table"

Let me begin with a division in writing, between Stevens's "The Planet on the Table" (1954) and Janet Epps's essay "Killing Them Softly: Why Willie Can't Write" (1985). Feeling more than a little frustrated by the lessons that black students have faced in learning to write, Epps takes up a side of writing missing from Ariel's celebrated words and self, all one under the sun, in Stevens's poem. In the course of her essay, she declares that "composition is the gatekeeper of the inequalities perpetuated in the American system" (1985, p. 155). This chapter concerns the meeting of these public and private questions in the New Literacy's efforts to ground the teaching of writing in the actual processes of writers. The New Literacy has the potential to house both of these impassioned sides to writing, but it has yet to act equally hospitable to both. Stevens's "makings of his self" is more than happily met by the New Literacy, if without his trace of irony over the naturalness of the process.

On the other hand, Epps's concern about the political function of writing classes and the powers of gatekeeping go largely unspoken in the annals of the New Literacy. Yet Epps sounds the more urgent note for the teaching of writing, just as she sets a different agenda for that program: "We have not been allowed to acquire true literacy. The acquisition would necessitate an analysis of who we are and would point a critical finger at the continued racist and classist nature of America" (p. 155).[1] It is a truth about literacy that will haunt this discussion of writing instruction, especially at its most euphoric moments. The New Literacy takes writing very seriously and does much to advance its place in the curriculum and in the lives of students. All that needs to be asked of this development is what would they make of the power and glory released through writing.

In this chapter, I wish to take hold of the spirit and substance of writing classes that have fallen under the spell of the New Literacy. Moving back and forth across the Atlantic and two decades of educational development, I will step over a good deal of interesting work in this busy area and pick up only five substantial but interwoven strands in the New Literacy: writing at the center of literacy; the Writing Process movement; both the London and New Hampshire Schools of New Literacy Research and Advocacy; and the Writing Across the Curriculum movement. Each serves to demonstrate in a different way how New Literacy programs address the unrealized powers of writing in the curriculum, how they are about teachers and students working together in new ways and toward new goals, and how they take their direction and drive from the world beyond the classroom. To these programs, I would pose the questions that have yet to be asked in the first blush of success, questions that fall between Stevens and Epps as the personal and public force of writing has only begun to be realized in these various programs.

The New Literacy brings more than a fresh teaching strategy to writing; it has heavily endowed writing with a profound moral and psychological thrust. It has found in the teaching of writing the means for restructuring the nature of work in the classroom, restructuring it around a new relationship between students and teacher, between students and text, between students and a self that can be written on the page. In its success as a program, it has yet, in my opinion, to adequately confront what it is up to in, as the rhetoric now runs, *enfranchising* the student population with its natural right to expression.

Bringing writing to the center

What learning to write comes down to, for an advocate of the New Literacy such as Frank Smith, is a matter which neatly dissolves distinctions between child and adult, student and professional: "Writing is learned by writing, by reading and by perceiving oneself as a writer" (1982, p. 199). Allowing, and even encouraging, this sense of *being a writer* is the radical moment for the New Literacy. At once so simple a move and yet such a departure for education—to teach them what they are and might be, in being a writer, rather than what they have yet to attain in order to be able to write. In the eyes of the New Literacy advocate, this amounts to "life's ways of reading and writing" (Heath, cited by Atwell, 1987, p. 22).[2]

The measure of this seriousness about writing for the New Literacy begins with pushing writing to the center of the language program in the schools. For many classrooms, this has meant a considerable distance to travel. In the United States, "creative writing" did not find a spot in the school timetable until the 1950s, although progressive education programs had experimented with it for some time before that. Even this official entry into the program was still by the backdoor for the most part. In my case and like many teachers, I scheduled a forty-minute period toward the end of the week for "creative writing." It was a very small part of a language arts program dominated by daily reading and spelling classes. In those not-so-long-ago days, I was proud enough that at least I did not resort to the predictable and sentimental *Saturday Evening Post* covers by Norman Rockwell from which as a child I had to produce a weekly composition. Instead, I offered my students Kenneth Koch's (1970) formula of writing poetry through sentence completion ("I wish . . . " repeated over ten lines) or tried to entice them with one of the endless stream of essay contests that show up at the school promising earnest writers easy money for pursuing themes related to the sponsor's interests. All told, it was one of the expendable periods whose absence did not raise the groan of a missed art or, worst of all, a physical education period.

The lesser place of writing among the language arts is a story that I'm sure has been told too many times, a story of teachers turning to a trick or treat activity which is guaranteed to carry a writing period with students' busily engaged. Like a good number of teachers, I had yet to imagine that there might be something more worthwhile or exciting to the time spent on writing. Composition was on the edge of the school timetable, and it was at the bottom of the job roster in the English department at the university. The marginal position of writing in the curriculum, however, is no more than an extension of its status over the course of this century in teacher education, language arts textbooks, and the research on education.[3] It is also no more than a representation of a certain receptive emphasis in the schools, as reading a text is to receive, while writing is to produce, express, and create. But perhaps the schools take their cue from the society at large in which we read our way through the day while writing very little as we fill out one form or another. The balance that the New Literacy strikes by elevating writing begins with educational research and practices, but it also seems to speak to the general lay of literacy in this land.

However overlooked it had been, in the 1970s the teaching of writing became a source of concern with the discovery of an American "writing crisis" by college and business leaders. Among the prominent indicators of trouble abroad in this subject area was *Newsweek*'s shift from the 1960s educational complaint about reading to "Why Johnny Can't *Write*," and books such as *The Great American Writing Block* (Wheeler, 1979) and *Empty Pages* (Fadiman & Howard, 1979) traded in on the public concern.[4] Although hardly of crisis proportions, the National Assessment of Educational Progress did indicate that a drop in the American standard of writing had occurred since the 1960s. From there it was a short step to declarations that "writing should be the center of schooling," which is what Theodore Sizer (1984) stated in one of the hard-hitting looks at American education that set the agenda for the decade. It wasn't long before this particular version of the perennial literacy crisis had insinuated itself into the public conscience.

The ensuing responses to this national writing block varied. Those given to conservative tendencies in education were quick to bring the testing of writing within their more general call for greater accountability in the mastery of the basics (without being discouraged in the least by what seemed to be the highly interventionist position in this request for government monitoring). They offered less guidance on what programs would be best, although "time on task" was a phrase that seemed at times to encompass the entirety of their curricular vision.[5] The New Literacy responded to this sense of crisis and the spirit of the times by pressing for a more focused and hard-working approach to writing with a special emphasis on understanding it as a laboring process, while at the same time building the process around a child-centered pedagogy of the 1960s, in itself an extension of progressive education. The New Literacy's solution was to develop a nearly new pedagogy of process for writing.

Given its commitment to students as a strong source of meaning in the classroom, the New Literacy has set out to recover writing as the literate equal of reading in language arts and English classes with increasing efforts to integrate the two into the full expression of literacy. This promotion of writing runs beyond language arts and English classes and moves across the curriculum; that is, the New Literacy has also introduced writing as an effective way of thinking out problems in mathematics, capturing the valence theory in chemistry, and bringing to life events of history. Through this new approach, literacy serves as both an *expressive* and an *interpretive* vehicle, whether students are taking their own stories across the blank page or composing their initial response to the French Revolution. As the New Literacy dares to have it, this emphasis on writing signals to students that they are primarily engaged in the construction of meaning, rather than serving as empty jugs waiting to be filled; they are meaning-makers, with the emphasis on *maker*. It is hardly surprising then that the stress on the powers of writing became the first line of attack in the manifesto of the New Literacy. Reading has not been ignored in this shift of emphasis. The image of reading as simply a receptive and decoding skill has itself been purged of its passivity in favor of an active reader constructing meaning in a transactional process.

The New Literacy encourages a more active voice for students that they might become outspoken on the page and in class. This further enfranchises students, giving them the power to actively write (and read) their own story, to feel a part and to participate in this public community of discourse and texts. Which is to say that the New Literacy runs, in part, on the language of political aspiration. This theme of the "right to write" serves as an underlying morality for advocates of these programs. It tends to figure in the opening rhetoric of their texts; Lucy Calkins, for example, begins *The Art of Teaching Writing* (1986) by appealing to something dwelling within us: "Human beings have a deep need to represent their experience through writing. We need to make our truths beautiful" (p. 3). That much said, what follows in such books is a revering of writing and the writer which sanctifies the teacher's work in providing opportunities for both to develop.

This new moral emphasis on writing has meant changes for the role of the teacher, the regard for the child, and the structure of the classroom. Where once, and still, the moral force of teaching literature was this urge to civilize, now the New Literacy turns to writing to enfranchise. The writing period has witnessed a move from direct instruction in the parts of a paragraph or theme to collaborative conferencing over the writer's work and the management of cooperative editorial settings.

What distinguishes these strategies from the more traditional classroom fare is not simply that students are moving about the room in a whole new way, although these structural shifts are very important, but that the New Literacy has drawn this new model of the writing class from the careful study of fluent student and professional writers. The lessons learned are now finding a surprisingly widespread application from the first grade to the college level.

One of the first things to establish in understanding the writing process movement is that the implied distinction of process versus non-process writing is misleading. The issue at stake for the New Literacy is not the traditional creative writing class's neglect of process, but that students were being asked to write by going through a process that has no basis in "life's ways" and the world outside of school. Donald Graves's (1983) reference to his work as part of the "writing process movement" is slightly misleading insofar as there had always been a process in the teaching of writing, as there has in something as prosaic as the manufacture of soap: the original writing process begins with learning the letter shapes and eventually moves to mastering the parts of speech; it relegates spelling, grammar, and creative writing to different periods in the weekly timetable to keep students and teachers from getting confused about the content of the language arts. At given points, a class is set aside so that students might apply the different aspects of this knowledge in a composition to be handed in at the end of the period or next class. As part of the New Literacy assault on this pattern and process, Tom Romano has cleverly termed this the "Due Friday Model of Writing" which he diagrams with a large "Mystery" step that stretches between "Topic Chosen" and "Final Copy" (1987, p. 53).

The results of this process are no mystery, but they are rife with social discriminations to which the New Literacy quietly speaks as part of its mission. The "Due Friday" writing is not much fun to read, as a rule, although it is certainly read *by* the rule. The grammar lessons come a little easier to those whose ear for standard English has been trained by what amounted to an immersion program in a middle-class life; these students also find that they have it in them, with a little work and attention to propriety, to write some of the best English compositions in the class. Gender plays its part in this process. Young girls, especially encouraged in this fidelity to propriety and given to a certain advantage in verbal skills, are likely to find greater success in writing only to discover later in life that this advantage can be frustrated by certain obstacles on the road to writerly, or many other forms of, success (Spender, 1983). However, the fact remains that a good number of students in this scheme of things learn they cannot write, period. The composition or creative writing class in such instances is rarely anyone's favorite. The importance of reiterating this familiar pattern once more is that the New Literacy not only teaches writing better across the board, but challenges this reflection of social privilege in those predictable results.

After teaching within this pattern of privilege and contradiction for a number of years, I found Pierre Bourdieu's work (1973; Bourdieu & Passeron, 1977) offered a coherent explanation of what might well be going on. I had already run into a gaggle of competing explanations for the continuing class-based differences in school performance, from Bernstein's (1971) differences in language codes, to which I was initially drawn, to Jensen's (1980) differences in the genetic pool of intelligence among racial groups, which I found particularly alarming. Bourdieu does not begin with the inadequacy of the victims' dialect or genes in searching for a structural relationship that has to do with the successful perpetuation of class in a society whose education system is committed to facilitating social mobility. He chooses to treat the reproductive process in terms of investment strategies: those students with childhoods in standard English might be said to bring a certain "cultural capital" to the school that has already been invested in a stock that pays the highest of dividends, a capital that will have realized a considerable profit under this writing process. If the schools have failed to teach all students to speak and write standard English, they have at least, according to Bourdieu, certified those students whose background merits it. Those students whose linguistic experience was rooted in other communities of discourse also bring a form of cultural capital to the school only to find their investments depreciated and their resources depleted, an accounting which they find confirmed repeatedly in English classes.[6]

I have played out Bourdieu's grand and dispiriting metaphor because the New Literacy proposes setting this writing business on another footing which does not depend on this single linguistic investment in correctness and propriety, in the advantages of a certain upbringing in the language. It diminishes the deceptive aspect of a "hidden curriculum" based on differences in cultural capital. With great panache, it first does away with the pretense that writing is taught by the schools (to those students "willing and able" to learn). The New Literacy is founded on the premise that, indeed, students have already developed profitable forms of communication when they arrive at school. As students show up at school with a variety of cultural resources, these diverse forms of capital become a rich source of learning and literacy, but this embarrassment of riches can best be realized through expression, through writing. The diversity is what gives it this potential for contributing meaning to the classroom and that diversity is simply waiting to be utilized by a program that understands communication to be a dual process of reaching in to reach out.

But I would pause for a moment here over the very persistence of the traditional process of teaching writing, before moving on to its reform. While the political machinations which Bourdieu has uncovered were not likely to be apparent to teachers busily correcting grammar and spelling exercises, neither had many teachers been deterred in the least by the large body of evidence attesting to the ineffectiveness of grammar instruction in improving writing. Given that this evidence against grammar began to accumulate in 1906 and has been building in various forms and settings over the course of this century, it should have been surprising that well into the 1970s I was still planning my language lessons in my daybook with the likes of "Commas: Take up Ex. 6–7 and assign Ex 6–8, No. 1–10, p. 123."[7] However, I can't help suspecting that I was well accompanied on a global scale, and certainly the fact that the principal of my school was teaching grammar in the grade ahead of me had something to do with my taking it up. Suffice it to say that we were motivated by something other than the evidence of improved writing from our classrooms or the research from abroad. We had other grounds as well. For one thing, spelling and grammar classes were the very stuff of good teaching; they lent themselves to an easy and systematic process of planning, delivery, and evaluation. But this was far removed from the daydreams of powerful writers and successful writing which many of us carried around with us from a time before we had become such easy and systematic teachers.

The New Literacy opened the door to this other sort of learning about writing. It opened the English classroom door to the richness of students' language and it turned the mystery of writing from its association with the teacher's authority to the world within the student and outside of classroom. The wedge that was used to open this jammed classroom door was often a matter of research into writing. If the old ways represented artifice and the new the natural, then it was incumbent on the advocates of the New Literacy to establish the true nature of writing-in-the-world. This pursuit of writing-in-the-world draws its lessons for the classroom from two sorts of writers who actually write in any quantity—the student writer and the professional writer.

The idea of pursuing the processing habits of the "serious" author has always brought to my mind an image of the intrepid researcher boarding a plane to Paris and finding a table at, perhaps, the Brasserie Rimbaud in order to closely observe the methods of a *real* writer on a *real* arts grant developing her *real* process, as it moved between cafe table in the sun and garret overlooking the Seine. The time at the cafe, why it must be prewriting! (I recall the parallel in my own life which was, I suppose, finding my writing process in a lunch booth at the Small Fry Restaurant tucked between the Trans-Canada Highway and the American border; I filled those small black spiral notebooks with a prewriting notation that was nearly sufficient to carry me, in poetic fashion, through the high school years.) However, rather than heading to cafes or greasy spoons, the writing researchers have spent more of their time in classrooms. They do turn for the processing of professionals to the *Paris Review* interviews where they can learn, among other things, how William Faulkner began his process with "paper, tobacco, food and a little whisky":

> *Interviewer*: Bourbon, you mean?
> *Faulkner*: No, I ain't that particular. Between scotch and
>   nothing, I'll take scotch. (Cowley, 1957, p. 125)

It is little wonder that the researchers have turned their eyes to younger writers who are more likely to tolerate, if not outright enjoy, the additional attention.

In this case, the effort to learn from the writing practices of students has proved to be a happy marriage of educational research and leadership. This is more than the old research story of the observer subtly affecting the observed. This research deliberately sets out to recover the lessons that might be learned from the under-utilized potential of these students' ability to make their own way as writers. The conception of language and literacy advanced by this process cannot help but undermine the traditional notions of literacy in the classroom. In this manner, an effective case has been built for programs that minimize the interference pattern that schools tend to generate against this natural progress.

The processing of a method

If there is but one specific teaching strategy of the New Literacy that has caught on in a generic sense, beyond any sense of identification with a single group or school, it is "writing process." Many teachers pick it up for their first taste of the New Literacy, and it has become something of its own orthodoxy in the teaching of instruction. But with this widespread acceptance of the concept, distortions inevitably ensue. New Literacy advocates have found it necessary to move on to a *post-process* approach in pursuing this elusive model of writing in the real world. A short history of the development of this process will be instructive in setting out the challenge to education the New Literacy poses and the challenges it has yet to face in its own development.

The writing process might be said to have evolved out of the relatively harmless introduction of a "prewriting" stage to the college composition class. Richard Rohman is given credit for this important coinage; it appears in his essay "Pre-Writing: The Stage of Discovery in the Writing Process" (1965). His original definition prefigures the expressive mode of writing and the student's independence, both of which later came to play such an important part in the New Literacy: for Rohman prewriting is "when a person assimilates his 'subject' to himself" (p. 106). This gradual taking in of the topic certainly made more sense than asking students to write by sitting before a blank page in a classroom of enforced silence, while waiting for the words to appear *ex nihilo*. The concept of "prewriting" allows for a warm-up exercise, which built up a little momentum and a few leads for the writing to follow. The quintessential prewriting exercise is what became known as brain-storming, with the ideas letting fly like bolts of lightning. This was enough to alter the structure of the classroom in the most subtle of manners—a little loose thinking and rough writing were to be allowed. That was the first step in suggesting that learning to write might be, in part, a process of learning from oneself.

But the New Literacy needed a bigger push than a little brain-storming to get under way. One breakthrough came from the Bay Area Writing Project which mobilized teacher interests in California and has since spread across the country in the form of the National Writing Project, in what has amounted to "the most positive development in English education during the 1970s," in James Moffett's estimation (1981, p. 81). With foundation and government support, the Project created summer programs at Berkeley and other sites that involved large numbers of teachers working and writing together. The two guiding principles of the Bay Area Project was that the best teachers of teachers were teachers themselves, and that teachers of writing should write. They do write and teach, producing newsletters, collections and booklets, professional pieces on teaching. A third principle of the Project has been its general eclecticism, its openness to a host of ideas and strategies for enhancing writing. It has taken up the writing process and done a good deal to promote it, and yet the Project has not become associated with the development of any one strategy; it serves as a model of grass-roots involvement and implementation which built on major statements in the field by others.

One of the early and one of the bravest of the statements from this period is Peter Elbow's *Writing without Teachers* (1973). In his work with college students, he dispensed with the authoritarian figure at the front of the classroom and the writing had bloomed. This attack on the divide between teacher and student was also on the relationship between meaning and language. In what now seems to be a fundamental challenge to a "meaning-first" tenet of the New Literacy, Elbow attacked what he identified as the commonsense, conventional "two-step process" in composition: "first you figure out your meaning, then you put it into language" (p. 14). The separation of these two concepts, which he saw afflicting college writing programs, also, interestingly enough, continues to be a danger for theorists of the New Literacy (although you will have to wait patiently until Chapter 8 for a full discussion of the point). For his part, Elbow sets writing first, while letting the refinement of meaning follow as a result of the writing; he dislodges the student-writer's block through the headlong rush of "freewriting"—just let the language within you pour onto the page—a technique which had also become widely known through Daniel Fader's *Hooked on Books* program (Fader & McNeil, 1968). Elbow removes the need for a "teacher" by treating each student as a reader/listener whose responses to a work can help the writer. This element of sharing your work remains a mainstay of the New Literacy. The persistent problem of how to teach writing was solved by going teacherless; Elbow found writing to be a matter of "growth," and more vividly, "cooking," with the word simmering upon the page.

The fact is that for many of us freewriting did work an initial miracle. Teachers who tried it experienced the pleasure of watching their students bent over their page, many for the first time, pouring out words pain-lessly. It had the distinct and appealing look of a classroom full of engaged writers. While freewriting helped students overcome the initial and formidable hurdle of getting underway on the page, it had little to offer in strategies for making something more of these pages of free flowing writing that soon began to build up in students' notebooks. This was an old problem of linking the productive exercise and the natural process. The exercise is in preparation, but then, one asks, what is the goal beyond that, the natural end of all this writing?

On returning to Elbow's text, I find that it proves short, in its anti-authoritarian pose, on a sense of purpose for writing. The mood is one of "let's get this writing thing going; it's easier than you think." Still, Elbow (and Fader) had with great simplicity undone the mystery and opened the gates of a writing process that could be shared by everyone. As it has turned out, freewriting was still too much like a practice exercise to survive the real-world emulation of the New Literacy; it was the substitution of one formula for another, and not yet the clear break with the old manners. Elbow offered his students a method that worked, and it remains one option for students freely writing their way into meaning.

The missing element in this sea of freewriting is the guiding light of the writer's intentions. Free as it is, the writing suffered a want of focus, to shape it into a steady stream of sense. Elbow's conviction that writing was a manner of self-discovery has held in the New Literacy, but introducing a greater place for the point of intention was a necessary and sophisticated advance for the writer in control.

However, during this period, intentionality in writing was finding a place across the ocean in Alan Bullock's now-famous report for the British government, *A Language for Life* (Bullock, 1975). James Britton (1982a) was a member of this Committee of Inquiry, and although he complains of the compromises entailed in arriving at consensus, the report provided a degree of official impetus to his ideas and those under discussion in this book, and to a surprising degree for a report commissioned by the then Secretary of State for Education, Margaret Thatcher.[8] The report offered a series of what might be taken as New Literacy responses to the literacy crisis which had sparked the official inquiry; it provided both substance and direction for the British schools in a manner which is not possible in Canada or United States, where education is a provincial and state matter. To use this example of intentionality and free-writing as an instance, *A Language for Life* brings together a strong sense of purpose to writing within a balance of personal and "corporate" interests:

> In our view the main stream of activity in the area of "personal writing" should arise from a continually changing context, not a prepared stimulus. The context will be created by the

corporate enterprises of the classroom and the individual
interests and experiences of the students, cumulatively shared
with the teacher and the rest of the group. Moreover, the
writing should be constantly developing in its capacity to fulfil
the demands this context produces. Whenever spontaneity is
exclusively valued this kind of development can be inhibited.
Children reach a point where they need new techniques, having
run through the satisfaction of their spontaneous performances.
. . . The solution lies in the recognition on the part of the
teacher that a writer's intentions are prior to his need for
techniques. The teacher who aims to extend the pupil's powers
as a writer must therefore work upon his intentions, and *then*
upon the techniques appropriate to them. (Bullock, 1975,
p. 164, original emphasis)

In pulling together these strands from Elbow and Bullock, and through
the benefit of hindsight, we can see the New Literacy beginning to take
shape around a scheme that placed intention before technique, but also
intention before the specification of meaning which might develop
through freewriting, brain-storming or whatever "prewriting" activity
might be undertaken. Think of it as unfolding an alternative road map
into writing which charts a new landscape for students and teachers,
beginning with Intention and moving through Exploration on the way to
Technique. It was quite the reverse of the tradition it was confronting,
and it promised whole new territories to explore for all concerned.

Although the Bullock report spoke against the use of "prepared stimu-
lus" for personal and preliminary writing, these early prewriting and
freewriting activities were still staged like formal lessons, to be completed before the actual writing could begin. The writing process soon
developed into something of a three-stage method, with classes set aside
for prewriting activity, for drafting and drafting, and for sharing and
editing the work. In sum, the writing had to come from something, had
to be worked, and had to be going somewhere as well. The variations
on this quest for the ideal writing process are plentiful; although nowhere
near as fully developed as the research industry behind developing
reading models which I will take a look at in the next chapter, the New
Literacy has produced a dozen different variations on the writing process
(neatly summarized in Boomer, 1985, pp. 132–45). The primary inclination is to represent it through a number of steps, between three and five,
with the more recent ones opting for a "recursive" element suggesting

a certain flexibility. Among the more organic depictions of the writing process, James Britton and his research associates offered the vital set of "conception," "incubation," and "production" (Britton et al., 1975).

However, as I indicated earlier, the danger persists of packaging the writing process into discrete stages and a 1-2-3 step sequence. This substitution of process exercises for grammar lessons does not encourage students to take charge of the meanings on the page. Teachers were turning process into a "recipe," and gaining little of writing's organic, fluid and, ultimately, recursive nature (Knoblauch & Brannon, 1984). For just such reasons, Applebee, Langer, and Mullis (1986), in their analysis of the National Assessment results, have come to question the effectiveness of "new instructional approaches" in the writing process: "Students are not learning to link process activities with problems they face in their own writing" (p. 13). The danger, as Donald Graves (1984) realized after a few years of promoting the New Literacy, is that the radical innovation soon becomes the new orthodoxy—with such distortions as "compulsory revision"—and what was once organic loses its lithe resilience.[9] This hardening of the categories and stages is to be cured by allowing the process to follow the rhythms and developing writing habits of students: they might, after completing a full draft, return to a prewriting search for new materials to bolster the piece; they might be encouraged to apply the process to writing in other subject areas or in their response to literature.

A second and related ailment that strikes the writing process is an over-processing of writing that might have been well enough left alone. To move across the Atlantic again for the corrective measure, James Britton rightly senses the contradiction, although he does not set it out in these terms, that has emerged between a trusting of the language impulses—"hearing an inner voice"—and the pervasive (and teachable) incursion of the writing process model: "And does our present concern with pre-planning, successive drafting and revision suggest that in taking oil-painting as our model for writing we may be underestimating the value of 'shaping at the point of utterance' and hence cutting off what might prove the most effective approach to an understanding of rhetorical invention" (1980, p. 65).

This evolving conception of the writing process has also influenced the researcher's perception of the pre-schooler. In *Language Stories and Literacy Lessons* (1984), Harste, Woodward, and Burke find an emergent literacy in the young child's mix of drawing and scribble-writing. Advocates of the New Literacy had already found this work to be promising instances of prewriting (Graves, 1983; Myers, 1983). But Harste, Woodward, and Burke are ready to find in it something more. After reminding readers early in the book that "language teaching and language learning are rooted in belief" (p. ix), they set out to alter nothing less than our beliefs about writing. They claim that this early scribble-writing is not prewriting, but writing itself, prior to nothing. It is "writing" as it serves to record semantic meaning for the writer. It seems worth noting that more than their powers of observation are at work in this discovery; it is part of the natural theoretical progression intent on the breakdown of the artificial distinctions which schools are given to perpetuating.

This blurring of the boundaries of literacy writing is part of the move away from the "pseudoconcept" of a stage theory that Knoblauch and Brannon have challenged with such pointed questions as "Does thinking casually about the subject while brushing one's teeth constitute prewriting? Is Life prewriting?" (1984, p. 89). It suggests that *all writing is real writing*. The extension work here is in line with Donald Murray's efforts to relate the practices of students with the work habits of accomplished authors. We have broken with the traditional containment of writing by the school and opened it at both ends. It is opened to the preschool literacy experiences of children and to the work and habits of the professional writer who works from beyond the end of schooling. The classroom becomes a station on the line of a literate life, a life that will not be so neatly compartmentalized in its learning.

The London School

The Institute of Education at University of London has been a center for such advocates of the New Literacy as James Britton, John Dixon, Nancy Martin, Margaret Meek, and Harold Rosen. Through the 1970s, their influence spread as the London School became the dominant force in the National Association for the Teaching of English, eclipsing "the Cambridge School" under the leadership of literary critic F. R. Leavis and those who carried his sense of English's moral mission to the schools, such as Denys Thompson, Frank Whitehead, and Fred Inglis (Ball, 1988). The Cambridge School saw instruction in literature as salvation against the deadening effects of a society in decline, and exhausting work it was: "We find ourselves compelled to expend much of our energy in a ceaseless struggle against the mainstream of contemporary 'mass-civilization,' and we may be forgiven if we are sometimes a little discouraged" (Whitehead, 1966, p. 57). In something of an about turn in the face of this discouragement, the London School embraced the living language and culture of students as the new point of engagement in learning for the student. And as educational historian Stephan Ball points out, "for the majority of London teachers, that meant primarily the lives, culture and language of the working class" (1988, pp. 21). It was a conscious political move that clearly promoted the stature of writing and self-expression in the curriculum.

Among the early and more influential research statements from the London School is *The Development of Writing Abilities, 11–18* (1975) by James Britton, Tony Burgess, Nancy Martin, Alex MacLeod, and Harold Rosen. The book is a major theoretical statement underwritten by the extensive research conducted on the state of writing and writing abilities among British students. We are encouraged to trust students as legitimate informants on the process of writing. Students are considered in control, making decisions about writing that researchers can learn from: "The strength of their conviction that a new start must be made, even though the teacher may have no complaints about what has been written, is sometimes remarkable" (p. 34).

But the lessons are bolstered by another, more powerful device for bringing about a change in the teaching of writing. Although the "writing process" is addressed in an early chapter in the book, what becomes the driving idea of this version of the New Literacy is that writing can be classified on the basis of its function and audience and that such divisions served to document the manner in which the schools failed to draw on writing's full potential as a learning tool, as well as making the most of students' potential as writers. As the book of Genesis demonstrates, divisions make all the difference in the creation of the world. Equally so, we are given to an epistemology by classification or the making of knowledge by the rule of divide and conquer. In this case, *Development of Writing Abilities, 11–18* opens with the caution that "we classify at our peril" (p. 1) and goes on to present what has proved to be the most pervasive classification system of written language in the New Literacy: writing falls into either an *expressive, transactional,* or *poetic* mode, while writers take on *participant* or *spectator* roles.

To briefly review these well-known divisions, the *expressive* encompasses writing in which the student is engaged in figuring things out on an informal and personal level. The *transactional* mode is marked by an impersonal and business-like nature; the writer acts as a *participant* in this mode (as a further, complementary category) by using writing to get things done. The *poetic*, while it may still retain expressive elements, has an artfulness prepared for public consumption, with the writer entering the *spectator* role, in which writing is an end in itself.[10] But of the three modes and two roles, it is hard to exaggerate the importance of creating a space for "expressive" language in the schools. Britton and company point out that the concept of an expressive mode is drawn from the work of the anthropologist Edward Sapir. In their words, "expressive language signals the self, reflects not only the ebb and flow of a speaker's thought and feeling, but also the assumptions of shared contexts of meaning, and of a relationship of trust with his listener" (p. 10).

Once they had pointed out the psychological and intellectual value of this expressive mode of talking and writing, the second step was to show its absence from current practice in the schools. The research team headed by James Britton gathered 2,000 pieces of students' writing from across the subject areas which were divided among the categories of the transactional, poetic, and expressive. They found that the majority of the writing (63 percent) was in the transactional mode including short-answers, essays, book reviews, and reports. The poetic or creative writing mode accounted for 18 percent of the sample, with almost all of it taking place in English class. The schools were paying little mind to the powerful area of expressive writing; only 6 percent of the writing had that personal, almost "inner-speech" quality, in which students are thought to be able to work out and integrate ideas, and that small percentage was also restricted to English class. The figures are meant to emphasize the imbalance and the missed opportunities to utilize and practice the very intellectual and communicating powers of the written word. The resulting increase in this mode of writing in British schools is attested to by the Barnes's study a decade later which found English classes did a good deal of their writing in this expressive mode. It goes a long way in establishing the power of a category, as it can create a new field of endeavor where it seems only to organize (Barnes & Barnes, 1984, pp. 80–84).

The London School had launched a substantial critique of modern schooling, not only for its failure to produce writing that has any heart or soul to it, but also, and more deeply troubling, for the school's tendency to set students off from their own experience, their own community of experience, and ultimately their own language. Although social class does not enter the discussion for the most part in Britton's work, it is clearly relevant as Peter Medway makes poignantly plain in his book, *Finding a Language* (1980). To suggest that not only is expressive language at the root of talk, but that it is the very manner of making sense of the world is, I think it fair to say, a large part of the educational accomplishment of the New Literacy. Out of this follows the possibility of creating a new situation for writing, students, and teachers in the classroom. The paucity of expressive and poetic opportunities in the curriculum was easily demonstrated and this proved a powerful way of drawing attention to the narrow and ultimately disengaging nature of writing in the schools. The school was simply wasting this educational opportunity, especially as the expressive lead so naturally led into such powerful language forms as narrative: "We also underestimate the somewhat mysterious power of story writing, which provides a drive which just is not there in transactional writing, a drive which gives greater length and fluency to slow learners and which carries them over some of the language barriers" (Martin, 1983, p. 166). Expressive writing has increasingly become a legitimate vehicle for learning in the classroom.

There have also been efforts to incorporate the American emphasis on the writing process into the London School: "Expressive writing is appropriate for first drafts and therefore offers enfranchisement—though more able students may get by without it—to all writers, but it is crucial for beginning writers and slow learners" (Martin, 1983, p. 163). Yet it is not a clean fit; the differences among the three London School modes are better thought of as matters of voice and audience rather than stages of manuscript processing. That is not to deny that much can be gained by comparing New Literacy innovations in both countries. The writing process has created a space for expressive writing in the American classroom, but it leaves the expressive as something unfinished, in need of revision, which is not Britton's intention for it at all. Equally so, poetic and transactional writing does not always begin in expressive writing, especially if students are interested in imitating a certain form and taking on a specific voice. And yet the possibilities for the writing process can grow by incorporating an easy flow between expressive and transactional or poetic writing. The enfranchisement is not only in retaining a degree of personal voice, but also in increasing power over the production of different forms of discourse for different audiences.

The New Hampshire School

In America there was a similar move to acquire detailed observation of what students were up to when they wrote things down. Janet Emig's close observation of twelfth grade students (1971) formed an early model for this work, but a more influential program was launched by Donald Graves, beginning the same year as *The Development of Writing Abilities, 11–18* (1975). Graves and his research associates at the University of New Hampshire have conducted a number of studies of students in the primary grades (Calkins, 1983; Hansen, 1987; Hubbard, 1985; Murray, 1982). The key to understanding this research program is its melding of innovation, implementation, and documentation. The studies are often collaborations between teacher and researcher as they fashion a writing process for students which restructures both the teaching and the writing around the unfolding of what is taken to be the child's discovery of meaning on the page. The student-writer finds a topic of personal interest and through prewriting exercises and conferences with peers and teachers begins to develop a piece which through revision and editing may make its way to classroom publication or performance. The researcher works with the teacher in building a supportive environment for these lessons as the students find and share their way in writing.

As teachers have worked with researchers in leading students to the pleasures of a writing process that begins with their own meanings, it has tended to rub off on the teachers who are soon writing and publishing their own reports and studies (Atwell, 1987; Giacobbe, 1984; Romano, 1987). Rather than a research intent on isolating the variables in this approach to writing, validating the measures of its performance and plumbing for significant differences, this attempts the self-demonstrating project. The work of the students and teachers speaks for itself. Yet I would not dismiss the charge against the New Hampshire School that they are speaking *to* themselves by ignoring the forcefulness in the educational community of quantitative research. But leaving aside the comparative research question for Chapter 6, this School has found a new writing process for children and found it by looking into the ways of their writing.

To take one important example, Graves discovered in his early work that young writers often rehearsed their work through talking or drawing before actually writing. Graves turned the gesture into the process; the child's habit is moved from disruptive or idle behavior into the realm of

44

"prewriting."[11] The students are informants for this research, but the researcher is building a new regime for the classroom, a new understanding of the student, out of the students' gestures. It is a recovery project of budding student competencies, as if they are already writers with something to teach other writers. This is, in itself, part of this shift in meaning as learning to write is to learn to find a process, a method, in oneself rather than in the method prescribed by teachers at the front of classrooms who do not think enough of it to try it themselves. Another element in this starting with a sense of students' competency is drawing the parallels with professional writers. Graves has pointed out that, just like professional writers, students have good and bad days, bursts of brilliance and agonizing slumps, with their writing. The characterization of the children in Graves's work—"six-year-old Dana speaks to himself as he writes" (1983, p. 61)—suggests that these students are writers who have begun to find their way and can teach us about writing in the process. They are credited with, by virtue of this research process, the idiosyncratic writing habits that mark the folklore of the author-artist. By watching these students closely for the first time, it seems, Graves is able to recover their writerly sensibility, treating it and its nurturance as the promising basis of this new program.

An interesting test of Graves's ability to harness this power of observation in his program's favor is with the mundane question of handwriting. The improvement of handwriting might well seem inescapably a skill and drill matter. Yet in response to teachers' concerns about developing a disciplined cursive writing style, he simply describes a scene in which a teacher is chatting with a student about how the student can use handwriting to exert greater control over meaning and space on the page (1984, pp. 82–91). Similarly with spelling, the process begins with the child's initial efforts at invented spelling forms. This sounding out in search of the letters creates its own phonic lessons for the young writer. But in this process, meaning is still to come before accuracy, and only gradually does the student refine the spelling in order to reach a wider audience.[12]

While certainly this keen observer of children knows what he is looking for and is adept, it seems, at noting engaging instances thereof, the result is that he has been able to offer something very convincingly like a "grounded theory" of the student as a writer. The work of this school remains sensitive to the practical demands of classroom organization and to the concerns of teachers trying to imagine how they will fare with this alternative practice. Yet there is less consideration given, with these teachers and children busily at work, to what they are eagerly writing toward.

Graves does turn to the importance of "voice" at one point: "Voice is the imprint of ourselves on our writing" (1983, p. 227). But this call to voice is ultimately tuned to advancing the work at hand; he illustrates the importance of voice by showing what it adds to students' writing. On the one hand, I admire the modesty on Graves's part, as he avoids making grandiose claims for writing in schools; he stays close, in this way, to what can be observed in the classrooms that he visited and helpful in his advice to interested teachers. As opposed to Britton, he offers little theorizing and no taxonomies of writing modes or stages. On the other hand, I think it a fair question to ask what a program of this potential makes of writing, as well as what it makes of the child and the teacher in the process, even if it is busy answering other sorts of queries.

Graves appears to find the importance of writing in a need the child has for expression. His initial premise is that "children want to write" (1983, p. 3) which may come as a surprise to many teachers (and students). He challenges the schools to find a place in the timetable for the expression of such a desire while implying that the schools have played some part in its typical and unproductive dissipation. In the development of this New Hampshire School, Graves has found a manner of bringing the child's desire in line with the work of the school. The literacy lesson turns from the acquisition of skills to the finding and expression of a meaning that begins within. As a result of sitting among these happily engaged student-writers, Graves has isolated the function of the writing class in its special service to the child.

Graves casts this expression of desire and desire for expression as the point of a personal and social realization for the child:

> Children need to write every day and receive a response to their voices, to know what comes through so that they might anticipate the self-satisfaction and the *vision* of the imprint of their information on classmates or the *vision* of their work in publication. It is the forward *vision,* as well as the backward vision, that ultimately lead to major breakthroughs in a child's writing. (1983, p. 160, original emphasis)

This cascade of visions results in "major breakthroughs in a child's writing." The process and the vision can easily seem trapped in the search for improved performance; writing meant to enhance writing. While this may be true to the temper of the times and its prevalent concerns with test performance, I still feel something more must lurk in Graves's work. Consider how in this passage cited above, he puts his emphasis on the satisfaction which the process affords the child, of something desired and met by the daily work of writing. It is the social location of this pleasure—in the smiles of classmates—that goes beyond Graves's more explicit and circular points about writing: we write out of a need to express, and that the process of writing leads to break-throughs in learning about writing. That sense of connection ("imprint of their information," if you will) can dispel what can otherwise seem the essential self-absorption or solipsism of the act. It holds the seeds of both Wallace Stevens's sense of poetry's complacent pleasures and Janet Epps's moral indignation at writing's place at the gates of a just society, both the personal and public elements of literacy.

Graves does set this child-writer within an educational landscape that can seem at times to be made up of aspiring professionals and their consultants. Together they confer, testing out their ideas about the production of this once rarefied commodity of student writing. But the underlying terms of support for this program remain highly individual-ized in the child; the teacher is self-effacing and the world beyond the classroom windows is completely out of sight, except as the child cares to bring it in and set it on the page. What more goes on with writing, as it acts as Epps's gate-keeper or as it tells the stories of some people over others, is left unspoken at this point by Graves's conception of the writing process. He has altered the social conditions of its production in imitation of how he believes writing might be thought to *naturally* occur. This lessons-from-a-child approach of the New Hampshire School has proven an effective means of restructuring the place of writing in the classroom; the next step is to learn more from the larger context of writing in the world, as literacy is the constant site of social struggle, empowerment, and disenfranchisement.

Closely watched students serve as one guiding light for the New Literacy; yet another light, if somewhat lesser in intensity, is the work of the professional writer. Among the most eloquent exponents of the take-it-from the-pros approach is Pulitzer-winner turned writing-teacher, Donald Murray. In an exemplary piece of New Hampshire School didac-ticism, Murray attacks the traditional writing class for demanding essays during forty-minute periods by calling on the appearance of the writer: "When publishing writers visit such classrooms, however, they are astonished at students who can write on command, ejaculating correct little essays without thought, for writers have to write before writing" (1986, p. 37). Murray follows this with a defense of such writerly foibles as periods of resistance-to-writing supported by cites from the personal experiences of writers Dillard, Kafka, Levertov, and Wordsworth. And although the list of notables goes on, what is also important to under-standing the ways in which the New Literacy rhetoric works is that Murray takes as his other source of authority the observations of his colleague Donald Graves. In this case his observation of children "re-hearsing" their work through drawings and talk can be fitted to the reflections of Edward Albee: "All of a sudden I discover what I have been thinking about a play" (p. 40). The humbling of the writer in this process—as Albee stumbles across the meaning of his work—must be seen as part of the levelling process, a redistribution of the goods on writing, which the New Literacy brings as part of its promise to teacher and student.

The honors that are freshly shared in this linking of professional and child writing within the setting of the English class are, I would argue, as much the teachers' as the children's. Murray elevates the teaching of writing with students of any age to an act of cultural participation with the pantheon of literary heroics; the struggles, the breakdowns, and breakthroughs that sweep through the classroom are connected to the literary activities that take place for writers in offices, greasy spoons, garrets, and cafes. The student is offered a new model to write by, but then so is the teacher; the teacher can trade in the role of lab-coated psychologist administering the proper sequence of learning activities in favor of the impresario assisting the artist wrestling with the soul of writing. In the first chapter, I alluded to the way in which the teacher in the New Literacy becomes literary agent, editor, and publisher—again note the emulation of the real world of writing—but added to this is a final element of commingled roles, as the teacher also becomes a student of writing and begins to risk that blank page in search of another voice not often heard in the classroom. And the student, in turn, becomes the teacher.

New Hampshire conferences and workshops

If there is to be writing without teachers, at least without teachers explicitly teaching, what becomes the new line of work? What are teachers to do after stepping down from the platform at the front of the classroom while the self-taught students pursue their own projects, stories, and voices? And if they do step down, is it still a classroom? Not to leave the teachers unemployed, the New Literacy encourages them to take up the pen and processor to work on their own stories. But more than that, they are invited to consult with the students—editor to writer, writer to writer—in developing their work and skills, as professionals often do, establishing a different relationship, moving much closer to one that works between client and professional. At the center of this relationship is the scheduled conference in which teacher and student sit down together to discuss the progress of the work at hand. The writing conference has been developed most notably by Donald Graves, again in association with the teachers with whom he, in turn, has collaborated in his research on writing. He places it at the heart of what he terms "the writing process movement." It is a one-on-one meeting with the student which is intended, through a cleverly staged collaborative process, to facilitate, nurture, instruct and ultimately clear the work for publication. Students, beginning in the first grade, are encouraged through these brief sessions to maintain control over their work while learning how to question and listen to it.

To assist teachers with the setting up of the conference in the classroom, Graves has provided his own set of scripts in *Writing: Teachers and Children at Work* (1983). He goes so far as to offer a schematic drawing of the seating arrangement showing both the right way to conference ("role of advocate"), with chairs side by side, and the wrong way ("role of adversary") with a desk between them (p. 98). The scripts of sample conferences between teacher and student emphasize the way in which the teacher repeatedly works her opening line ("How is your piece coming, Greg?") and other stock questions. Students are led to tell their story as well as their concerns with the work, and the teacher stays focused on the writing task ("There is good specific information here"). The teacher deliberately avoids responding to the content, which seems a little odd in the case of an excited description of the damage the weapons of war can cause (pp. 120–23). Graves stresses the limited duration of the conference which is indeed crucial to consulting with a classroom of writers; he provides the times for the scripts and they tend to range from half a minute to four minutes. The longest in this series involves a student punctuating sentences by ear in preparation for publication, as the teacher challenges these writers with "Convince me that it is ready to go as it is."

While the conference offers the most individualized of learning situations, it also takes on, in Graves's presentation, a certain formulaic
aspect; the teacher's scripted parts seem to rely on the same repeated
prompts. The student cannot help but eventually internalize the pattern,
which may well result in the odd case of parody—"How's *your* piece
coming, Dr. Graves?" (to which Graves might point out that he has
addressed the book *A Researcher Learns To Write* to that very question).
Yet this repetitious aspect is intended to engrain in the writer the sort of
editorial questions that are bound to be asked of a text. The student can
figure out that, ultimately, it's all on the writer to ask of the text and
decide its state of completeness, although it is good to have someone
with whom to hash things over.[13]

The conference is a first step in redefining the classroom. A further
move in evolving a suitable environment for the realization of these
lessons from real and student writers is the setting up of a writing
"workshop," with all its implications of productive labor and craft. The
workshop has become something of a classroom ideal from the primary
classroom to the college composition course. But also consistent with
the New Literacy theme of deschooling/reschooling, Lucy Calkins describes the writing workshop as the classroom practice which can break
through all that has made schooling inimical to the life of the student:
"The workshop has none of the emotional flatness that characterizes
most of the school day. The content of the writing workshop is the
content of real life, for the workshop begins with what each student
thinks, feels, and experiences, and with the human urge to articulate and
understand experience" (1986, p. 8). The idealism of this workshop
connects the individual to the real life of work and production.

Among teachers who have taken up the workshop, Nancie Atwell
provides an important document in the implementation of the New
Literacy with her book, *In the Middle* (1987).[14] A student of the New
Hampshire School like Calkins, Atwell describes the development of
her program teaching junior high school students in Boothbay Harbor,
Maine. She began with what I take as the opening moves of the New
Literacy, from "enforced ten-minute 'free' write" and her own writing
in front of the class—"But I wasn't writing; I was performing"—
followed by working through the writing categories of James Moffett's
"universe of discourse" with a new adventure scheduled each week in
the exploration of the galaxies within this universe in star-trek fashion
(Atwell, 1987, pp. 7, 9). With a little outside help and a good deal of
her own insight, she made her breakthrough into the workshopping of

writing, followed by parallel developments in reading, which I will take up in a subsequent chapter. The workshop in writing was much as one might imagine it, with students coming together to work on their own projects in this hobbyroom of tools and resources with the teacher taking her cues from student initiatives and interests to facilitate their work.

Atwell makes her case for workshopping on both pragmatic grounds (it is organized to work well) and on what I consider a psycho-ethical basis (this is closer to how students naturally learn and live). In terms of organization, she introduces a lesson infrastructure for her workshop period that begins with a "mini-lesson," conferences during the middle, and group sharing of work at the end. By way of record keeping, she maintains a set of "Teacher's Conference Records," "Skills Lists," and "Status of Class" sheets. Atwell is not afraid to deal with the institutional questions of time and motion management.[15] What has developed into the structuring of the daily hour-long workshop becomes a wholesome compromise with the nature of schooling and its need to organize time. She is very clearly drawn to the way the workshop brings the class and herself together, and she appreciates the psychic nurturance the writing provides one and all. Yet she remains sensitive to the charges of escapism laid against the similar education experiments of the 1960s.

She makes the case that this is indeed an engaging and workable recasting of possibilities in pursuit of a literate goal. In this spirit and following the pattern set by packaged reading programs, Atwell offers long lists of skills, goals, and questions that constitute her program coverage; she illuminates her work with strong examples of the students' and her own writing, from poems of despair to parodies of parents' letters to the teacher. She bolsters her case by citing increases in the test scores and the number of titles read by her workshopping students, if, perhaps, more often than necessary. But one cannot help feeling that her case for workshopping rests in its appeal as "a way of life" (p. 17).

As Atwell turns increasingly to the students and the workshop in her development as a teacher, her account becomes a story of shifting roles for teacher and student: "What I learn with these students, collaborating with them as a writer and a reader who wonders about writing and reading, makes me a better teacher . . . " (p. 3). The workshop offers her students a new level of responsibility: "Freedom of choice doesn't undercut structure. Instead, kids become accountable for developing and refining their own structures. Everyone sits at the big desk and everyone plans what will happen there" (p. 15). As part of the New Literacy's liberalizing transformation of the classroom, her own structuring of the class slips from view as she focuses the students' and our attention on their new responsibility.

Students busily taken up with their publishing projects in the workshop setting seem to have dissolved any questions about power and authority in the classroom, questions that tend to disrupt other classrooms at times. The workshop is following a pattern which the intellectual historian Michel Foucault (1980) has identified as an invisible circulation of power that has marked the rise of the middle class since the sixteenth century. This may be reaching a bit, in trying to find the sense that draws teachers to this form of education, but I feel it does rest in this manner of restructuring the institution and the work that goes on therein. The power which makes this space a classroom rather than coffee shop is still present but the teacher has found a way to circulate it through all the participants rather than lord it over them. I do not mean to condemn Atwell's writing program by this comparison, but it may prevent it from misrepresenting itself, from slipping into the magical thinking of the 1960s in which authority is thought to be dispelled and the classroom removed from the political state of education.

The fact is that Atwell moves in fashioning this program among the spirit and politics of different decades. She draws on what might pass as the executive-class language of these times—with the "accountability" of "the big desks"—while she builds her case for the workshop on an attack of schools which act as a "holding tank" for the young. The attack does sound a bit like a remake of such educational hits from the 1960s as Friedenberg's chart-topper, *The Vanishing Adolescent* (1959), if without something of the original sting: "Our junior high schools," she declares, "are structured to deny, or at least delay the satisfaction of our junior high students' needs, physical, intellectual, and social" (p. 36).

She also brings John Goodlad (1984) into her New Literacy critique, as he takes issue with the ways in which the tracking of students in high schools does needless damage to them for the convenience of programs (Atwell, 1987, pp. 38–40). Atwell points out that the workshop makes the homogeneity of the group pedagogically superfluous; but more than that, I would add, the workshop implicitly promises to undo the differences in students' relationship *to* language which the streams have tended to foster in students. The academic students have tended to work on building their case, fashioning their argument around the liabilities of kings and princes Macbeth and Hamlet, while the non-academics learn to practice their deficits in language (Oakes, 1986; Willinsky, 1988a).

Yet Atwell's comments on streaming are made only in passing, although her program contains this substantial critique on this structural aspect of schooling. She seems to forget that the student named Jeff, from whom she learned her first lessons in the New Literacy, was a candidate for the non-academic stream. The workshop approach grew out of a need to meet this sort of student, and more importantly, perhaps, the workshop could be the difference for Jeff between finding a voice on the page and remaining silenced, in a literal way. The workshop is more than an attractive method of having students learn to write with confidence and interest; it is part of a larger politics of the educational promise which Atwell has only begun openly to address through the New Literacy.

One way of continuing to explore this promise is to consider how the workshop fits within the New Literacy's effort to emulate writing-in-the-world. Where in the world, one might ask, is the model for this writing workshop to be found? They fall for the most part within the sponsorship of educational institutions, from The Bread Loaf Conference set in the Green Mountains of Vermont to The Writer's Studio at Banff in the Canadian Rockies which dominate the horizon outside my office window. But I would offer another, less comfortable and romantic, workshop model for the New Literacy. This one comes closer to the sense which Jeff offers of a student gaining a new sense of power in a system that had previously tended to deny any basis for it. Gerald Gregory (1984) has described the emergence of a small "community publishing" movement among working class groups in Britain who have taken up the writing, editing, and publishing of voices otherwise unheard. It returns a certain justice to the original sense of workshop, and picks up on William Morris's revival of the concept with his Kelmscott Press and other craft ventures in response to the de-skilling of the trades by industrial forms of mass production. Toward the close of the last century, Morris used the workshop in his effort to restore a medieval sense of craft as the basis of a socialism that stands against the commercial degradation of art and life for the worker.[16]

Although there is just as great a temptation to romanticize the writing of workers as there is with young students, Gregory speaks of the factors that motivate this writing and publishing as deeply felt and highly politicized:

Passionate conviction about the intrinsic value of working-class culture . . . especially those solidarities that underpin its outstanding and unique institutional achievements (e.g., of

trade union, political and mutual help associations); a
determined refusal to stay marginalized; indignation and
impatience at being represented, misrepresented, patronized and
abused by outsiders; these have fuelled the drive to write rather
than be written (or not), publish rather than be published (or
not) and, increasingly, to theorize rather than be theorized.
(1984, pp. 222–23)

The points of appeal bear an unmistakable connection with the work of
New Literacy. This seems more like what is meant by the deep need to
write which the New Literacy calls on, especially compared to preparing
efficient memo-drafters and brief-writers able to work to task with their
colleagues after a short conference with the authorities. That does seem
a little unfair, and I do not mean by this to be unduly hard on the
intentions of those promoting the New Literacy; I only wish to press
ahead with the unasked questions about what we do intend by this work
with writing.

In *The Republic of Letters* (Maguire et al., 1982), the authors make
it clear that the worker writers, of the sort that Gregory describes, are
prepared to confront the marginal status of their work as a lesson about
literacy which they feel they must challenge. They attempt, by their own
example, to "disestablish" literature whether in the unconventional form
of their writing or by directly addressing the complacent state of literature
within the schools. Such is the mission and inspiration of this series of
workshops and writing organizations.

But it is not only a class issue, as the publishing workshop has been
equally taken up by feminist writers and publishers. Again it serves to
extend the degree of literary enfranchisement through the sort of collective sensibility and strength that can be facilitated by a "workshop"
setting. For Atwell, the workshop is a redefinition of the traditional
classroom; there is something to be found in this way of working with
language and writers that otherwise goes missing in the classroom. The
same is true of feminists' response to the publishing industry; Lynne
Spender has found that feminist publishing projects had also turned to
the workshop for those special qualities that Atwell sought: "The shared
commitment and the co-operative nature of the process produce rewards
that were not mentioned by the people involved in other publishing
organizations" (1983, pp. 103).

These modern instances of worker and feminist collectives pose one
possibility as a model of the writing workshop. If we have, as I believe,

a better way of teaching writing with the New Literacy, we still need to explore the limits of what we would dare in our classrooms when we begin by saying that "human beings have a deep need to represent their experience through writing" (Calkins, 1986, p. 3). The energy of the "political concern with cultural and personal dimensions," as Spender (1983, p. 103) refers to the feminist publishing project, has its parallel in the workshops of the New Hampshire School. Yet a look at these adult and political workshops also tests the limits of commitment of these junior versions to writing as a critical social enterprise as well as a project in individual development. This critical aspect is not so much absent as waiting on development. Atwell, for one, refers to her students' awakening interest in social issues of peace and pollution, and these interests are welcomed as sources for inspired and committed writing. It is carried even further by Ira Shor's (1977) work with open admissions college students; he turned the issues in the students' lives into directed inquiry and a writing project that produced documents on marriage, work, and other civil relationships. These documents were more than an expression of voice, more than a breakthrough in student writing. These students had entered a new public arena in which they had the opportunity to work out their ideas and make their case into a coherent statement. The writing out and thinking through was, in itself, a power of literacy that they had been missing and one that led to a critical recasting of the important structures in their lives.

The New Literacy has shop-floor aspirations. It transforms working conditions for student and teacher, as it moves the classroom into a collaborative and collective worksite. Not without a trace of irony, then, it might be said that the New Hampshire School offers in some ways a better apprenticeship for the community publishing projects of workers and feminists than for working within the competitive writing and publishing practices of New York City. However, as both the New Hampshire and London Schools still conceive of writing principally in terms of the individual's project, they leave behind the New Literacy's latent concerns with the social situation of the individual. That missing or at least underdeveloped element returns us to Janis Epps's concern with what writing must do for black students—"an analysis of who we are" (1985, p. 155)—with which I began this chapter. The workshop settings I have just described are motivated by more than a desire to foster the individual's story. They represent a common, critical project in the social dimensions of literacy and voice that begins with the students' own situation as writers and readers. Without the development of this critical element in the New Literacy, learning through expressive writing and the writing process, through conferences and workshops, will continue to leave much of the world untold.

Writing across the curriculum

The ethnographic research conducted by the advocates of this new approach would demonstrate, above all, that students have this great potential for expression in writing, and that rather than searching for the best technique of teaching writing, we need to set up an environment in which writing can be pursued and learned as a craft of practice and experience, rather than direct instruction. But in finding that writing has this untapped power, it becomes imperative to allow it to be realized more often in the school day than during English classes. As I intimated at the beginning of this chapter, the second element in the claim of writing has been its powers across the curriculum, given the right working conditions, as an engaging means to learning and knowledge.

This movement to encourage writing in the subject areas other than English and language arts suggests yet another way of looking at the project of the New Literacy. As I have described the agenda of these different programs up to this point much of what they intend appears to be boundary work. New Literacy programs are intent on diminishing the boundaries between home and school, teacher and student, speaking and writing, as it attempts to integrate these traditional dichotomies into the students' project with literacy. If writing can become a method of connecting, of integrating the learner into what is to be learned, then surely, the reasoning goes, this new form of writing could advance the state of learning in other subject areas. And likewise it would set in motion what Michael Marland has termed a "virtuous circle" as this new wave of writing would also produce more literate students (1977, p. 3).

As it turns out, these movements variously known as Writing Across the Curriculum or Language Across the Curriculum have won a good deal of official support which moved it to the policy level, and yet a policy that was to be developed by teachers in their own schools. The model here was the work of the London Association of Teachers of English (L.A.T.E.) which initiated its policy with the premise that "boys and girls in their attempts to master the school curriculum and in their process of growing up have to call upon their language resources"

(Rosen, 1969, p. 160). To assist in this marshalling of resources the policy outlines what have become the trademark strategies of language and writing across the curriculum: first there was to be talking, real talking, exploratory, speculative, fantastic talking in groups with some reflection on the language of the discipline; writing is to move toward the real and intrinsic in motivation, form, audience with much sharing and, again, reflection on the process and form; reading, too, should move beyond the traditional texts into the real and various world of print (pp. 162–68).

Following the L.A.T.E. work and the call for school language policies in *Language for Life* (Bullock, 1975), educational jurisdictions began to ask teachers in Great Britain and Canada to set about developing statements about language in the schools. On the positive side, this mandate to create policies gave rise to powerful discussion over the initial premise that language was at the center of learning, or as Douglas Barnes puts it with disarming simplicity: "Schools are places where people talk to one another. And where they write for one another. Nothing could be more obvious" (1975, p. 10). For the science and math teachers, what is not so obvious is that this language is at the center of learning and intellectual activity. Sure, there is talk, they would hold, but doesn't it get in the way of actually investigating and thinking through problems. This contrary position to dominates the professional literature in science education: "For scientists, answers are reached through scientific investigation, and rhetoric serves to provide a clear format for the presentation of findings. Scientific discovery precedes the writing, and the writing itself does not produce the discovery" (Lablanca & Reeves, 1985, p. 401). In the schools I have worked in, I have seen the debate grow into a contest between those schooled in Britton and those in Piaget, as language can be said to lead or to follow in learning, and for that kind of heady discussion and articulation of theories of learning in the staffroom, one can be grateful. Still, I think from the New Literacy side of things it has to recognized that this "language first" pedagogical stance is a point to be demonstrated with students' classroom work rather than virtuously assumed as a first principle.

One result of this pursuit of a language policy was a surfacing of regressive measures decidedly *against* the spirit of writing and language promoted by the New Literacy. I can recall in my own school meeting with teachers to discuss their interests in enhancing the use of language across the board which amounted to developing a standard policy on marking spelling and notebooks, as well as having students answer in full sentences; it happened often enough that the policy meant policing the standard, a process that Nancy Martin (1983) reports on in England and that Roger Simon and I (1980) have written about in Canadian schools. It seems clear that the New Literacy is not going to find a place in the schools through the actions of conscripted policy teams.

Even where it is not a policy issue, but one of private initiative, the danger remains of misapplication. Looking at the American instance, John Parker and Vera Goodkin (1987) have found that "in many WAC (Writing Across the Curriculum) programs in American schools and colleges, forms of writing rather than situations for writing are taught because of society's need to test students for mastery of these forms" (1987, p. 7). Rather than writing for thinking—exploratory and speculative—they see this passion for assessment promoting "the view of language as being solely for communication" (p. 7). Martin notes this problem as well in her work with London schools, suggesting that it is not simply an American problem: "We had observed that innovations in schools which are the result of a new theoretical position tend to be taken up as if they were just an alternative *method,* and the theoretical implications which could have more far-reaching results get lost" (1983, p. 104).

Where the movement has amounted to more than an alternative method in America, it has been spread more by force of workshop and example. Toby Fulwiler (1986) has led here with most of the work going on at the college level. The principles and practices are the same as in the British instance, although he sets out three specific goals for this work with teachers: 1) "writing is a complex intellectual process," 2) "writing is a mode of learning," and 3) "that people have trouble writing for a variety of reasons" (p. 21). The last point seems oddly set with the other two, but speaks to Fulwiler's great practical concern that teachers fear the degree of writing apprehension in their students. The published work in this area is rich in illustration, and although Art Young and Fulwiler (1986) subtitle one collection *Research into Practice,* it does seem to run the other way as practice is way ahead of anything conclusive on the art of the research.

The studies reported do indicate that writing apprehension is lessened in a writing across the curriculum program, although students did not care any more of writing after the four years of the program (Selfe, Gorman, & Gorman, 1986); they provide evidence that the writing of biology lab reports was improved by peer critiques and modeling (Flynn, McCulley, & Gratz, 1986); and that math students who kept a journal in which they reflected on their work did no better than other students on tests nor felt any better about writing (Selfe, Petersen, & Nahrgang, 1986).

The case for writing across the curriculum and the New Literacy in general hangs more on the instance itself, as illustrated by this sample from a journal of a high school physics student:

> The Greeks had an interesting, although completely fallacious, concept of how objects fall. Their concept, especially that of Aristotle, was formed because of observations. Aristotle, without a doubt, observed that a feather fell to the ground much more slowly than a rock. He came to the conclusion that, the heavier an object, the faster it falls to the ground. This is a very simple but logical conclusion that can only be refuted by very careful observation. I, myself, when very young, came to the same conclusion. It seemed obvious to me that the heavier the object would fall faster. I guess the Greeks were really the children, while we are now the adults. (Grumbacher, 1987, p. 325)

Grumbacher notes that among her physics students, the "successful problem solvers" use "their logs to synthesize their new knowledge about physics with their prior knowledge and experiences" (p. 325). This is the New Literacy claim and too often the extent of its substantiation. For it may well be that these students simply solve the log problem with as much success as the others they face. This student does bring the experiences of her childhood to physics, if at Aristotle's expense, as well as introducing a measure of ethnocentrism. Yet in terms of the gravitational problem, she is wrong about the carefulness of Aristotle's observations, rather than taking issue with his choice of objects to compare. Grumbacher does not comment on the logic, for the value of the excerpt is its demonstration of a form of integrated knowing, of connection, that is rarely found in a physics lab, a sense of connection, I would note, that runs between the student and the physics, but also between the student and the teacher. Rather than supporting a claim to learning or problem-solving, the new *form* of this knowing and its vital *sense of personal connection* constitutes the strong force in the particle physics of the New Literacy across the curriculum or at home in the language arts.

In a major study of the impact that writing has on thinking in the content areas, Applebee and Langer (1987) found that writing did make a difference, a difference in both the level of thinking and the nature of teaching. The relationship between writing and thinking proved to be complex. Although it is very tempting to assume as much, the study found that it is specious to expect writing, of itself, to help the mind develop in some general sense. Applebee and Langer found instances, when the material was already in hand for the students, that writing about the topic was no better than simply reading it over. Yet as a rule, writing helped understanding and retention and did so best with more extensive "manipulations of the materials," as in an essay, which proved to be a significant factor in improving test scores. On the other hand, the carryover to a larger grasp of the field, to integrating what has been learned, was limited. Applebee and Langer offer the clever and memorable formulation that "writing is not writing is not writing; different kinds of writing activities lead students to focus on different kinds of information, to think about that information in different ways, and in turn to take quantitatively and qualitatively different kinds of knowledge away from their writing experiences" (p. 135).

A few of the teachers who took part in this writing across the curriculum research were impressed by this approach, even without benefit of the statistical gains, some "minimal," which the study eventually produced. Three of the seven teachers no longer saw their primary roles as imparting information; rather they understood teaching to be about helping "students interpret and reinterpret what they were learning for themselves" (p. 87). Part of that change in perception was in how the teachers viewed knowledge in their subject areas of science and social studies. Applebee and Langer describe the shift as one from "accuracy of the students' recitations to the adequacy of their thinking" (p. 137). It seems a positive move in the relationship between student and teacher, and is obviously the one that I am identifying as at the heart of the New Literacy.

Writing across the curriculum opens the door in other subject areas to the sort of changed work with literacy which this book has been describing. It does so by suggesting to educators that in the first instance writing is good for a whole lot more than simply recording or reciting, and that through new forms of writing a different relationship can emerge between teaching and learning, teacher and student, especially as students are challenged to wrestle on the page with what they think they know, turning to the teacher in a new way to share and test that process. Writing across the curriculum carries with it a different set of ambitions, more modest than the writing workshop, more focused on the instrumental uses of writing to further learning of a given subject area by individual students. Yet even in these other classes, it clearly possesses the power to gently shake the definition of literacy and teaching. The New Literacy moves between these private and public aspects of writing and reading, as its introduction into any classroom constitutes a subtle critique of schooling and speaks to taking literacy and student seriously in a new way.

Notes

1. A third and cautionary perspective on this issue comes from June Jordan writing about her work as a poet-teacher in the schools and writing against the assumption "that black people are only the products of racist, white America and that, therefore, we can be and we can express only what racist white America has forced us to experience, namely mutilation, despisal, ignorance and horror. . . . there really are black children who are *children* as well as victims" (cited by Livingston, 1984, p. 269, original emphasis).

2. Don Gutteridge (1988, p. 134n) accuses the New Literacy programs of making a "fetish" of this concept of working in the "real"; he points to the inefficiency of pursuing "real" writing situations compared to what can be done with prepared classroom materials. The point is well taken. The "reality principle," as a touchstone for the New Literacy, does go beyond efficacy; that is part of the New Literacy's challenge to the nature of schooling.

3. Donald Graves has attempted to document the marginality of writing within language arts programs. He found some years ago that among 36 New England universities which he had inquired after, there were 169 courses on reading instruction and only two on the teaching of writing; in another study (1984, pp. 52–60), he examined the treatment of writing in language arts textbooks only to find that in the early 1980s, writing did not take up more than 10 percent of the major texts in the field. In the area of research, he found that for every $3,000 spent on the investigation of reading, there was *one* dollar spent on writing.

4. For a balanced summary of the 1970s' writing crisis see Fadiman and Howard (1979, pp. 13–20), with perhaps the most telling data coming from the National Assessment of Educational Progress sponsored by the Education Commission of the States which does indicate something of a decline on standardized test scores over the course of the decade.

5. Aronowitz and Giroux (1985) establish an interesting link between these conservative interests and their own left-wing call for a radical "critical education" both of which begin from the "fact" that literacy is a problem and see the solution in something other than a student-centered approach,

although they differ over what constitutes the missing basics: "Critical education agrees [with the conservatives] that the [literacy] problem exists; but it is less a question of *functional* illiteracy than historical and critical/conceptual illiteracy" (1985, p. 66, original emphasis).

6. Bourdieu's work has since been attacked for its sense that social reproduction overly determines individual lives and is blind to acts of resistance, subversion, as well as fully willing compliance; his exclusive interest in a social class analysis also misses out on gender as a cultural capital which teachers and parents have tended to channel into different markets (Apple, 1981).

7. One of the best summaries of this extensive research remains Andrew Wilkinson's (1979, p. 123).

8. It is worth noting that the dissenting voice in the report, Stuart Froome, defended traditional educational concerns with maintaining standards in the language and placing an emphasis on reading and listening, as receptive activities, rather than writing and speaking, as expressive ones. Britton (1984) comments on the irony in the intentionality quotation that I offer at the end of this paragraph by noting that the report, even in its promotion of student and teacher intentions, represents the imposed intentions of others (1982a, p. 186). For reflections on this important document from both British and American educators, see Davis and Parker (1978).

9. Among the criticisms that have been offered of the writing process, there is Livingston's attack on the undue hastiness in sharing and publishing children's poetry (post-writing). In her concern that students "translate their personal images into universal symbols and thereby, to communicate," she worries that publishing will "replace the absent symbol with audience" (1984, p. 301). The dangers of compulsory revision, in this case, are replaced by forms of compulsory sharing without questioning whether the piece has that public quality of universal symbol, whether it warrants the distribution. To publish it without this quality, Livingston implies, is to mislead the writer and do a disservice to the readers. The writing process does not preclude such quality control, although it depends, as Livingston points out, on the teacher's sensitivity not only to the needs of children, but to something like the qualities of poetry. I might add that there remain New Literacy advocates who continue to represent the process in an easy-to-follow, step-by-step manner (Atwell, 1987, p. 127).

10. I might add at this point that I have always found the participant-spectator division especially perilous as classifications go. The distinction is introduced in *The Development of Writing Abilities* as "a digression" (pp. 91–94), although it figures elsewhere in Britton's work. The danger of Britton's division is in what it would describe for language and literature. In an earlier piece, the part he describes for literature, which is said to take up the spectator role, would seem to deny its ability to affect the world, as "the utterance is an end in itself and not a means" (1971, p. 213). On the other hand, language in the participant role, with its power to do things in the world, seems to be denied its rhetorical element; in this mode "attention to the forms of language is incidental" (1971, p. 213). The point is well taken that in telling a story we are taking a spectator's role toward the life

we would tell from the stands, as it were, and that we employ transactional writing to get things done. My concern is rather with the diverting effect of suggesting to teachers and students that the poetic does not do anything in the world or that the transactional does not take up the play of form. It seems a disservice to the nature of both, and thus to the student of writing.

11. Janet Emig provides another good example of how the observation process advances the program; she found that self-sponsored writing tends to involve far more "prewriting" than school-sponsored writing (1971, p. 92). It is in this way that the recognition of categories such as "self-sponsored writing" build the case for the New Literacy.

12. Linnea Ehri and Lee Wilce (1987) found that teaching students to spell in the first grade assists students in their reading of word lists and spelling of nonsense words. But this is precisely the sort of evidence that does little to move the advocate of the New Literacy, for whom something else is at stake than lists and nonsense. As Marjorie Fields (1988) makes the New Literacy case, spelling can be seen to follow, in an organic manner, the natural progression of oral language: as the child moves from babbling, through native language sounds, words, and creative grammar to adult speech, so the young writer moves from scribbling, to letter-like forms to invented spelling and finally something approaching standard spelling. With results on both sides of the question, Jeanne Ormond (1986) holds that students do learn spellings from seeing words as they read, but that direct instruction is still of benefit.

13. There has been some research done on the effective conference. Carolyn Walker and David Elias (1987) found that how much students talk is not an important factor in the perception of a successful conference by participants. Contributing to the sense of a "successful conference" was the "formulation and articulation, by both participants, of the principles of good writing and evaluation of the students' work against these criteria" (p. 281). Another important factor proved to be the focus "on the student and the students' work" (p. 281). Because the study did not consider whether the conference helped the students' writing, the results are rather predictable and of limited value.

14. While Atwell's example strikes me as a perfect instance, I would acknowledge other versions of more formal and structured workshop approaches, among them, John Parker's *The Writer's Workshop* (1982) for high school students and for teachers Harvey Daniels and Steven Zemelman's (1985) *A Writing Project*. Because these versions lean far on exercises to teach the students or teachers about writing, they represent less of a challenge to both the classroom and the nature of literacy being taught.

15. Calkins (1986) proposes a similar routine of a four or five minute mini-lesson, followed by "transition time," then the workshop proper, and finally the sharing time or response groups (p. 26); yet she sets out this breakdown only after complaining that "the entire school day is fragmented" which "Graves describes as the cha-cha-cha curriculum" (pp. 23–24). She makes a sound case for "why I now spend so much time addressing classroom management" (p. 183) and she does address the management issue with an eye to detail as she cites, for example, one teacher establishing

the ground rules for the mini-lesson: "And second if you are wearing those sneakers with Velcro strap, could I ask you not to play with the straps during the meeting . . . " (p. 176).

16. Morris's efforts lent inspiration to the Arts and Crafts Movement in the early part of this century and his Kelmscott Press did produce some beautiful editions of his work as well as Chaucer's (Thompson, 1967); these neo-medieval illuminated manuscripts served as models in my work with children working up their own illuminated manuscripts in my efforts to build poetry publishing workshops (Willinsky, 1985).

3
Reading Lessons

"The death of Lucien de Rubempre is the great drama of my life," Oscar Wilde is said to have remarked about one of Balzac's characters. I have always regarded this statement as being literally true. A handful of fictional characters have marked my life more profoundly than a great number of flesh and blood beings I have known.

Mario Vargas Llosa, *The Perpetual Orgy* (1986)

Reading is a basic life skill. It is a cornerstone for a child's success in school and, indeed, throughout life. Without the ability to read well, opportunities for personal fulfillment and job success inevitably will be lost.

Becoming a Nation of Readers (Anderson et al., 1985)

For a second time, I would start a chapter with a contrast that marks out the necessary reach of the New Literacy. Mario Llosa speaks to a reading that is larger than life, that ranges beyond the "personal fulfillment" referred to by the commission that produced *Becoming a Nation of Readers* which regards reading as a life-skill. In reading, Llosa enters into a state of intimacy with the sensibility of another, with the characters and ideas created on the page by that other, sitting alone with the words, and without the tiring sociability of being with another. In such cases, the text seems to ask nothing of the reader except to drink it in at pleasure. This is the literary experience as Llosa would have it, turning to Flaubert's expression for indulgence in it—"the perpetual orgy." Recalling Freud's *Civilization and Its Discontents*, we seem destined to live outside such an exhilarating and exhausting state; we are fated to live the better part of our days, for the sake of a civil society, with reading as a "basic life skill." Literature is a leisure-time activity, among the hobbies one lists, a way to set the day to rest before going off to sleep. The reading that goes on outside of literature is the enormity of the real world, the traffic-jam of texts—notices, forms, accounts, reports, proposals, contracts, directions, manuals—which is the life of reading for us all, as professors of English literature tell me over lunch that they have no time during the term to "read."

The two sides of reading appear divided. There is the reading that reaches intensely within us, and the reading that we turn to, like the road sign before the highway exit ramp, to guide us to our destination. Over the next two chapters, I explore New Literacy programs in reading and literature. The distinction between the two is easily declared a false dichotomy; after all, reading is reading. But this division between reading and literature has a history in the schools, just as it has a certain distinctiveness in the social lives of our literacy. This chapter takes up the New Literacy position on learning to read, encompassing psycholinguistics and whole language, although this often runs to the reading of literature. The following chapter looks at the reading of literature under the influence of reader-response theory which comes closest to representing the educational ideals of the New Literacy.

In writing this chapter on reading, I found myself trying to keep to the prosaic, working sense of reading. But if you listen closely you will detect a preference for the literate moment, a bias born out of the formative period of my own literacy, when I would slip out of my parent's house and down into the wooded gully with a small stream still running through the suburbs, to sit with my feet in the water and Joyce's *Ulysses* on my lap, as afternoons passed one summer with little more than a sense of the book's acquired greatness speaking to me in tongues I grasped only in flashes.

That time in the gully is a long way from my own forgotten days when I was learning to read, worksheet by worksheet, in the primary grades, and it is a long way from the classrooms where I eventually taught others to read and "do" literature. I found that my teaching of reading was often enough a teaching against those who had enough of reading the assigned literature, letting their heads slip to their desks in tired frustration with this tough labor of the page, which nowhere in their lives seemed ready to pay off. Sometimes when I taught, they would catch the enthusiasm in my eyes and voice for that stream-fed literacy and off we'd go; sometimes they found it hard to credit; and sometimes it simply wasn't there on anyone's part. They were learning the lessons of literacy.

Yet as I began to write this chapter, I also had the chance to look across the room to my youngest son sitting and reading to his mother. He read and stumbled along, not much enamoured by the stories, except at odd moments; but then neither were we thoroughly engrossed in listening to this plodding through the ways of a little bear. In this way, he cautioned me against writing this chapter as if reading were something that children just step into, like talking or walking. The New Literacy can make it seem that way at times, and it is undoubtedly like that for a number of children, but not, by any means, for all of them. (Yet by the final draft of this book some months later, my son seems to have lost most of the hesitation in his reading and has begun writing and illustrating comic books that he is able to sell to his older brothers.)

The New Literacy has always had a different challenge on its hands with the teaching of reading. As the teaching of writing suffered a lack of attention in the curriculum, reading never wanted for support. The daily reading period in the elementary school is readily supplied with a rich field of ideas and strategies, programs, and packages. There has rarely been a question for the teacher of what to do in reading. On being transferred to a new school, for example, one inevitably finds a reading program already in place, with sets of readers and workbooks ready to hand out or at least covertly photocopy. Writing is there, too, as some of the activities in the teacher's guide to the reading series will touch on composition, some of the photocopied worksheets will have prompts for writing, complete with illustrated borders and lines to fill, all tied in to the selection read. But these are still very much reading programs. After elementary school, there is the secondary school literature program based on bookrooms lined with anthologies, novels, plays, with supporting question sheets. And, finally for some, there is the college reading list and essay topic sheet. To introduce a new program in reading, a new approach to literacy, at any of these levels, is not to begin something anew with students, as it is with writing. It is to set something aside. In most cases, it is daring to go it alone on the teachers' part, as I pointed out in the preface to this book, without the enormous support structure of the developed and packaged program.

As you may be able to guess by this point, the reading programs that I am terming instances of the New Literacy are based on the assumption that we read to find out, moved by a simple desire to make sense out of that part of the world represented on the page. Learning to read is finding a meaningfulness in print that is rooted in students' experience and grows through students' engagement in texts that are ends in themselves rather than exercises in improved performance. Among the theories of reading posited by those whom I consider to be advocates of the New Literacy is the psycholinguistic model developed through the work of Kenneth Goodman (1985) and Frank Smith (1978). As will become apparent, this model of the reading process stresses the importance of the knowledge that the reader brings to the page in search of meaning there. It is sometimes termed a "top-down" model in comparison to the more prevalent "bottom-up" models.

This top to bottom difference is an important, although not readily apparent, distinction between these two fundamental orientations toward literacy and learning. The competition between models is a telling battle given Frederic Jameson's apt formulation that "the history of thought is the history of its models" (1972, p. v). In this case, the contest of the reading models is part of the historical division between organic and the mechanical explanations of reality. The guiding "natural" phenomenon for these metaphors might be taken as the flower and the computer. However, I think it would be a mistake to see one model overtaking another, as Jameson suggests is the usual historical pattern; the field of reading is *not* undergoing a "paradigm shift" in Thomas Kuhn's (1962) often-cited sense. I do not see any clear evidence, in this case, of one model or paradigm of reading eclipsing the other. They have coëxisted in various forms, if not always on friendly terms, for the better part of this century and will continue to do so, I imagine, well into the next. The New Literacy has taken on a certain momentum and expanded scope recently, which is the reason for this book and its identification of the phenomenon as the New Literacy, but the coexistence of competing paradigms remains the rule in education. The strength of this paradigm contest and coexistence is the wealth of choice it offers to the educator, a choice that I have been stressing is both philosophical in its orientation and material in its structuring of the workplace.

Of the two competing models of reading under consideration here, the dominant one is the "bottom-up" approach with its focus on the mastery of specific skills in sequence. This model begins at the "bottom" or smallest units by teaching students letter and sound correspondences; the learner then moves *up,* using this knowledge, to reading words and sentences and texts. The assumption is that it is necessary, for young and old readers, to recognize the letters and the sound those letters make in order to read w-o-r-d as "word." The research suggests that phonics programs give students the decoding skills to tackle new and unfamiliar words; they become independent and accurate readers (Chall, 1983).

On the other hand, the psycholinguistic model assumes that reading begins, for beginner and expert alike, at the "top" level of *meaning,* with a sense of the text. The child's sense of story is a good example of an understanding about literacy which children bring to school, as Carol Fox's (1988) research has demonstrated.[1] Using this knowledge of the story form as well as knowledge about things in the world like wagons and trees, the novice reader proceeds to work *down* from this general level of expectation to a reading of the individual words with increasing accuracy, based primarily on expectations of what would follow in the story and the sentence. Rather than decoding words, letter by letter, there is a "guessing game," in Goodman's famous phrase, guided by clues from story, sentence, and letters.

The bottom-up model leads to reading lessons that exercise the specific skills which will eventually add up to effective reading. It is a mechanical conception of learning insofar as it assumes that when all the right parts are in place, the machine will run. The top-down model works from an organic conception of learning in which reading grows out of what the child already knows (about story, for example) and what the child needs (greater meaningfulness).

This division over how best to go about reading is part of a larger philosophical struggle over the nature of the child. How are we, as educators, to take and fashion this creature? Is the child a blank slate, the empiricist's tabula rasa, that must be carefully inscribed with the needed information and procedures to operate in this world? Or is the child an autonomous meaning-maker in search of increasingly more sophisticated ways of developing a sense of the world? This casting of the difference between models of reading holds no less for the New Literacy approach to writing than reading. The real model here, in a philosophical sense, is that of the child. These conceptions of the child represent a contest of ideas which education can take on when concepts of literacy and learning are at stake.

The solution to this difference in the *direction* of the reading models, at least, may seem obvious. Compromise and bi-direct. Make reading dialectical, both top-down and bottom-up in some sort of reciprocal motion. There is, in fact, such a model of some stature circulating at this point in the professional literature on reading research. David Rumelhart (1985) has brought forward an "interactive model" which is considered by some to be "the dominant view of reading today" (Spiro & Myers, 1984, p. 483). This model awards an equal position to the different levels of knowledge entailed in reading ranging from low level concerns, such as orthography, to complex questions, such as syntax. The interactive model may well offer a resolution to this dispute, as well as a more comprehensive view of the reading process.[2]

Yet the New Literacy is not drawn to the pyrotechnical quest for multi-faceted models that occupies a good part of the reading research community. Smith and Goodman are not simply after a model that is somehow more comprehensive or finely tuned than the numerous other contenders. They begin with a different premise about what reading and the reading lesson are about, a premise that shifts attention away from model-building and to intentionality, to the purposes and meaning of reading. For one thing, this brand of psycholinguistics rejects "information processing" as a helpful metaphor for understanding reading. Certainly, the computer engaged in information processing seems to be the guiding light for the construction of two-dimensional flow-chart models of reading. Smith is most adamant about rejecting this approach: "The model from which I want to escape perceives language as synonymous with communication and communication as the transmission of information, the exchanging of messages like sums of money or bags of oranges" (1985, p. 195). Rather, reading is embraced as a creative, critical endeavor that entails the meeting of *intentions,* as a missing organic element in many models, that occurs between reader and writer (Goodman, 1986a).

A third New Literacy figure capable of throwing considerable light on this alternative in learning to read is Margaret Meek (1988). She comes through with a "model" of the reading process that appeals directly to our experience of texts and people. She holds that time spent with good books is the best lesson in reading. Although this may strike some as too culturally cozy with a certain kind of literacy whose time has passed, it is because she speaks to this literary quality in literacy that she is able to tap this power that resides in texts. That power has been assumed in many cases to be missing and, thus, must be supplied by the teacher and the lesson. Rather, this is a literacy that emerges out of the organic relationship that evolves between readers and texts:

> We learn to read, competently and sensitively, because we
> gave ourselves what Sartre called "private lessons," by
> becoming involved in what we read. We also found we could

share what we read with other people, our friends, our
colleagues, our opponents, even, when we argued with them.
The reading lessons weren't part of a course of reading, except
of the course we gave ourselves with texts. (1988, p. 7)

Among the reading programs that seek this state of literacy among
the young are those that fall within the designations of Whole Language
and Real Book approaches; these tend to start students off with books
and stories that are written for children and not for reading programs,
books that allow the children some choice and control over their reading.
The Shared-Book Experience or Big Book programs are another variation on Whole Language that uses oversize versions of contemporary
children's literature with accompanying class sets of the books which
the class reads together and apart (Holdaway, 1979; I will offer a
classroom instance of one such program in action in Chapter 5). With
older students, the corresponding reading programs remain centered on
the students and their work with literature, with the guiding light provided by "reader-response" theories such as the Transactional Theory of
Louise Rosenblatt (1978) and Subjective Criticism of David Bleich
(1978) which form the subject of the next chapter.

The idea here, to return to my thematic concern with the shop-floor
dynamics of the classroom and the working conditions of literacy, is to
shift the production and economy of meaning. The New Literacy is
attacking a circulation of meaning that begins and ends with the teacher.
The teacher assigns the reading selection, preparing the student to dive
in for a specified set of meanings with a few directing comments and,
perhaps, a set of leading questions. Once into the text, some students
do get distracted by the writing itself and fall under the author's spell,
with others finding powerful wells of private associations are lead away
from their assigned destinations. But then, like divers on a mission, the
better students set aside these extraneous artifacts and return with the
bits that were planted for them to recover which the teacher then examines and declares to be, yes, the very thing that had been sought or, no,
something immaterial and foreign. Many reading programs go a step
further and do not leave this search and recovery method up to the
teacher's direction, but plot their own set of skills to be exercised with
each selection, from finding details to detecting emotions. The teacher
administers such a program, keeping students on track and keeping
record of their progress.

The New Literacy gives the teacher of reading a different role than director of meaning or program technician. Send those literate divers after their own treasures; upon returning to the surface with their finds, allow them to share their findings with the others. Reading becomes the experience of discovery, of uncovering this range of meanings in the texts and relating of this meaning to others. The teacher can help the student expand the range of meanings by sharing and discussing the reading experiences with students and by opening new vistas in the variety of sources to which the student can turn. This approach represents a blending of a learning theory based on the integration of self and knowledge, and a policy on literacy which declares that reading should be a source of pleasure, insight, and self-exploration. But I realize that this makes it seem too easy a contest in favor of the New Literacy, and that the dominant model of reading under challenge from the great contender should be given a fuller and fairer showing of what it has to offer.

The mainstream account of reading

The most comprehensive of recent public statements on reading in the United States is *Becoming a Nation of Readers: The Report of the Commission on Reading* (Anderson et al., 1985). It was produced under the auspices of the National Academy of Education and sponsored by the National Institute of Education as one of the wave of blue-ribbon commissions of education in the 1980s which included the federal government's *A Nation at Risk* and the Carnegie Foundation's *High School*.[3] It is a highly readable effort "to summarize the knowledge acquired from research and to draw implications for reading instructions" (p. 3). But more than that, it clearly has taken it upon itself to set the tone and agenda for the teaching of reading. The report attempts to bring to bear all that is known about reading, helpfully gleaning the best that has been thought and tested in the teaching of reading; it is guided by a sense of literacy's importance to the nation and an interest in the dissemination and application of knowledge. From another point of view, however, the report represents a consolidation of the reading research industry which continues to shape the teaching of reading.

The report gives ostensible credit to the teacher as the source of good teaching: "If the practices seen in the classrooms of the best teachers in the best schools could be introduced everywhere, improvements would be dramatic" (p. 3). But the comment is made in passing, while the report goes on to take its lead from the work of researchers and research teams in establishing what can be learned by those who have turned the psychology of reading into their science. The opportune moment which the report takes advantage of is one in the state of research and scholarship in reading:

> The last two decades of research and scholarship on reading, building on the past, have produced an array of information which is unparalleled in its understanding of the underlying processes in the comprehension of language. Although reading abilities and disabilities require further investigation, present knowledge, combined with the centrality of literacy in the educational process, make the report one for optimism.
> (p. viii).

Before going on to the report's reading of this work, it should be noted that this optimism over the current state of knowledge about reading is not universally shared. John Chapman (1987, pp. 31–32), in describing the British perspective on the teaching of reading, takes a more humble tone by citing another recent report which concludes that "little is known about the processes that underlie efficient reading" (Gorman, 1986, p. 5). What disturbs Chapman is that there is not yet a single or adequate model that can explain how readers do make sense of what they read. The equation of how much we know with the achievement of a single model may be to rely too heavily on the example of the physical sciences, with their widespread acceptance of models for the atom, evolution, and light, if not yet gravity. With human behavior and culture, the concept of competing models has its own history in human knowledge.

Yet, as if conscious of how important striking a chord of consensus among the experts is to establishing a convincing position on literacy, *Becoming a Nation of Readers* begins with a small but important point of agreement: "The majority of scholars in the field now agree on the nature of reading: Reading is the process of constructing meaning from written texts" (Anderson et al., 1985, p. 7). Indeed, as I have already argued, *meaning* is the fulcrum on which literacy balances while dipping in different directions, toward different models of how we read. This chapter is, in a sense, about different models of reading drawing in part on the same body of research, models of reading that differ most obviously not on how reading is accomplished so much as on the point of what is reading and what needs to be taught to students about it. What needs to be attended to, then, in examining these approaches to reading is what they make of this activity. What is important about reading?

In trying to capture the nature of the reading act, *Becoming a Nation of Readers* compares reading to the working of a symphony orchestra (Anderson et al., 1985, p. 7). In spite of its artful associations, the metaphor suggests the considerable mastery of subskills and the endless rehearsal sessions which are necessary for the public performance. Not only does it take hours of solitary practice before taking a chair with the woodwinds, few symphonies get it all together for their own pleasure on a Sunday afternoon. This is a serious and considerable accomplishment, and the report treats reading as nothing less: "It is a complex skill requiring the coordination of interrelated sources of information" (p. 7). I find that this definition bears the stamp of the research mentality struggling to map and make perfect sense of this process, rather than that of either the reader with a book or the teacher sitting down with a child who reads, stumbles, repeats, skips, and laughs her way over the pages. The complexity is undoubtedly there in what the child is attempting; it is there in the effort to guide her attention and listen for what's giving her a problem. But as the reading eventually comes to the child through time, hints, guesses, and more time, the complexity is absorbed seamlessly into the act. The "complex skill," "coordination," and "interrelated sources of information" sound more like the discourse of the research investigator and the corporate executive, rather than either the reader or the conductor of a symphony orchestra.

To understand the difference between this approach and the New Literacy, between the "complex skill" and the "social practice," it would be worthwhile to examine the critical question of *phonics*. The question is whether to instruct the child in the rules of phonics, of how letters relate to sounds, which can lead to such delightful ditties as "when two vowels go walking, the first one does the talking" (as in w*ai*t, if not w*ei*ght). Learning letter-sound relationships is the cornerstone of a parts-to-whole, bottom-up, approach. *Becoming a Nation of Readers* would "lay to rest" the old debate, deciding in favor of phonics, if in a qualified way: "Phonics instruction is just the first step toward the ultimate goal of fast, accurate word identification and fluent reading" (Anderson, 1985, p. 46). One strong source is support of Jeanne Chall's (1983) examination of what she has tagged "the great debate"; she finds that the research clearly supports the phonics side against the whole word or "look-say" methods. The benefits are most apparent in word attack skills, but are also found with sentence and story comprehension especially in the early grades. The paradox of phonics instruction, Rod Maclean (1988) has noted, is that it appears to be beneficial to teach the young a skill that they will later have no need for as competent readers, and that it can be taught on a letter-to-sound basis which bears little relationship to how phonics is employed in practice. The report recommends that the first two years of reading include phonics instruction and that the rules be kept fairly simple (Anderson et al., 1985, p. 43).

The report also has the good sense to foresee the complaints against phonics by advocates of the New Literacy; it makes reference to "a false dichotomy between phonics and meaning" (p. 42) suggesting that the problem of phonic-without-meaning worksheets lies with the faulty de-sign of specific programs. For the New Literacy, however, phonics still symbolizes the very sort of interference that schools can run against children becoming literate. Phonics is regarded as too much for the student, by way of complex rules to be mastered (with 73 rules for the 6 vowels), and too little by way of meaningfulness in exercising those rules on worksheets; and it is ultimately irrelevant for the nature of reading in which sounding out the word is not how reading is carried out, except on occasion with an unfamiliar word. Kenneth Goodman and Frank Smith led the attack on phonics instruction in the 1970s, with a strong alternative reading of the research literature. The resulting psycholinguistic model of reading, with its own claims to a science of reading, shifted the emphasis from the decoding of parts to the prediction of meaning—Goodman's "guessing game." They envision reading as "the reconstructing and comprehending the writer's meaning" with the clause rather than the phoneme acting as the unit of most importance for the reader (Goodman, 1982, pp. 26–27), which Goodman later expands to the "the text" as the basic unit of meaning in language (1985, p. 817).[4] Frank Smith, for his part, concludes that "spelling-sound correspon-dences are not easily or usefully learned before children acquire some familiarity with reading" (1978, p. 150). This hardly refutes Chall's findings that phonics programs work, but then neither does Chall's work demonstrate to what degree or how these phonics principles are acquired. Yet my point remains that there is more than a research question at stake between these two models of reading.

Another key issue in the challenge presented by the New Literacy is the role of the text in the teaching of reading. The report notes that basal readers, which have come a long way since *Fun with Dick and Jane,* constitute 75 to 90 percent of what goes on during reading periods in elementary school classrooms (Anderson, 1985, p. 35). They have developed into total management and testing programs which "would make a stack of books and papers four feet high" (p. 35). *Becoming a Nation of Readers* stresses the business of this highly influential enterprise, citing figures of 15 million dollars in development costs for a single series. It adds a word of caution against underestimating the influence of these programs. Although the report finally arrives at the key concept of meaningfulness, it is clearly not the starting point, but another application: "No matter how children are introduced to words, very early in the program they should have experience with reading those words in meaningful texts" (p. 43). The report is quick to admit that basal readers may want for such moments and yet it seems resigned to the continuing dominance of the basal reading series. Limitations are recognized and calls are made for improvements in the quality of the stories. Ultimately, the report acknowledges that the reader will remain a mainstay of reading instruction and asks that better stories might be commissioned for the books (p. 48), but so have many others since Huey's (1968) turn-of-the-century appeal for more realistic language in readers.[5] Incipience continues to rue the reading period, abetted by the single-skill worksheet as an accomplice to the banal reader. Here the figures on American teaching practices suggest that students spend 70 percent of their reading period on this "seatwork" which requires minimal reading and involves less meaning (p. 74).

The report gives some recognition to the fact that "Real Book" programs have found their way into the schools. It reports on the use of "more natural selections that do comprise complete stories" (Anderson et al., p. 45) by New Zealand, which has earned the label of "the most literate country in the world." Yet the report points to the mixed results this approach has experienced in the United States, citing the Cooperative Reading Studies by Bond and Dykstra (1967) of some twenty years ago which compared programs on the basis of first- and second-grade reading achievement tests.

The report goes on to deal with the importance of integrating writing into reading, curtailing the use of ability grouping, and balancing the reliance on standardized tests. It is a powerful, reassuring statement about the path to a more literate society. It is not completely removed from what the New Literacy would have for the classroom, in the way it embraces an integrated approach to writing, calls for better literature, less busywork and less ability-grouping. But a difference still remains.

The New Literacy calls for a reading that is driven by a search for meaning rather than a skill.

The New Literacy account of reading

I do not want to leave the impression that New Literacy programs are turning their backs on the research enterprise in a gesture of anti-intellectualism and outright disdain for the scientific world view. Advocates of the psycholinguistic strand of the New Literacy, principally Kenneth Goodman and Frank Smith, clearly draw on the research literature to build an alternate paradigm of how reading operates, and how it is to be encouraged in the young. If eschewing, for the most part, experimental methods and standardized measures, advocates of the New Literacy have remained empiricists, as they sit with the child as informant, observing the processes of reading in action.

The strongest example of this meeting of research interests between New Literacy and the other traditions in reading is the work on the active contribution of the reader to the construction of meaning. Among the landmark studies cited in Harry Singer's (1985) review of reading research in this century is Bartlett's (1932) work on memory which posited the use of "schemata." A schemata amounts to a network of ideas associated around a certain concept such as ordering a meal or reading about vegetable gardening.[6] The research on its direct relation to reading is found in the work of Pichet and Anderson (1977), among others, who devised experiments which demonstrated that different schemata colored the sense that readers make of what they were reading. This work on schema theory provides an excellent example of how this research can be applied to the classroom: in the impressive work of Isabel Beck and Margaret McKeown (1984), these improved reading lessons offer more active roles for children, who are now asked to bring the relevant schema into play or are provided with the needed schema. But again, as the research is set to measure efficiency of processing, this upgrading of instructional practices is an extension of the reading-technology model of literacy.

On the other hand, the idea of prior knowledge has a rather different ring to it in the hands of the Brazilian literacy educator, Paulo Freire: "Reading does not consist merely of decoding the written word or language; rather, it is preceded by and intertwined with knowledge of

77

the world" (Freire & Macedo, 1987, p. 29). What that intertwining can mean for Freire is a transformation of the world: "reading the word is not preceded merely by reading the world, but by a certain form of *writing* it or *rewriting* it, that is, of transforming it by means of conscious, practical work" (Freire & Macedo, 1987, p. 35, original emphasis).

Equally so, the psycholinguistic wing of the New Literacy takes this research on the importance of the reader's schemata in yet another direction. For this group, it lends support to an upending of systematic instruction about features of the words on the page. Frank Smith refers to what the reader brings to the page as nonvisual information and after his careful review of the literature on perception, cognition, and linguistics, he leaves little doubt about the challenge he would pose to traditional methods of teaching. This is the use of research against direct teaching, rather than its deployment to advance instruction. Smith represents the New Literacy as the position of informed common sense against the monolith of the research and instruction enterprise that tracks the details of reading and misses the lesson that "the essential skills of reading—namely the efficient use of nonvisual information—cannot be taught":

> There is only one way to summarize everything that a child must learn in order to become a fluent reader, and that is to say that the child must learn to use nonvisual information efficiently when attending to print. Learning to read does not require the memorization of letter names or phonic rules, or large lists of words, all of which are in fact taken care of in the course of learning to read, and little of which will make sense to a child without experience of reading. Nor is learning to read a matter of application to all manner of exercises and drills which can only distract and perhaps even discourage a child from the business of learning to read. (1978, p. 179)

Smith's forthright challenge to the entire instructional apparatus which has been constructed around the reading lesson has been essentially ignored by the research community. Working from this community's findings, he has essentially theorized away the existence of what is at the center of the teaching day, the reading lesson. This was somewhat more than anyone had asked of the scholar. It was as if he had proposed to the cereal companies that breakfast was an unnecessary distraction in getting on with the day.

By way of an instance of this stepping over Smith's challenge, Jana Mason (1984), in her review of instructional practices in early reading for the massive *Handbook of Reading Research,* suggests at one point that "it may be very difficult for many children to figure out how printed phrases and sentences are related to meaningful speech. This is perhaps the point of 'reading for meaning' stressed by Goodman and Smith" (p. 522). Actually, the point of reading for meaning was to turn distracting if not discouraging instructional time into the active expansion of meaningful language through speech and print. In the *Handbook*'s 350 pages on "Instructional Practice—the State of the Art," Smith's challenge to the teaching of reading does not come up.[7]

Yet for all of that, he has not been without effect. What he did do for those educators who were drawn to his work was very much tied to their perception that teaching may not be as beneficial as teachers often hope; this perception has been captured by Margaret Meek (1988) who starts with an acknowledgement of Smith's work on her way to describing "how texts teach what readers learn":

> By reminding us of what we know [that children learn to read
> by reading], Frank Smith reclaimed reading for learners, freed
> teachers from enslavement to pedagogic methodology, and let
> us rediscover reading as something with language at its core. It
> then followed that children's aptitude for learning language,
> early and well, guaranteed that reading and writing are obvious
> social things to do in any community where written language is
> part of our function as human beings. (pp. 3–4)[8]

In this way, the New Literacy proposes an alternative sense of reading which rests on two principal dimensions of meaning. The first is rooted in students' experiences with the text. The second is set within the sociability of the classroom setting. Under this disposition toward reading, the classroom takes on a different atmosphere; literacy is something to share and language for connecting with others, all in the amplification of meaning. Goodman's work in defining this approach takes on the psychological trappings of the American research tradition with his proposed "transactional-psycholinguistic model." He examines the nature of reading only to arrive at an organic sense of this meaningful process:

It is the search for meaning which preoccupies the reader and
unifies the use of strategies and cycles that the process requires.
Meaning is both input and output in this process. That is why
aspects of the process and how it works cannot be isolated
from the construction of meaning that is the ultimate goal.

Learning to read involves getting the process together. That
is harder if instruction takes it apart. (Goodman, 1985, p. 839)

Goodman would also undo the instructional strategies of the dominant
programs that get in the way of meaning, of texts and language. He
posits a model that is still grounded in cognitive strategies and optical
cycles, because he is working within a tradition that seeks a science of
model-building, as part of a search for a unified theory. But his work
seems capable of moving in and out of that tradition, as he suggests that
what the student puts together instruction should not rent asunder. While
it may be tempting to accuse Goodman of endowing the drive for
meaning with spiritual or metaphysical dimensions, as meaning is input
and output in something of mixed metaphor, I think the simpler explanation is that Goodman is guided by the accord he would pay to the students
he visits in their classrooms: it is their right to meaning that he defends
so vociferously, as people who deserve to be doing something more with
their time.[9]

Yet another contrasting statement to the "What is Reading" manifesto
of *A Nation of Readers* is Collin Mills's "Making Sense of Reading"
(1988). In something of the British tradition within the New Literacy,
he stresses the social life of the literate primary classroom with a concern
for the place of spoken and written language:

Reading requires children to make sense, explore possible
worlds, invent, sort out what is not said. Real, lively texts
connect all that with the polyphonic and diverse social
interaction that goes on in lively infant school classrooms ("Oh
no, I can't stand it!"). It is the lively mix of varied voices that
links literacy, literature and talk with social practice. (1988,
p. 50)

In contrast to the American pattern for both models of reading, Mills is
not intent on catching a glimpse of the cognitive mechanisms involved
in a student's reading. The focus shifts here from a complex, interrelated
set of cognitive skills, to an equally diverse and intricate set of social

ones. Mills's classroom may seem far too absorbed in a certain dramatic liveliness—the unwelcome mark of the 1960s ("Oh no")—which tends to overlook the individual child struggling with word after word in *The Little Train that Could*. But what is kept present and accounted for is this sense of reading's purpose and place in the life of the classroom. The classroom is not cast as a convenient housing of individual cognitive practices but a community of readers with something to share and talk about, with a reason to read.

Top-down or bottom-up, psycholinguistic or phonic-based, the educational spotlight has been on the student with the book, the basal reader, the worksheet, or even the teacher; Mills and this British perspective dissolves the false sense of isolation, by turning on the house lights which reveal a room full of readers. The New Literacy, as I am reading it, is about restructuring the life of literacy in the classroom and the nature of the work which teachers and students do together. The reading lesson that Mills describes is clearly about extending and enriching the social, intellectual, and aesthetic exchange which literacy affords with texts and language. This manner of perceiving the classroom community could add to Goodman's sense of intentionality as a social enterprise; it could add to the New Literacy conception of reading as a socio-psycholinguistic activity.

But apart from Mills's cheery conviviality, there is another sociable setting for reading lessons that also needs to be recognized by these reading models. This other scene opens onto a vista larger than the classroom and in harsher tones speaks forcefully to ways in which reading lessons are implicated in the perpetuation of poverty and the failure of schooling to make a difference. *A Nation of Readers* only addresses this other social fact about reading lessons in an afterword by Jeanne Chall. Yet many of the successes and problems in the teaching of reading can easily be described in terms of the social order and the fate of minority students and what seems to amount to the reproduction of "pariah status" among them, in the words of Ray McDermott (1985). This is not simply an American or British problem, by any means, and McDermott provides disheartening instances from Japan, Norway, Ireland, India, and Israel, all of which speak to the manner in which learning to read is caught inexorably in a larger social process: "Many pariah children adapt to the senseless and degrading relational messages given them by unknowing teachers with different communication codes by shutting down their attention skills in response to teacher tasks as reading" (1985, p. 559).

Reading lessons are no less a social process for all of the children in school, although in many cases it may well be a far less costly one. The problem is not simply that the social situation of the classroom is too often lost to view by the researcher who focuses on the individual students' processing of the text, but that in ignoring this issue, the very causes of failure and continued inequality are too conveniently overlooked. The work of Kamehameha Early Education Program (KEEP) in Hawaii demonstrates that the use of reputedly efficient instructional strategies, of the time on task variety, did not succeed in raising the test scores of the Hawaiian children, while the introduction of culturally sensitive programs that included co-narration with students and interested non-threatening adults succeeded in bringing them up to grade level (Tharp, 1982).

That these cultural factors fall outside the dominant models of reading seems increasingly irresponsible. Both McDermott (1985) and Courtney Cazden (1985) offer detailed reviews of their own and others' field research on the social dynamics of the reading lessons which minority students face. The lessons are easily read as negotiations of power and subordination for teacher and student; they may entail learning and resisting the designation of place through such subtle cultural communication systems as eye contact, focus of instruction and time on task, testing situations, and grouping. It works by less subtle means, as well, through commanding the students' attention and calling their very use of language into question. These studies offer poignant pictures of classrooms in which teachers do treat students differently. McDermott (1976) found in one study, for example, that interruptions in reading lessons for the low-achievement group were 20 times more frequent compared to the better group, and it was the better group which initiated, along with the teacher, a good number of the breaks. Much time was also lost to the "negotiations of embarrassment" by both teacher and students in the low group in avoiding the task of reading out loud. In trying to convey the anguish of the situation, John Ogbu (1983) has argued that black children are living with what is in effect a caste system in which it is all too apparent that learning to read does not offer adequate compensation for the humiliation it can cause.

The classroom caught up in these social dynamics calls for a model of reading that goes beyond the psycho-mechanical processes of one person making sense of print. It is well to recall that one of the strands of the New Literacy began in a setting of social exclusion with the development of a Language Experience program by Sylvia Ashton-

Warner (1965) in her work with Maori children in New Zealand. She began with the words that were most ripe with meaning in their lives— *kiss, fight, beer, hit, Mum, airplane, fast car, blood, skeleton*—and built a blossoming literacy out of the shared stories that filled their lives. Equally so, we have the reading lessons of Paulo Freire whose work began with impoverished Brazilian communities in the early 1960s. His lessons with adults hinged on the generative powers of keywords which students could offer in their discussion of the striking pictures with scenes from their lives which Freire used: A barefoot man stands under a slight tree and before his field, with a open book and a hoe in his firm hands; behind him is a mother and daughter holding hands and looking on beside a well and a small house. The teacher asks "who makes the well" and the group sets out to discover how people "modify reality" through their work. These sessions became the sources of what Freire terms "annunciation" and "denunciation" in a reading of the world that was fully intended to become a form of cultural action (Freire, 1974). The power of literacy that these two programs draw on begins in the meeting of personal and public elements of meaning, the one reaching in very deeply and the other reaching out to others in this experience and culture. The idea is that once stated and read in this way, the world will be as changed as the new reader.

But one can easily spot the objection that these communities, in New Zealand and Brazil, are far removed from the suburban and city classrooms that this book addresses. Yet they remain models of the New Literacy in their resetting of the educational agenda for a reading that comes from the student, and more to the point, that take up reading as a cultural enterprise that can work with or against the life of the student and the community. Smith's psycholinguistic model of reading gives this cultural element little enough recognition, and Goodman (1986a) brings it in as an appendage, although an important one, to the search for meaning. Mills's lively classes are running on a self-contained assurance that would also seem to have yet to fully reckon with the world, even if only the smaller one which students face after school each day. Freire's program is a political reading lesson for student and teacher, as reading the word is reading the world, in his terms (Freire & Macedo, 1987).

It is an interactive model, but one that *interacts* with a world larger than the one inscribed by the mind of the reader and the words on the page. Its influence among reading theorists has been especially felt in conjunction with Lev Vygotsky's work (1962) on the integral role of social engagement and dialogue in the learning of the young; but in the process, the emerging understanding of literacy does lose its radical edge: "When people are convinced that they can shape their social reality and that they are no longer isolated and powerless, they begin to participate in dialogue with a larger world, first orally and then through writing" (Elasser & John-Steiner, 1987, p. 51;). But this engagement is not so removed from the understanding of reading advanced by Smith, Goodman, Meek, and Mills. Certainly, Freire does not shy away from exhorting teachers to teach; he refers to it as their "indisputable responsi-bility" in a "Letter to North-American Teachers" (1987, p. 213), and he has worked very hard with literacy workers to bring literacy to the untaught in Brazil and elsewhere. Smith and company, on the other hand, would serve the young and somewhat over-taught with a restoration of their native abilities to learn.

Among those who have recognized Freire's powers as a teacher were the military leaders of Brazil who took power in 1964; they recognized that this was indeed to teach a literacy that re-read the world. Freire was imprisoned that year for 75 days for employing an educational program that was clearly opposed to the "national interest" (Mashayekh, 1974). For one thing, his programs were beginning to add a considerable number of voters to the rolls. But if we are working with a different level of enfranchisement here in our schools, I am concerned that teachers see that the same seeds for cultural action reside in other versions of this approach to literacy and the learner. As removed from the forests of Brazil as these other classrooms may be, their embrace of the New Literacy remains a radical act of challenge against the established author-ities. It begins with simply deciding to put away the basal reading program in favor of real books freely selected by the reader. Let me make the case for an incipient radicalism—of a "cultural action for freedom," in Freire's phrase—at the root of a domestic version of the New Literacy which is run for young students in the vales of New Hampshire.

Jane Hansen (1987) has worked with New England teachers to develop a model of the teacher's role within what I have termed the New Hamp-shire School of the New Literacy. Of special relevance to our discussion here is her work with teachers of disadvantaged children. As she de-scribes it, the teacher's job is a matter of listening to, receiving, and accepting a child's choice of texts. The teacher also "shows the child ways to solve problems when reading—e.g. context clues, picture clues" and "refers the child to peers for help" (p. 187). The teacher "provides opportunities for children to share successes and knowledge" within the classroom and with other classes, by tutoring, or with other adults. Hansen concludes this summary of activities by describing the process of evaluation conducted by teacher and children under this new system: "At the end of the project when Millie interviewed her students, they labeled themselves as readers because they read a lot of books, chose their own books, and their reading was like everyone else's. Millie's own comment was, 'I wish I had learned this years ago. This is the best thing I've ever done in my career' " (p. 187).

This is a form of reading without teachers, after the original fashion of Peter Elbow's (1972) work with writing, and not only is it the best thing for Millie but it is virtually a new career for her. Recalling Frank Smith's liberating influence, the teacher is freed from the constant ordering and evaluating of literacy in the classroom; the autonomy of the student is encouraged and the classroom is made over into a community library and intellectual meeting place for the young. The disquieting shift here is for the teacher to hand over a part of the intent of literacy to students, that is, the principal thing about reading is that you are to read for yourself, for the sense which books can make of, or add to, your own experience and understanding, which you then have a responsibility to share with others. Part of this responsibility is not to assume that students can discover the various ways of reading, on one hand, of entering into the life of a text and, on the other, of feeling confident about arming yourself against its persuasive reasoning. There may need to be some modeling of reading postures, directing of tentative first steps in having students realize these textual interests. After a year of this work, students might begin to figure that one enters these officious buildings known as schools because they are convenient places to pursue personal projects with texts and people; that one turns to those who have power to more easily realize the goals one has selected; that one meets with others to work together on these projects or to share the wonders of what has been found.

Students are to have within them, not only the resources for sharing their knowledge with their peers, but also a sense of cooperative work and how people in authority act in a helpful manner. With a little luck, it will serve them with something less than a rude shock when they have to leave this haven for literacy. Yet it remains a substantial attack on the foundations of schooling. After all, how different is this from Paulo Freire's efforts to allow adults to rethink the structuring of their farms and jobs, how different from "Freire's conception of *writing* as a figure

85

for *transforming the world,*" as Ann Bethoff has put it (Freire & Macedo, 1987, p. xx, original emphasis)?

While there remains this radical element in this concept of literacy, I cannot help suspecting that it suffers a certain simple-mindedness over how power and social structure are brought to the classroom. The anthropologists of the inner-city school have brought home to educators how complex and deeply ingrained are the processes of stratification that teach students the boundaries of their lives, often in the neighborhood outside the school door. How goes the New Hampshire school of literacy in downtown New York or London? Lucy Calkins (1986), for one, has found promising success in New York City with her writing programs drawn from work with Donald Graves in New Hampshire. But as she represents her work with these students and their teachers, the social issues of the troubled city do not emerge, and more work will have to be done to development a literacy that is prepared to speak to the differences in the meaning and lives of its students. The question is, in part, whether the teacher would turn over to the students the power necessary to somehow transform the world, or is it enough to provide a momentary refuge from that world? I tend to think that it can run both ways; although the one is less certain than the other. To what ends these students will turn a literacy that is made theirs remains an open question, one that makes these programs so fascinating. They will allow for different senses of literacy to emerge or we will have to once more temper our talk about the power of reading and writing.

Yet to work at transforming the classroom into a place that dares to explore and negotiate the demands of such a literacy on the institution, teacher, and student is in itself to create a refuge for the teacher and student. The educational experience of literacy is not a period of preparation, but the actual practice of a personal and public power. Is it allowed to speak to how literacy might also work in the larger world? Does it press ahead with its own implied critique of schooling, a critique posed by the New Literacy that too often goes unspoken, which also might lead to a re-reading of the world? Without this critical edge on the part of the New Literacy, I think that the familiar criticism of progressive experiments in education, from those who would hold to the basics, is a fair one to consider: Are these students being set up for a world that does not exist?[10]

The charge against New Literacy programs is one of misleading students. Yet it is not simply deceiving them about what is important about literacy, as these critics of progressive education might contend.

The point of the New Literacy is that it speaks to what is indeed important about reading and writing at some of its most interesting and intense moments. Yet this personal sense is only part of the story for literacy. The question that remains is whether students are prepared for handling the difference between the literacy they have begun to work with, in which they pursue their own meaning, and the reading expected of them outside these classrooms, in which they are sent hunting for the meanings of others.

Students need to have literacy set in the larger context; they have to be let in on the challenge that it can pose to the reading of others. They have to learn to play with the politics of reading, the contest of meanings and sources of authority. For it to work, this critical stance has to begin in the classroom with the fact that the New Literacy is itself a critique of meaning and authority in education, and one that students, with any experience of schooling at all will quickly recognize and begin to wonder about. In my experience, students will test this sense of difference with an odd comment about the way things are run—"Why are things *different* in this class?" The question deserves some thoughtful reflections as a way of understanding how literacy operates in different contexts. This could form the first step in a larger lesson on the nature of reading, a lesson which I think is a necessary addition to these programs.

While I do not want to engage here in the design of curriculum supplements for New Literacy programs, a number of other starting points come readily to mind in sharpening this critical edge to the New Literacy. One instance might be to have students examine how textbooks operate to establish the nature of meaning and knowledge within a discipline; it is an understanding of the nature of text that would serve them across the curriculum. They could also examine the prevalent reading programs of their own education for its designs on them as readers, by virtue of selections and questions. These selections can be understood as official lessons which are meant to situate their own community and understanding of themselves; they can begin to advise the school and the school library about alternatives and think about redressing imbalances in the representation of the world as a reading lesson. Students, in moving from response to interpretation, might explore related questions about how literacy works; there is already much work underway on the style of representation and the nature of bias in the press and other media. Or more broadly, an area I have begun investigating for possible classroom application is the question of how standards are set in the language, and how the dictionary is constructed as a comprehensive authority in the language. In each case, the idea is to study and realize literacy as a social phenomenon, a work out of which there is a meeting of meanings, as the text is written to convey a sense of things and as a reader turns to it and to other readers to make a greater sense of things.[11]

In this way, students might be better prepared to defend the realms of meanings that they are interested in pursuing or in the works of others, but also to understand the external contexts which can further shape the sense of texts. Students see that literacy is a matter of contexts and intentions. Reading in specific situations for different purposes—sitting an exam in a gymnasium; sitting with a book by that proverbial stream—always contributes to the meaning of literacy and is thus also subject to inquiry into literacy.

The reader is empowered from the first day of school simply by being treated as competent in new ways and being considered in a position to contribute to the meaning of the text, the text gives something up to this reader. This great and lively endowment in the primary classroom, happy in its free pursuit of meaning and story, can be lost as the more serious business of reading begins in the later grades. I can do no better with the drama of this change and the very dichotomy between private and public meanings which the New Literacy would crack, than to offer Madeleine Grumet's (1988) warning of the loss to the classroom as students are forced to go public. She envisions the "body reader" as the figure of wholeness in early literacy who must learn to discriminate between readings that are within and readings that are out there:

The body reader now is still alive and well in many elementary classrooms where language experience, directed reading/ thinking activities, and phonics provide a rich and varied sensory and interpersonal ground for learning soon gives way to the reader who discriminates the private self from the public text. When it is in here, it is identified with feeling, sensuality, and imagination that cannot be communicated and cannot be negotiated into any statement that deserves the status of knowledge. When it is out there, it belongs to the text and to the teacher, and understanding means that the reader stands under the text, under the gaze of the teacher, and learns to anticipate and repeat the interpretation that is the index of comprehension. (1988, p. 142)

Here is a deeply felt lesson in literacy. It may be more than the New Literacy can overcome, but it still needs to be named as Grumet names the acts of discrimination and displacement that the school teaches the student about reading. The language experience gives way to the literature lesson. While literature might seem to hold the power of running deeper, of reaching within, it has nonetheless spelled the end of such engagement for many readers in this public setting with public texts. But that brings us to the subject of the next chapter.

The psycholinguistic model, with its top breezily down and its engine tuned to the desires of the child, promises to cover a lot of ground in the making of a meaning, full of feeling, sensuality, and imagination. It can be sounded out in that sensual way which Grumet alludes to with a conciliatory gesture toward phonics. But to that private realm to which the New Literacy has sought to open the classroom, there needs to be added the public elements of the classroom as a community of readers and writers, of reading as the beginning of an exchange that encompasses larger communities, that can form the basis of engagement and critical challenge. And once the social bond among these readers is grasped, then this literacy can also be seen as a reading that dares to reach out into the world. This is to question how this world is written and how it can be critically read as a means of rewriting it, in Freire's terms. As I noted, I remain unsure about how far this New Literacy reading will go in undoing or altering the world, once it has been freshly read. But at the very least, it has begun with an interested inquiry into what a re-reading and re-writing of the child's world will bring about in the classroom. This change in the ways of authority and order is one way of reflecting on the powers of literacy with students. Beyond that point lies the current edge of the New Literacy horizon, the point at which questions need to be raised and the debate among these programs' advocates renewed.

Notes

1. Fox's work with children's story-telling has demonstrated how book-like their language can be as it moves within traditional structures of narrative; she finds that the children's stories "are metaphorical mirrors which are able to reflect several aspects of their inner experiences simultaneously" (1988, p. 62). Rumelhart (1977), using a theory of "story grammar" based on the way stories are put together, has made explicit the case for children's

"top-down" reading of stories that begins with their "grammatical" knowledge of what to expect.

2. Rumelhart's (1985) interactive model works on a number of levels bringing to bear orthographic, lexical, semantic, syntactical knowledge. The positing of these entities is based on considerable experimental testing of readers and are backed by a number of algebraic equations which describe "a system of evaluation for the optimal use of information available at any given point in time" (p. 749). However, in terms of an interactive model that reaches out to the social context of reading, there is Ruddell and Speaker (1985). They add a conception of the "reader environment" which includes the three elements of textual, conversational, and instructional features that match my concern in this chapter with reading as something that must be understood as a work process in a classroom setting. For a review of the fascinating and ongoing quest for a satisfactory model of reading see the survey of Samuels and Kamil (1984). They point out that for want of a common focus among the models, as one looks at word-recognition and another at comprehension, comparison is superficial at best. The other important point they make from my perspective is that the models do not spring up in isolation from each other but must be understood as different responses to the field of model building in reading, each vying for their own place and contribution. Other sources on the question of the model are Massaro (1984) and Singer and Ruddell (1985).

3. See The National Commission on Excellence in Education (1983); Boyer (1983). For a discussion of these and a dozen other reports from that heady period, see Symposium on the Year of the Reports (1984).

4. Goodman's (1965) famous "guessing game" study, which found a 60 to 80% improvement when children read words in sentences rather than in lists, has been challenged and most recently, perhaps, by Tom Nicholson and David Hill (1985). They found that good readers are still distinguished by their decoding skills of words in isolation, and that context did not assist them with reasonably difficult words such as "weaver" and "obstacle." Their work is another reminder of the relatively weak experimental base on which the New Literacy rests in many instances; the question is addressed more fully in Chapter 6, but generally teachers follow Disraeli's advice with statistics and follow the implications of their beliefs about education; William Rupley and John Logan (1985) have found that in teachers' beliefs about reading, those who think of themselves as student-centered avoid programs with a stress on decoding skills. The statistics be damned.

5. Francis Kazemak has accused the report of being an "apology for the continued use of basal readers," as it "virtually ignores the whole issue of linguistic diversity in reading and writing education" (1986, p. 262). While the readers are racially mixed, that is only the first step in preparing the students for a society: "What do kids learn about linguistic diversity from basal readers? With very few exceptions, they learn that everyone in the United States speaks the same!" (p. 261). Allan Luke has noted how the basal reader has been both responsive to reading theory and social movements such as Progressive Education, using the example of *Fun with*

Dick and Jane as instances of "adaption to social environments and creative development" (1988, p. 97); in the process, a contradiction emerges between these interests and what he terms their "technical and dramaturgical form" (p. 181)—they leave too little to chance and that overwhelms its other intentions.

6. For a complete overview of the schemata approach to comprehension, see Anderson and Pearson (1984), and in the same volume for some of the difficult questions that this scheme of things has yet to face, see Kamil (1984, p. 43).

7. Ignored on the instruction question, Smith is given little on the theory side as well. In Samuels and Kamil's (1984) review of reading process models, Smith's description of reading is denied the all-important status as a model of reading with the suggestion that this was not his aim; Smith is credited, however, with explaining "how the redundancy inherent at all levels of language (letter features, within letters, within words, within sentences, within discourse) provide the reader with enormous flexibility in marshalling resources to create meaning for the text at hand" (p. 187).

8. Christine Pappas and Elga Brown (1987) have taken the lessons learned from reading one step farther with their case study of a child *pretending* to read a story: "Her three pretend readings, we believe, provided her with an access to written language. In the context of learning to read by reading, she learned how to extend the functional potential of storybook language" (p. 175).

9. The contemporary case in favor of retaining an element of "direct instruction" in reading, which takes aim at Goodman among others, has been forcefully set out by James Bauman (1988). Bauman would dispel the myths that give direct instruction a bad name, but he concedes that such bad instances as "teacher-proof lessons" can become the reality unless care is taken.

10. Although it would seem to be common to the conservative critics of education, this question of preparation is raised on both sides of the political spectrum, as Roger Simon makes clear: "If we do not give youth a sense of how to 'make it' within existing realities, all too often we doom them to social marginality: yet another high-minded way of perpetuating the structural inequalities in society" (1987, p. 375).

11. By way of bibliographical support for the development of these ideas, I would begin with Apple (1986) and Luke, de Castell, and Luke (1983) on understanding how texts operate as authoritative, ideological, and economic forces; on the nature of reading programs, Luke (1988) offers a critique of the basal reader and other textbooks for literacy, while Segel (1986) examines reading selections and gender among the young; Herman and Chomsky (1988) provided a richly illustrated example of the "political economy of the mass media"; I have done work on the formation of the modern dictionary (Willinsky, 1988a), and its structuring of sexual difference in the high school (Willinsky, 1988b).

4
Literature in Response

In one book I read, I really learned something: I learned that it
doesn't really matter what the guy looks like, it matters what
their attitude is, and what they're like is really what matters.
                    Alice, age 12 (Willinsky & Hunniford, 1986, p. 23)

Literature is experience not information.
                    Robert Probst, *Response and Analysis* (1988, p. iii)

Let me begin this look at the teaching of literature with Alice's sense
of engagement and learning. At one point in this pursuit of the New
Literacy, I had the opportunity to work with Mark Hunniford, a junior
high-school teacher, on the reading habits of twelve- and thirteen-year-
olds in his classes. We discovered that his students reached for one genre
above all others and were inclined to do so on a daily basis. The young
adult romance novel, as it is known, held sway among the girls in his
classes in a way that no other book did. In fact, we found that close to
90 percent of the girls in the two grade-seven classes he surveyed took
time to read these books every day. Hunniford and I had both seen the
books around the schools over the last few years, but we hadn't paid
much mind to them. At this point, we read a few of the books and began
to ask questions about how the students viewed these formulaic stories
of the bad and the good, the mischievous and the misunderstood, all on
their way to a happily resolved romance sealed with a chaste kiss. What
emerged from the discussions with the students was a picture of thorough
literary engagement and absorption; their reading struck me as an intense
form of reader response. These students were constantly talking and
sharing these books; the young adult romance had become a form of
cultural communication and exchange among them, bonded as these

students were in a collective and anxious knowing. The students formed something of a "textual community" around an arcane and personal sharing that has always marked societies of the book.[1]

To gain some perspective on the response of these students to the young adult romance, Hunniford and I used Janice Radway's (1982) close and careful study of forty adult women who read romance novels with devotion. The girls in Hunniford's classes enjoyed the books for some of the same reasons given by the adults, turning to them for relaxation, to escape daily problems, and because these books are never sad or depressing. But one thing set these two groups of readers apart, namely the seriousness with which they took the literature as prophetic. More than half of the girls indicated that they were hoping for a romance like the ones in the books—something the adult readers didn't express an interest in—and in their interviews with Hunniford, the students expressed a further sense in which these works served as a preview of the romance and novelty to come in their own lives (Willinsky & Hunniford, 1986). The books provided them with a script for an initial reading, a rehearsal for the big production that they face in the high school years ahead: "It gives me ideas about how I can meet boys" (Isabella); "I think, well, one day, they'll happen to me and I really like the stories" (Alice); "It always says near the beginning what she's wearing, and I get ideas, like, I should wear that next time I go out" (Jane; pp. 23–24).

We were more than a little surprised and puzzled by the element of credulity in these responses. Puzzled not because we couldn't understand them taking the books this seriously—the books were rich in verisimilitude, full of the suburban detritus of these reader's lives—but by how, as educators, we might best react to this particularly intense form of reader response to a genre with which we were uncomfortable. The students saw the books as mirrors, it seemed to us, mirrors in which they believed they could find themselves and which, like portable periscopes, afforded them a glimpse of what lay around the next corner: "That'll probably happen in grade eight or nine," one of the students predicted (Janis, p. 22). They are selecting an immediate future out of the easy impossibility of fiction that is sold in designer covers and colors and is available in the perfectly hypothetical world of the shopping mall. It is a maller's genre.

We could not help suspecting that this was a *new* literacy that was blowing no one any good. Yet what could we make of a reader's response that represented an absorption into *a* literature, if not *the* literature, and into an active culture of literacy? This absorption in text still represented an ideal for us as teachers of the language arts; it bespoke a change in fashion among the fashion-conscious young, that perhaps we should have been applauding; yet we were more than a little baffled and frustrated by it.

This issue of self-directed reading and response for the teachers of these readers of the romance is a part of a broader concern for the New Literacy which this chapter approaches. The New Literacy has set for itself ideals of engagement and self-expression and when these ideals are realized in sudden outbursts among students, we are sometimes surprised and taken aback by the unforseen complications of engagement. In the next chapter, I will examine a further example of this problem of self-expression by looking at the question of what we should to do if the self finally expressed in student writing is not the one we were hoping to see emerge. In this case, these young women are taking these books as seriously as I could imagine anyone taking a book at their age. They are reading their *own* way into the world; they have found a language and a master narrative through which to associate and connect both, in the immediate sense of a literate community of friends, and in a larger sense as these books bring them to the idealism of youth and as they are quick to take the simplifications of life as the thing itself.

But if they are being misled by the young adult romance, in their more-than-willing suspension of disbelief, how are they to be guided into a dispassionate, less engaging response, in what they were so freely reading? Hunniford and I did not arrive at a safe and sure answer. It posed a different kind of challenge to the New Literacy than the ones I have posed up to this point. We were lucky enough to find in one student a double stance that moved between engagement with the text and detachment from it through her close friendship with another student:

> I read them and I discuss every book with Edith, my friend.
> I'll read it, then she'll read it and we'll discuss it together. And
> we talk about what we saw to be true in the book and what is
> totally unbelievable and couldn't happen to anybody. (Cara in
> Willinsky & Hunniford, 1986)

These critical acts of reflection that deal with the text seemed the critical pose that we tend to encourage. Cara and Edith were making something of themselves as "resisting readers," in Judith Fetterley's phrase (1978), for avoiding coming under the spell of romance which is how the text would have itself read. But we needed to understand better the nature of response, to understand how to work with the pleasures of the text, and in this way educate or better arm these readers, not solely against the genre of their first choice, but more generally across the range of their textual experiences. Reader-response theory provides a critical vehicle for just such an educational operation.

Reader-response theory

I open with this incident of engagement to introduce, in an odd and disconcerting way, *reader-response theory* as my candidate for a New Literacy approach to the teaching of literature in the schools.[2] Reader-response is a theory of literary criticism which focuses on the way in which texts work on readers (Tompkins, 1980). It dares to fly in the face of what New Critics, Wimsatt and Beardsley (1954) identified as "the affective fallacy" which warned readers not to be mislead by how they were affected or moved by a work in the careful and systematic labors of an unaffected, close reading. As many readers will recognize from their own school experiences, the close readings of New Criticism dominated the teaching of English in the colleges and schools since the 1950s, and in many instances continues to do so. Reader-response is its undoing. Rather than hold that there is "a confusion between the poem and its results" or deny "the psychological effects of a poem," as New Critics did in their efforts to create a science of their trade (Wimsatt & Beardsley, 1954, p. 21), reader-response criticism speaks to the literary experience, to the pleasurable and stirring times spent with books, rather than an analysis of the artifact. Terry Eagleton has suggested that after the Romantic and nineteenth century interest in the author and the New Critics attention to the text, the reader's turn has indeed arrived (1983, p. 74).

Not surprisingly, I feel that reader-response theory has more to offer the New Literacy than timeliness. As I have intimated, it is this experience with books that brings teachers to language arts classes in the first place and it is what they affect in the class in the hope of offering as much to students. We may wonder if this is too much to hope for: is the classroom the right place for literary experience? We might compare Robert Frost's confidence that the "earth's the right place for love: / I don't know where it is likely to go better." If I'm not as certain about literature in the classroom, I at least hold that reader-response theory offers to make literature go better for students. If the classroom can be transformed into something close to a community of readers finding their own way into literature, then the classroom seems a likely spot to work with a text about which so much can be said of the great deal that has gone into it. The classroom may also be a better spot with the New Literacy because there students are reading as writers, as those who are working the same ground in different ways. Writing is a common medium for author and student under the New Literacy, which gives reading a different significance than watching a video.

But before going any further into reader-response theory, I need to add a word or two about two problems that the New Literacy has with literature. The study of literature in the schools has often meant a reverential deference and silence before the mysteries of the great work; at best, one might emulate the teacher's critical comments on the text's meaning and significance. Although this is a caricature, one can see that such an approach runs contrary to the intentions of the New Literacy. In attempting to find the curricular value of students' language, experience, and culture in the New Literacy, literature teaching suffered a certain neglect. It was still heavily taught, but it did not benefit as much as writing and early literacy from the attention and innovations of those heralding the New Literacy.

This was especially true in Britain. A kind of democratic urgency in education swept through Britain in the 1960s and 1970s, although it is certainly under devastating attack now. It was this concern with making education more accessible that warranted leaving literature aside in the development of new and innovative approaches to an education in the language. To put all too briefly what was introduced in Chapter 2, the rising influence of James Britton and the London School marked a turning away from the importance placed on instruction in literature; the new focus was on the learning fostered by the use of talk, students' own writing, and the language of the immediate culture. The traditional methods of teaching literature were implicated in the social class discrimination perpetuated by the British schools. Although this turning away from literature can be set out in those stark terms, Britton (1984) did, in fact, write about the powers of poetry, and Barnes (1975) brought the force of small-group talk to bear on literature classes. Which is to say, that literature has retained a place in this British form of the New Literacy, albeit without the benefit of a singular champion such as F. R. Leavis provided for a generation of teachers before the New Literacy.

If the study of literature is no longer safely ensconced as the highest point of an education in the language, reader-response theory gives it a second life as a means of learning more about the world and art both outside of and within the student.

A second difficulty is that the study of literature, as it has developed in high schools and colleges, remains a discipline apart from reading and writing. The university is especially notorious for maintaining a two-level hierarchy between those who profess the glories of literature and those who toil in composition. My division by chapters of writing, reading, and literature remains a backward-looking convenience, a setting of boundaries that in many instances the New Literacy is trying to erase. From the previous chapter, it should be clear that Margaret Meek, for one, would end the division between reading as a skill to be mastered and literature as a recreation to be appreciated after the reading lessons are mastered. These efforts at bridging the three areas of writing, reading, and literature are a natural outgrowth of New Literacy efforts and collections on this topic have begun to appear (Petersen, 1987). Reader-response has its own history as a critical practice removed from classroom concerns, but there remains an arm of it given to the responses of students and of fostering that response through writing. This look at reader-response theory as a New Literacy approach to teaching literature will thus move in its own way to that moment of integration among the language arts that form literacy.

It follows from the case that I have been making in this book that the New Literacy will ask of literature what it has asked of the teacher, that it defer some part of its authority as a source of meaning in the classroom to the student. In just this way, reader-response theory is the perfect complement of the writing process movement and the whole language approach to reading. As Robert Probst (1988) presents it in his excellent guide to reader-response teaching in junior and senior high school, "response-based teaching" is simply a realistic solution to what might be taken as the larger response statement that has already been delivered by the student population. They may well be little interested in academic questions in literature and care less about literature class, but "they will read because they are interested in themselves, and because in the reading they may become the focus of attention" (pp. 3–4). He warns against self-indulgence, even as he capitalizes on it by suggesting that "at its best, it is an attempt to see more clearly who one is and where one stands" (p. 4). This method stretches and scrapes clean the rough and superficial self-reflection, as one tans leather to realize its beauty and usefulness. The emphasis on response works from a double assumption that literature works by affecting readers and that teaching literature works if the student connects with the text. It is a promising approach which speaks as well to the issue of accountability. In their assessment of American achievement in reading, Applebee, Langer, and Mullis identify the lingering problem of students failing to think more deeply and relating to what they read: "All students need to develop effective strategies for thinking about, elaborating upon, and communicating what they have learned" (1988, p. 25).

Still, before growing too sanguine, there are a couple of tendencies in reader-response criticism that I want to warn against. The first is the habit of turning the reader into a critical tool or lens which ultimately reflects the critic's own good sense. Umberto Eco speaks of the text producing Model Readers in which case "the reader is strictly defined by the lexical and syntactical organization of the text" (1979, p. 10). Stanley Fish, in what he calls "an early manifesto" for this critical school, refers to a "super-reader" who, in essence, embraces the entire range of traditional literary questions of genre and conventions *"redefined in terms of potential and probable response"* (1980, p. 49, original emphasis). But what, one may well ask, of the response of real readers? They are often too busily engaged in reading itself to carry on the sophisticated and sensitive annotation of the super-reader. This does not deter Fish from arguing that his method is a pedagogical boon for the college classroom, as it "breaks down barriers between students and the knowledge they must acquire" (p. 22). However, I still suspect that students are little comforted by the prospect of imaginary Model Readers or super-readers looking over their shoulders; the New Literacy has a need for a reader-response grounded in the practices of mortal readers.

A second tendency to watch against is the treatment of a reader's response as readily apparent and accessible, rather than something seen through a glass, or more often a class, darkly. The idealism that can plague reader-response theory at times is its ready assumption that it is working with the totality of response. We cannot thoroughly render or articulate the experience of reading; we can only sketch out parts piece-meal with perhaps a little imaginative filling-in for what goes missing.[3] Certainly, every moment that we are engaged in reading elicits a response of some sort, but writing about that experience brings on a different set of responses. In a theme that becomes pervasive in this book, we might say that there is no such thing as an "essential" response located in the individual reader, that is, one that is private, unmediated, and removed from the circumstances of the reading and the social history of the reader, as a student, lover, or a research subject in an undergraduate literature class experiment on reader-response. Rather than futilely seeking a thoroughly natural response from students—"What does the poem make you feel?" (Probst, 1988, p. 10)—it is more realistic to provide a shared focus or set of foci around which students' responses can gel in this social setting of the classroom.

If the classroom barrier between student and literature, which Fish refers to, is to be breached and the response of the reader not unduly idealized, it is more likely through a direct assault on specific traditions in teaching literature. To that end, I am offering over the remainder of this chapter the reader-response work of Louise Rosenblatt, David Bleich, and the textual community of feminist literary criticism. Rosenblatt has long been a prominent figure in promoting a teaching of literature that entails the meeting of the reader's own experience with this new or renewed moment of the literary work in a "transaction" between text and reader. Bleich encourages both the meeting of self and text in a more specific classroom program in response and a communal sharing of response that leads to an understanding of other readers as well as the text. The feminist developments have taken place in every corner of criticism; but in the house that reader-response built, I want to focus on the work of literature classrooms that moves through language, literature, and other media. Here connections are struck between the personal and the public, the private and the political, in a manner through which the New Literacy could profit and prosper. We need to explore an agenda for restructuring the climate of response in the English and language arts classroom, an agenda that might move readers to work with the personal and public elements of literacy. Rosenblatt, Bleich, and the feminist critics, each in their own way, provide aspects of that missing agenda in nurturing and challenging the response of students to literature.

Louise Rosenblatt

Rosenblatt is an apt starting point, as she began her long and outstanding contribution to an education in literacy by trying for a balance between individual meaning and development and the social responsibility of literature. She also provides a direct link between the New Literacy and its immediate educational roots in the Progressive Education movement. Thus I wish to take a somewhat different tack with her work, portraying its historical development since the 1930s. Over the course of this career, her theory of literature has undergone its own transaction with the changing interests of progressive educators and the increasing professionalism of English studies, as she has increasingly drawn away from her original reconciliation of the aesthetic and political roles of literary education in favor of a narrower concentration on the reader's experience with the text.

To appreciate how progressive this precursor of the New Literacy was, we need turn no further than to Rosenblatt's first major educational statement, *Literature as Exploration* (1938). It opens with the pressing needs of the world beyond the school: "In an unsettled world, our schools and colleges are confronted with the demand that they prepare the student directly for living" (p. 3). The book was sponsored by the Commission on Human Relations which was founded by the Progressive Education Association. The Progressive program introduced into the curriculum new concerns about health and vocation, family and community; it promoted an increased sensitivity to individual differences and represented a vibrant educational force during the first half of this century only to meet its official demise in 1955. Educational historian Lawrence Cremin (1961) has described its vision as "part of a vast humanitarian effort to apply the promise of American life—the ideal of government by, of, and for the people—to the puzzling new urban-industrial civilization that came into being during the latter half of the nineteenth century" (p. vii). A cover story in *Time* magazine in 1938, the year of Rosenblatt's book, confidently reported that "no U.S. school has completely escaped its influence" (cited by Cremin, 1961, p. 325). While I am not sure that urban *post*-industrial civilization is any less puzzling today, I do think that the New Literacy is no less a response to it than other programs of that period, and one that will exert an influence in schools everywhere.

In those early years, Rosenblatt built her theory of literature out of a pragmatic concern for how the text could work as a progressive force at every level of education, an education to "be judged in terms of its effect on the actual life of the student; the ultimate value of any knowledge depends on its assimilation into the very marrow of personality" (1938, p. 215). In *Literature as Exploration,* Rosenblatt sets the task for a progressive literary education "in our present era of social change" using the broad and ambitious terms of American pragmaticism:

1. To supply youth with the tools and knowledge necessary
   for a scientifically objective, critical appraisal of accepted
   opinion . . .
2. To . . . predispose the individual toward working out a
   basis for a more fruitful living. (1938, p. 212)

The contribution she made to the Progressive Education Association
was to specify how literature could facilitate the achievement of what
might be seen as broadly liberal goals in the "exploration" of human
relations, particularly as literature serves the individual in advancing the
democratic state. They promised that a well-armed critical reader intent
on working toward a better life was an ideal democrat in the voting
booth or an elected position. Literature's service to the development of
the whole and healthy child was also to be a means of entry, of getting
the child more fully into this burgeoning American society: "Books are
a means of getting outside the particular limited cultural group into
which the individual was born" (1938, p. 228). It was clear to Rosenblatt
that while reading had its place with the social and psychological services
rendered to the citizenry of this democracy, it also engaged the reader
in a private and aesthetic experience of the text: "The reading of any
work of literature is, of necessity, an individual and unique occurrence
involving the mind and emotions of some particular reader" (1938, p.
32). It might be said that the democratic role that she first imagined for
literature hinged on a *respect* for the integrity of the individual's response
to the text, combined with a collective *responsibility* to pursue, through
the social and natural sciences, a more "fruitful" life for all.

Her second major statement, *The Reader, the Text, the Poem* (1978)
has served the New Literacy as her first book served the Progressive
Education Association. Yet in this work, she attempts to step over the
educational and political mandate she had once embraced. She does so
in favor of the seeming maturity of literature read within the realm of
academic theory and criticism: "Eschewing further educational themes,
I concentrate on presenting a matured and more fully developed theory
of the literary work of art and the implications of criticism" (1978, p.
xii). The resulting insularity of interests which the progressive career of
Rosenblatt represents is a real and pressing danger, in my eyes, in the
development of the New Literacy. In her second book, the reading of a
poem is above all else a private and a literary event. Rosenblatt not
only sets aside her earlier stress on the social sciences as sources of
understanding, but she also discards the *vicarious* powers of literature

through which a work could bring readers the experiences of their fellow citizens in a sympathetic framework, making it the very tool of a diverse democracy.

Her debt to Dewey also shifts from his attempts at reconciling the individual and social interests in education to his formulation of *transaction* as a way of knowing, which in her terms indicates "an ongoing process, in which the elements or factors are, one might say, aspects of a total situation, each conditioned by and conditioning the other" (1978, p. 17). Yet this concentration on the reader's transaction with the text meant a certain narrowing of her original scope—"the text becomes the element of the environment to which the individual responds" (p. 18)—and the social function of literature becomes somewhat more introverted: "Literary texts provide us with a widely broadened 'other' through which to define ourselves and our world" (p. 145). Her circle of interest at many times in the book, though by no means all, closes in on the circle circumscribed by reader and text, as the title of the book suggests (in contrast to the outward looking *Literature as Exploration*). Yet this closing in on the literary event marked a renewed interest in her work which has reached into the curriculum of English-teaching with a new forcefulness.[4]

One strategy she has shared with James Britton is the creation of divisions where none had been thought worth noting. She, too, builds a New Literacy critique of teaching through the particular efficacy of terminology and taxonomy. And like Britton in spirit and number, Rosenblatt approached the task apologetically, stressing the fact that she requires only a modest set of three new coinages—"it is the only jargon I think I've indulged in" (1981a, p. 5). Her *transactional theory* of the literary work was based on the distinctions that could be made between an *aesthetic* and *efferent* reading of a text. As is now well known to English teachers, the aesthetic reading was distinguished from the efferent one by its concentration on the "experience" being lived through with the text, rather than in what can be "carried away" in an efferent reading (1978, pp. 24–25). While it can argued that we take something away from the most aesthetic of literary experiences and can find literary pleasures on the sports page, the two terms are effectively used to attack a pedagogical tradition which was satisfied to teach literature by asking students twenty questions about the poem's form and content. Such an approach is clearly attempting to teach literature efferently, with an eye to what students could cart away from the work to the examination. What was missing, the use of the two categories made clear, was any form of encouragement for students to *experience* the text in an *aesthetic* manner, an experience which was, after all, what art was all about and which might in the context of the classroom be profitably shared, refined, cultivated, and still, ultimately, examined.

As for actual teaching methods, Rosenblatt has not been as forthright as David Bleich who provides three stages of response and voluminous examples of students' responses. Rosenblatt has offered the sort of prompting questions she would use with children, and in them one can hear the effort to elicit nothing more than a form of out-of-school response to the literary work. She seems to envision it as a drawing-room conversation or wherever it is that children and adults sit to query poetry.

> What caught the interest the most? What pleased, frightened, surprised? What troubled? What seemed wrong? What things in the child's own life paralleled those in the poem or story? As differing responses are heard, there can be a continuing return to the text, to see what in the text led to those varied interpretations or judgements. (1980, p. 393)

But classroom methods are not what has drawn Rosenblatt to this work, and although she has reported on her own in-class work with students (1964), a detailed and sophisticated study of how students do respond to poetry has been left up to researchers in education such as Patrick Dias (1987) who demonstrates precisely how much a student can make of a poem.

Rosenblatt has been able to establish, through a concentration of critical energy, the importance of the reader's experience of the poem as an educational ideal. That in itself is worthy of note. Teachers drawn to Rosenblatt's work hear in it an echo of their best moments with literature, breath-taking and chilling; they also hear in it the de-schooling of literary study, of books and works that matter to the teacher. Between her work and that of Britton's, a space has been opened for what has become known as "personal response" to literature and that place signifies a different orientation to the child and the nature of literacy in the schools. I only ask that her earlier vision of literature and the state, as a political responsibility of the schools be kept within the realm of educational experience, response, and transaction. She closes the 1978 book on her transactional theory of literature with Walt Whitman's "vision of a great literature for a truly democratic society" which required strong readers: "Not the book so much to be the complete thing, but the reader of the book" (p. 175). My point remains that this vision suffered a certain tunneling as Rosenblatt pursued the completeness of what the reader "*is living through during the reading event*" (1981b, p. 22, original emphasis), rather than developing the broader social mandate that she had originally pursued.

A second point worth adding to this consideration of the intellectual shift in her work is that although literature's political role was to slip from the progressive education agenda set by Rosenblatt, the topic is far from moribund in literary and educational circles. Had she searched in earnest, she might have found pockets of supporting interest for her initial explorations of literature's political role, pockets that I am asking the New Literacy to attend to in continuing to develop as a source of innovation and reform in the schools. Among the New Critics, whom Rosenblatt has set herself apart from, Robert Penn Warren continues to declaim the critical democratic function of the literary text: "Our poetry, in fulfilling its function of bringing us face to face with our nature and our fate, has told us, directly or indirectly, consciously or unconsciously, that we are driving toward the destruction of the very assumptions on which our nation is presumably founded" (1975, p. 31). From within the ranks of the English professoriate, Richard Ohmann has always been quick to keep the politics of literature teaching present as part of its constant responsibility: "There is just no sense in pondering the function of literature without relating it to the actual society that uses it, to centers of power within that society, institutions that mediate between literature and people" (1976, p. 303).[5]

Rosenblatt has kept these two elements of the personal and the public alive in the rhetoric of her work; yet she has failed to give "the human condition" the same degree of energy, vision, and theoretical development that marked her later work on the transactional theory of literature. Through the development of this concept Rosenblatt was able to offer a new degree of enfranchisement for the student as a reader capable of participating in the literary experience, even if the important role this might play in a democratic society was not to be fully realized or explored. If she failed to fully develop how the transactional theory was to work in the class, Bleich has built around his own theory of response a practical three-step pedagogy which links the experiences of isolated readers. And if the political mantle has slipped from Rosenblatt's shoulders, it has been willingly taken up by the feminist critics who are asking, "Whose texts, whose response?"

David Bleich

In her introduction to a collection of reader-response criticism, Jane Tompkins offers a brisk summary of Bleich's stance, at least in its political dimensions: "He wants to take responsibility for the production of knowledge away from traditional sources of authority—texts, teachers, institutions—and place it in the hands of all who are engaged in seeking it" (1980, p. xxi). It is a New Literacy formula. But only one of many, as even those few figures assembled in this chapter are not in agreement; Rosenblatt, for example, has taken a swipe at Bleich and this "unfortunate pendulum swing to an excessively subjective approach which neglected the responsibility toward the text" (1980, p. 392). Yet, however subjective the response he was interested in, Bleich went about establishing his theory and his practice with a great deal of structure and objectivity, providing a much more explicit agenda than Rosenblatt devised and one that lends itself to sequence and development.

It begins with the nature of the response to the literary work: "It is the reader who determines whether a piece of writing is literature" (Bleich, 1975, pp. 20–21). We have decision here rather than an experience. And out of that "private decision," we find that the essence of a poem is in what Bleich terms "its subjective re-creation by a reader and in his public presentation of that re-creation." He then neatly divides the re-creation into three phases—"perception, affective response, and associative response" (p. 21)—which he elicits in turn from his students. The "perception" becomes what the reader "sees in the work," a restatement of the work as the first step in taking ownership of this new knowledge; the "affective response" becomes a re-creation of the reader's feelings during the reading as if to explore and nurture the bonding to the work, the identification in feelings; finally the "associative response" brings the work into the reader's history. There is room here for evaluation as well as engagement; Bleich holds that "critical judgements are implicit in emotional reactions," thereby paving the way to supporting and warranting these judgements as a means of assessing both the value of a literary work and a student's *re*-creation of it. More specifically, he identifies two principles for grading a student in response: "(1) the amount of work produced by the students, and (2) the seriousness of purpose in the production of that work" (p. 107).

Bleich provides examples of college-level students' responses which show a deep level of engagement as well as the expression of personal meaning and often a certain flair. Rather than offering an extended excerpt from one student—and Bleich provides and examines a good number of these in some depth—let me try to capture the range of response by pulling sentences from five students longer responses to *Vanity Fair*. Bleich sets the extra agenda of commenting on what was Victorian in this novel, again suggesting a necessary meeting of interests from the reader, author, and class: "I became immediately attached to William Dobbin, first out of a kind of pity and then out of respect"; "It was the continual rigidity—like being suspended in a sexual climax—that dragged me down and made it hard for me to read the novel"; "I can only vomit at the characterization of our wealthy old maid Miss Crawley"; "Since *Vanity Fair* deals with such topics as hypocrisy and social climbing, one could detach himself from the story and sit back and enjoy it"; "I could grasp a bit of myself in Thackeray's injected statements" (1975, pp. 82–85). I selected a range of concerns from their remarks to suggest the different directions the responses can take and be encouraged to develop.

Bleich clearly encourages students to move with literature in a whole new, more writerly way. The students find it easy to draw the work within the hold of this personal response, while the challenge remains in building their case for convincing others of how this response is rooted in the text and circumstances of the reading. One source of inspiration is the teacher, for as we saw in the non-teaching of writing with the teacher writing, Bleich, too, engages in this process of response. He offers his own readings on many of the same stories that the students have worked with; the change in his voice from the main exposition is dramatic: "My mother is fond of repeating that an old school chum of hers became Kafka's last lover. I imagine that poor tubercular hero trying desperately to make it with this girl a failing because of the arbitrary virulent disease" (1985, p. 258). Out of this arises those secondary statements which amount to evaluating and interpreting the craft and skill of the story through a reading of the response. These readings become the basis of understanding within the classroom. Without having to go beyond the classroom to the critics, the classroom becomes the site of a "new authority in producing knowledge of language and literature" (p. 272).

Bleich offers students three large steps away from the loss of personal meaning which, as you might recall from the conclusion of the last chapter, Grumet identified as the typical fate of the classroom reader. The sense of a text's meaning that arises inside readers can become the public discourse of the classroom along more than one dimension as it moves from the immediate experience of the story or poem and back through the reader's personal history. But Grumet also warns of an ineffableness to meaning, a resistance to its communication and its refusal to become a certain knowledge. It is as if to remind us that what does reach the page is not simply a response to the text, much of which is ineffably lost, but to the exercise of engagement which Bleich is structuring in the classroom. The nature of the knowledge represented on the page is not a question that Bleich shies away from. A science of subjectivity and knowledge is precisely what he does claim as the product for this subjective knowing. In *Subjective Criticism,* Bleich builds a philosophical foundation for his knowing on such seemingly solid ground as the science of quantum mechanics with Einstein and Heisenberg, the political science of Habermas, the psychology of Piaget and Freud (1978, pp. 10–37). Bleich does not let this reading program hang by a thread, but as the least Romantic of New Literacy theorists, he fixes it with the more secure knots of modern times.

A second strength to Bleich's program is its second level of association among readers—from their own associations in response to reading to the association that can be struck among readers. This sharing of meaning as a means of knowing has always been a part of Bleich's work, beginning with chapters like "Interpretation as a Communal Act" (1975). But more recently, he has taken to speaking of "intersubjectivity" as the basis of knowing for the reader. He speaks to "intersubjective reading" in terms similar to those I used in proposing a literacy more conscious of itself toward the end of the previous chapter: "Intersubjective reading starts with recognizing the community ('thought collective') in which individual readings take place: for example, the family, the classroom, the academic meeting" (1986, p. 418). He turns this acknowledgement into a prescription in which intersubjective reading is something one nurtures in students, as it "utilizes the incremental growth processes that are at work in any group," "includes reactions," "an ongoing exchange," "seeks to secure a palpable social basis for continuing reading projects whose collective authority may then approach other communities and wider populations" (p. 419).

From the three-phase lessons of a re-created response to the projects of reading communities, an education in literature becomes an association among texts and readers; in this way, response becomes connection. This classroom strategy makes bold strides toward the classic humanist call of "only connect," and it makes them through this essential connection between the associations of self and community. In this intersubjective understanding, which entails learning from what we freely share, the world can seem to work in this personal, explorative way. But as it is, there is a world and an authority outside of the classroom; readers bring it in with them. Bleich may close the classroom door as he picks the texts and frames the inquiry, but no community is completely safe from the contentions of the larger world. More than that, readers need to see how that reading connects not just with themselves, but with their place in the scheme of things.

Gender and the reader

Where Rosenblatt leaves off worrying the place of the literary within the polis, and Bleich hopes to have it in the communities of response, feminist critics are rewriting lessons and literary canons within a constant worldliness. Over the course of the last three chapters, I have returned to a singular difference in a literacy that falls between the personal and public, the individual and the political. In writing, it begins with the distance between the private pleasures of creation and the public passkey of standards in literacy. With reading, this division moves between models of cognitive mechanisms and a reading that means a rewriting of the world. And literature offers private transactions and public pursuits with texts that range from prescribed text to teenage fantasy. In each case, the New Literacy has engaged this range of personal and public experience; its promise is not in turning these two spheres into one, but in seeing the ways in which they are connected, sharing a single surface as soap bubbles can do. The slippery arrangements among the personal and public can vary a good deal by situation, and are sometimes exceedingly fragile. But these varied situations for literacy provide strong lessons about how to read and write. In searching for a model that speaks to the ways in which literacy works both within and without the classroom, and a model that supports change in the manner of teaching, we have the unmistakable contribution of feminist literary criticism, especially the feminist literary criticism that has helped to shape reader-response theory.[6]

With a certain obviousness, this contribution begins with the feminist commonplace that "the personal is political." But it goes much further than catchy slogans or even definitive assertions; the field is formative, uncertain, explorative, and filled with difficult questions that begin to hint at post-feminist readings. It is a specific response to the times, to women making the world over in the study of literature and beyond. It is the response of readers who have found themselves at stake in the reading of the text. Feminist literary criticism has successfully turned the study of literature on its head and in the process—perhaps through improved circulation—has invigorated both the teaching of classic texts and opened the classroom to new and overlooked ones.

However, only a small part of this concern with gender has focused on classroom practice. The *English Journal* has done a special issue on women's studies and the high school English teacher (Metha & Rothschild, 1985). Elizabeth Flynn and Patrocinio Schweickart's *Gender and Reading* (1987) provides a comprehensive collection of reader-response perspectives on gender which I will draw on in this section; however, I have found that the English Centre of the Inner London Education Authority has provided the most helpful guide for realizing the place of gender in the language arts curriculum. Their collection of essays and short pieces, *Gender: Material for Discussion,* (1984) along with other curricular support documents, draw from the work of teachers with the following questions, which if not specifically attuned to reader-response, certainly speak to the issues of literacy as a response to texts:

> For work on gender asks the question, "who are you?" in a
> form which implies other questions: "how are you seen by
> others? could you be different? what's stopping you?" These
> questions. however affably put, are sharp ones, even
> threatening ones, since they reach at the heart of much that is
> uncertain and unknown, especially in the adolescent. (*Gender,*
> 1984, p. 39)

Turning to this book and my own curriculum work with gender and response, I review the course of this topic as it moves from language to literature, from the close work of words to the ways of finding and learning a literature.

This renewed response to literature might well begin by raising questions about how language contributes to the significance and meaning of gender by virtue of grammar and diction, as we fall back on the propriety of the manly generic. But this look at language extends to the writing of the character in literature. The English Centre's booklet on Steinbeck's novel, *Of Mice and Men* (Ashton, 1980), points out that

Curley's wife lives and dies without a name beyond that possessive form that stakes her out as property. Here the English Centre booklet asks the student to respond to the author's intentions:

> Just as Crooks is the only black person on the ranch, Curley's wife is the only woman. She suffers from isolation from other women and her inability to lead the kind of life that she wants for herself. She has no name in the book; she is always called "Curley's wife." Why do you think Steinbeck did that?
> (Ashton, 1980, p. 16)

The questioning leads up to more general and contemporary concerns: "How many things can you think of, in the way men live and work, that might shape their attitude to women?" I envision these as options for response, as part of a far-ranging commentary that can move from what Curley's wife can be said to "suffer" to Steinbeck's treatment of her in plotting of the novel. For interested students, the text provides John Steinbeck's letter to a Miss Luce who is playing the part in a play: "I've known this girl and I'm just trying to tell you what she is like. She is afraid of everyone in the world . . ." (p. 18). So begins an inquiry into representation and the manner in which we know and judge others in literature and beyond.

The problems of representation are not restricted to gender. Language is far busier than that with meaning, but gender has earned a place as a model of re-responding, of learning a critical response, not necessarily self-defensive, but one open to reading and literature as a rewriting of what one knows. The English Centre book has students working with their reading of the language in taken-for-granted expressions and stereotypes, in looking at how conventions in the language work in textbooks, literature, and in the schoolyard. Response begins with the language, by looking at it, not as a window on reality, but as a way of constructing that reality, whether for Curley's wife or for those students who get called names in the schoolyard. Yet if response to gender is not to become the sole end of this exercise, students need to see how it leads to other engaging questions over the style and substance of representation in the text. Nor is this simply a negative venture, on the attack and blind to the arts and craft of the literary work. This look at language moves among the accomplishments of style, as it typifies a character and as it seems to transcend the unduly conventional, to offer a renewed vision of what people can be, in a phrase or metaphor. The danger is in finding literature's labor lost to this approach, but then so is the potential for making sensitive, critical readers of students around a common starting point in their own experiences.

The second aspect of this response falls more fully within the literary text, in selecting a new range of literature and in a renewed reading of the classics. Teaching in a London comprehensive school, Barbara Bleiman and Keren Abse describe in *Gender* how they moved from a unit on sexist language to investigating gender as a framework of meaning and typification in a variety of literary forms. They discovered that the students were interested "in comparing their own experiences with accumulated experience in their culture," and that in doing so "they are sometimes taken by surprise in noticing the differences between a stereotypical character and themselves" (*Gender,* 1984, p. 59). Among the literary responses we might hanker after with our students, "taken by surprise" seems an attractive one. This comparison of experiences can work between students and literary characters, but the literature also needs to be explored as a human artifact as well. As writers themselves, students can begin to appreciate what the author is up to with these characters in a story, play, or poem. This response to the author's intent and craft, and not just to the story alone, adds up to a reading that does not stand removed from students' own experience of the world. Gender provides a starting point of shared ground and vested interest.

But let me offer a few examples of the sense that tenth-graders in Richland, Washington made of a unit that Jim Bedard and I developed on a feminist approach to *Romeo and Juliet* (Willinsky & Bedard, in press). In this booklet, we shift the critical spotlight from Romeo, where it rested in some of the instructional material we examined, to Juliet as the play's center for courage and intelligence. Against the sense of an ill-fated love, our unit prompts responses from the students to the role of opportunity, friendship, and duty as Shakespeare gives expression to these in the play and as they speak to our own times. In Debbie Lee's Richland class, the students kept a diary of their responses to the play as they read it in class: "Act V: I hate this whole act. You'd think after all that has gone wrong with the two, *something* could go right!" During the "writers' workshops," the students responded to questions of gender and characterization out of their own reading, experience, and judgement:

> Shakespeare seems to think all young men should be brave and
> tough, like in the fight in the beginning. But men should cry,
> like Romeo did in the Friar's cell. Shakespeare women were

sometimes brave in a very gentle way (perhaps even wimpy).
The girls could say things like Juliet did in the Friar's cell, I
would rather die than be without Romeo, but when she got the
chance to she thought twice before doing it. Today it seems
young people can be sensitive, brave or tough without any
matter over their sex. I don't think Shakespeare's ideas would
work at all today. (Alice)

In the assessments of these sixteen-year-olds, the author is often
conflated with the society he represents and made responsible for the
characters' lives. But the literary naivete aside, the level of engagement
and subtle discernment is the measure of success. In a workshop that
considered how the play was driven by obligations to parents, the students' responses began to suggest re-reading as the crucial point of
developing insight in reading, as re-vision is for writing, and in this a
few of them realized the principles at stake in this play:

Juliet's parents expect marriage from her. Capulet wants Juliet
to Marry a man that will give her a place in society. (Like my
parents don't want Beth to marry a garbage man.) Capulet
thinks of Juliet as his little girl and he wants her to stay his
little girl even if she is a married lady. Lady Capulet agrees she
should marry a man for a place in society but she thinks she
should get prepared for marriage. (Stan)

At best, these model responses, and certainly I have been selective, can
serve to initiate and drive this community of readers. Recalling Bleich,
the meanings explored here can grow in the class's search for intersubjective points of agreement and divergence, points that require re-reading
and elaboration. The critical gems that the students do hit upon—"I
think that violence serves men as a means to masculinity"—are less the
goal here than finding a basis for meaning and engagement out of their
reading stories of young love. Students can find in this community of
text, experience, and discourse, a new level of earnestness which might
begin to spread out from the story:

It always takes tragedy to open people's eyes. Montague and
Capulet would never settle their differences if Romeo and Juliet
did not die. People are never appreciated until they are gone.
Sometimes it's too late to tell them that. (Sara)

After using this theme of gender to prompt a second look at language and literature, a third and final arena of literary response is our own reading histories in which we explore the ways in which our literacy exists within a matrix of texts and stories: "One of the most obvious ways gender influences our experience as readers is when it determines what books are made available to us or are designated as appropriate or inappropriate for our reading" (Segel, 1986, p. 165). We can re-trace our wanderings along the bookshelves and along the path that has been chosen for us; we can compare them to those taken by others, other generations and genders. This asks for a critical treatment of literary response in ourselves and those interested in promoting literacy. It creates critical readers not of the assigned text in isolation, but as reading and texts exist within a textual community, a discourse of literacy. In the *Gender* collection, Marion Glatsonbury has offered a memoir of early literary response, "What Books Tell Girls," which suggest how far back this response to literature can begin as a telling: "From the start I was recognized as a character in search of an author, forever wanting to be someone else, and pretending to read and write. At the age of three, I asked who was the most famous writer ever. 'Shakespeare' they said, and I announced my intention of marrying him. That he was already dead seemed a minor obstacle which could be readily overcome by a really determined bride" (1984, p. 43).

There are more than a few determined brides of literature, daydreaming of a literary romance, just as there are those who have not taken to the book for one reason or another which, one imagines, need not always fall on them in a blameful way, although it often does. As Probst (1988) has pointed out, even these reluctant readers have that smoldering point of literary interest, interest that begins in themselves. To examine these aspects of personal history is to discover that a response to literature, like literacy itself, is a social enterprise, and one that may well gain in re-examination. To dig through this literary and academic past produces the basis of its own textual community. Readers can also return to those earlier texts to see now how they originally worked their wonders, and to have readers consider redirecting their readings to new literary areas to see what has been missed, to challenge the conventional canon of literature in their own reading and see what else lies beyond the edge of the familiar page. Readers in such a class can begin to see how literature and life go together, and how the answers which they have been taught are deeply embedded in the text are only one aspect of what literature asks of us or tells about us.

Feminist criticism can make these three aspects—of language, literature, and life—the basis of a response to literary works that can begin
to shift the center of meaning from the teacher's reading to the student's.
Yet without question, this feminist perspective, with its intense concentration on gender, still strikes some readers as unconvincing, if not
patently absurd, and it does so with readers and writers whether they be
men or women. One irony to this approach is that a theory that calls
itself reader-response must in this way attend to the response of those
who say "no," who deny, or in the terms of the theory as it has developed,
who *resist* this dimension of gender in their reading, who ask if it has
any basis in fact. The research that establishes the gendered pattern of
responses to literature has drawn on two disciplines—psychology and
literary criticism. Employing the research methods that have been
developed around the cognitive psychology of schema theory, Mary
Crawford and Roger Chaffin found that "the effects of gender and
gender-typing, while reliable, are small" (1987, p. 21). While they
recognize that "so salient a factor as gender and so pervasive a process
as sex-role socialization" should have a more profound influence on a
reader's schema, they attribute the slightness of the findings to the
reading lessons women have learned, to what they refer to as "muted
group theory" which makes reference to the manner in which women
learn to read as if they were men.

More notable differences have been located in the findings or more
accurately the "reading" of students' responses to literature. Elizabeth
Flynn (1987) has studied the differences in response to short stories and
poetry from undergraduate students; she found a certain detachment in
the men and sense of participation in the story by women. The readers
resisted or were absorbed in the literature on this basis of gender, but
the nature of the story played an important role. The men resisted
engagement with stories that centered on the experience of women.
These two patterns in the reading can become the source of interest in
a class at any age level that is interested in how literature works, that is,
works on readers. The object remains one of using gender as a means
to engage the reader in the making and sharing of meaning, of "transact-
ing" with the text and the class.

Certainly, no one is claiming that being raised a girl or a boy is the
only thing that counts or comes to mind in being drawn along by the
ways of a book. Gender is but one source of difference and meaning,
yet one that has profound political and personal implications for the
world at large, for the young coming of age, and for the community

known as the classroom. In no sense, then, is gender to be taken as the sole source of meaning in the text. But it is a common, accessible basis for shaping and sharing a response to literacy; the form of response nurtured by this criticism can serve as a model of inquiry into literature that works between text and reader without losing sight of the fact that both are situated within a realm of differences. To see feminist criticism as blind to other elements of response is unfair. Feminist critics have attacked what seemed to be an initial single-mindedness of interest with the plight of a universalized woman, which may well have been necessary to give the concept a certain critical mass; in doing so it failed, however, to take into account that women's experiences greatly differ by class, race, and sexual orientation (Cotes-Cardenas, 1980; Kennard, 1986). The *Gender* material includes a collection of educational papers on "Sex, Race, and Class" (1984, pp. 88–105). These pieces move from encouraging a critical and independent stance in learners to helping them face the difficult truths in living through these issues. Rather than simply striving to ensure equality of opportunity in the classroom, the call is for deliberately "anti-sexist, anti-racists and anti-classist teaching and learning and this involves the critical examination of issues relating to race, sex, class and it means analyzing oppression, past and present" (p. 89).

Feminist reading begins with this very matter of difference as the source of renewed meaning, a difference in gender, certainly, but also one that works across a number of dimensions, each with its own social meaning, in anyone's life. This sensitivity to difference, I might add, has been the tool of the previous two chapters for getting at the sources of meaning for a New Literacy. It is enough to say that we live with many categories, many differences, which are sources of meaning in our lives. We are also distinguished by the broad fabric of our experiences which defies such narrow classifications but which greatly enriches our readings as both Rosenblatt and Bleich have demonstrated. Yet we read as we live, not solely as individuals, but as part of different frameworks of meaning from within the social situation and individuality of our lives.

Gender provides one framework that student and teacher knowingly share and of which they are trying hard to make complete sense. Of course, there are other helpful frameworks—such as Northrop Frye's (1957) cycle of genres and myths that govern literature—and these, too, can form the basis of leading response within the community of readers, but gender remains a pressing framework that is especially lively today

115

on literary and social fronts. On the other hand, I am not convinced that to eschew such frameworks and then imagine that one is reading the text straight and true is advisable or helpful to students trying to find their way into these texts. I also recognize that this may seem a questionable territory for a man to be treading on, if not peddling in. Once the issue is raised, the reader cannot help but wonder about the influence of my gender, as a man commenting on this recovery of a reading dominated by men. This attention to the writer's gender falls within the theory of response. I have been drawn to feminist literacy theory because it has put so much into question, and all of those questions seem to successfully bridge the personal and the public in the asking, if rarely in the arrival at satisfactory answers. It has that element of the unknown, of questions for literary works and readers that lends much to the sense of a common community and interest in this literary enterprise.

Reader-response theory, through Rosenblatt, Bleich, and feminist criticism, is one means of shifting the meaning in the study of literature. Literature can bring together individual experience and social action, as Rosenblatt originally proposed; it can mean students writing in response to the work of others through their own experiences and on to critical evaluation, as Bleich proposes; and it can pose questions to the reading which guide our own sense of ourselves, as feminists have offered. In all cases, the reader reads as a writer, as one engaged in some of the same problems of language and representation. Working from a response to literature raises to expression the barely articulate in these readers and writers and creates a combined reading, writing, and literature project in the classroom. On this theme of integration, it is a small step from a critical response as a reader of literature to one as a viewer and listener of popular culture, for which "reception theory" might be the better label. And as it turns out, the English Centre's *Gender* collection also has a chapter on media that moves from billboards and advertisements to magazines and television scripts; it begins with the strong interplay of media and meaning in our society: "that the media do not simply reflect back unmeditated images of reality but contribute to the construction of our reality is nowhere more striking than in the representation of women" (*Gender*, 1984, p. 63). The path of critical response, with a little encouragement and practice, is bound to move outward.

A reader-response approach to literature is concerned with how texts work on readers; it takes the response as the key to a better understanding of how texts operate, from Shakespeare to Margaret Atwood, from young adult romances to music videos. The sharing of response as a source of meaning about the text redefines the workings of the classroom. In this way the New Literacy establishes a literary community in dialogue with the individual's textual transaction. The theme of literary study becomes this intense pursuit of connection and meaning that extends beyond the page. But to be realistic about this aspiration, it has no greater hope of reaching the escape velocity necessary to lift it above the confines of the school than the writing workshop or the choose-your-own-book programs of earlier chapters; these are educational moments that must remain grounded in classrooms even as they transform them into a new images of literacy and literature.

Notes

1. The term "textual communities" is cribbed from Brian Stock (1983) and not without a touch of irony. Stock uses it to describe an implication of literacy in eleventh and twelfth century Europe as a way of capturing the nature of reformist and heretical religious organizations that formed around a literacy and an interpretation of text (pp. 88–240). One might claim that the young adult romance is a heretical text in the classroom and that the interpretation of these readers has its own devout twist to it.

2. William Powers makes a similar nomination by connecting the work of Kenneth and Yetta Goodman to the interests of reader-response theory. He points to their studies which establish that readers "read because in reading they make meaning for themselves" and "reading is carried out and meaning made in social contexts" (1983, p. 34). However, the association among the leading New Literacy exponents of writing and reading, as discussed in Chapters 2 and 3, and those involved in reader-response theory are rare.

3. This problem of what is experienced in reading is shared by all reader-response theories and speaks to its essential idealism. The physiological analysis of the reading act, conducted by Nell (1988), demonstrates that readers do enter something of a trance state, or at least an engagement to a degree that would seem effectively to preclude a self-conscious reflection on the response. Among reader-response theorists, Norman Holland (1975) has employed that blend of the imaginative and empirical to delineate four stages of this absorption through which the reader is ultimately said to be seeking an "identity theme" in the text. In treating the issue of gender, Holland portrays in his own reading a matter of different themes that comfort and that confront the identity (Holland & Sherman, 1987).

4. In the province of Alberta where I teach, the Department of Education has issued a new *Junior High School Language Arts Curriculum Guide* (Alberta Education, 1987) which pays tribute to Rosenblatt. The *Guide* stresses that "in junior high there needs to be a greater emphasis upon reading literature aesthetically, since lifelong reading is an objective of the Alberta language

arts curriculum, and most lifelong readers read aesthetically" (p. 42). The *Guide* goes on to state that to "understand and appreciate imagery or figurative language in a passage is part of an efferent analysis" (p. 42), which is not only misleading but carries with it the implication that such "appreciation" is not the sort of thing that lifelong aesthetic readers do. I think that the nuances are obscured because the purpose here is not so much to clarify the literary experiences of students but to further specific progressive pedagogical ends. The province's curriculum committee appears to employ Rosenblatt's distinctions to steer teachers away from a reading skill and drill approach to literature that goes after the *facts* that a poem teaches, as Rosenblatt has put it with some indignation (1980).

5. In seeking instances of this continuing political concern with literature, I was surprised to find Paulo Freire and Donaldo Macedo innocently citing Rosenblatt as a "seeming liberal approach to literacy [which] fails to make problematic class conflict, gender, or racial inequalities" (1987, p. 149). The fact is that, while she did celebrate the aesthetic moment, she also dealt with those problematics in her early work and more importantly, like Freire, she demonstrated how the power of the word was a political force which began in the reader's experience in language and the world. One need not subscribe to Rosenblatt's sense of literature's vicarious function in a democracy, which is clearly more than "seeming" liberal, to note that her original work on the politics of literature was a promising starting point and worthy of development.

6. Rosenblatt and Bleich should not be regarded as removed from the concerns of feminist response theory. Elizabeth Flynn (1983) has written about Rosenblatt's early acknowledgement of women's experience as a source of response. Bleich (1987) has written directly about the differences in students' response based on gender; he finds an intriguing pattern that divides women and men in their relationship to the narrator, as women find themselves in the teller and tale, while men remain apart. But he seems to place this response beyond the reach of the classroom by preferring to ground it in what he declares to be the biological fact of gender: "alongside the many common interests men and women have in language and literature they also have interests that are permanently tied to the biological fact that they are also of different genders" (1987, p. 266). The feminist reading that can advance New Literacy work with literature is not primarily rooted in biology but in the social meaning that tends to be fashioned out of this difference.

5
The Troubled Romance of Expression

It is the third commonness with light and air
A curriculum, a vigor, a local abstraction . . .
Call it, once more a river, an unnamed flowing,
      Wallace Stevens, "The River of Rivers in Connecticut"

It is not enough to describe the programs of the New Literacy in their splendor and shortcomings. There is a need to get closer to the work of the classroom, to the daily energy and exchange of a class taken up with this personal and public project in writing and reading. I want to offer that in this chapter by turning to the work of an innovative teacher who taught down the hall from my classroom in a rural school nestled in the hills above the Goulais River in northern Ontario. One fall, Ruth Fletcher gradually found her own way into a new kind of literacy program for her grade one and two students. We worked together on creating a record of what she was attempting when she let the basal readers slip from her program and turned increasingly to the literary resources of the blank page and library books. The students repaid her courage with wonderful literary acts, some of which will figure in this account as a demonstration of the New Literacy at work. The question I was left with was where did she get this faith in the children's ability to learn, to trust their own instincts, as she increasingly learned to trust her own? At first, she seemed to be running alone with these ideas about literacy in lessons that built on students' interests in reading and writing. It did begin to appear that they sat before blank pages, instead of skill-sheets, and they wrote their way into the world of books.

In this chapter, I want to draw close to a specific, limited instance of the New Literacy based on my work with Ruth and the subsequent efforts to measure the impact of this program in different classrooms. This composite picture works from three different sorts of discourse: 1) my field notes from the center of Ruth's classroom will be interspersed between sections on 2) the subsequent and critical reflections on the dilemmas we found emerging in that class on the issue of self-representation and gender, and 3) a report on a follow-up statistical study comparing first-grade classrooms which were working in the New Literacy with classrooms that were not. This chapter unquestioningly romances the classroom experience of expression, taken as it is from my deep immersion in its wonders at the time, and it then asks difficult questions of this expression, questions about its roots and implications that will only receive an adequate treatment in the chapters that follow.

Field notes from the New Literacy, part I

The goats

The children have been filing in, chatting, and hanging up their coats as I finish writing the description of the classroom. When I arrived the room was empty and now the class is reassembling after a morning field trip. Ruth calls out, "Boys and girls, sit on the rug." "The rug!" The cry goes out among a number of them. Ruth's "Let's go group" is met with a student's, "Anyone know where *The Black Stallion* book is?"

They have assembled on the small section of rug near the windows. The primary rug holds the eighteen children like an island, though the palm tree in this case is Ruth sitting in a tall-backed rocking chair with her elbows on her knees. She leans forward to discuss with the children their trip to Ted's farm, which is just up the road from the school. They have visited the farm to see Ted's two goats there and their newly born kids. The children's voices swirl around the rocking chair; one voice begins and they all feel compelled to follow.

"I liked Sammy."

"Ya, I really like Sammy."

"Me, I . . . "

Ruth raises a question, attempting to move on, about the mother goat's horns. "A chainsaw, ya, they cut them off with a chainsaw." The image catches their imagination and one boy adds, "Hey, ya, a chainsaw."

Ruth laughs, holds back, then tries to get them to speak in some sort of order, speaking with patient deliberation to signal to the children the virtues of control. But there can be no natural flow of conversation or discussion with eighteen children on a rug. It is, from this island of carpet, as if they cannot resist diving into the language, especially to ride the wave of affirmation, of "I liked, oh, I liked . . . "

[Ruth writes in the margins of these field notes: "Sometimes it seems that these discussions are the true point of learning— there is so much color and vibrancy and interplay of thoughts."]

"Okay everybody, in through your nose," Ruth says in a tone that cuts through the conversations. "Out through your mouth. In through your nose and out through your mouth. In through . . . "

There is silence again, with only the sound of this nasal breathing, as some of the children sitting on the soles of their feet, rock gently back and forth. Ruth then invites Carl to comment, and he carefully begins, "What I liked about the goats was the . . . " The others grow slightly restless at this deliberateness and Carl stumbles on for a bit about the goat, Sinbad, and the rest of the class is off again into the noisy surf, as everyone comments on Sinbad.

It is a reigning in and letting go. We would have them talk something like this in primary classes, have them call out to the world what they like. But not to get carried away by it. For though language is good, and to use language is good, there must be an ordering if what they say will be heard, if we do indeed say things to be heard. At this point, it seems enough to just say things, to state what you like right out loud.

Ruth gets up from the rocking chair and the students return to their desks, set in groups of four or five facing each other in pairs. If there were instructions given, they have slipped by me; the class is moving, it seems, under its own direction. Ruth hands out paper to each child, one sheet lined in blue and red and the other one blank. She then writes on the board in a list: like, goat, the, lazy, Sinbad, tongue, stuck, is, was, one, day, wild, baaaa, stable, pen, caught, saw, strong, Tyler's barn, bite, went, fishing, heart attack.

"I need 'saw,' " one student almost immediately asks.

Ruth takes a moment to ask for his best guess, adding that "you don't hear the *w*."

"Where's 'fishing'?" another student calls out to no one in particular. "F-i-s-h-i-n-g," comes the answer from a few desks away.

The students have begun to write of goats and fishing trips and heart attacks.

"Hey Carl, what's your title?"

"The 'I Like Goats,' " Carl replies; he has written:

> *I like goats*
> and he Caught a fish
> and he went home he his friend
> and he ate it

"Can you write 'died'?" Allan asks Ruth.

Death, she later tells me, is his constant theme and he finds a place for it in all his work. After another moment Allan is back up to Ruth's side, "Look how much I write; could you write 'be'?"

Ruth also tells me later that Allan's writing moves like this, word by word, one block at a time. After five months of grade two he does know "like," but it seems as if he should know "died" too. Only recently, she told me, has he been able to carry two words back to his desk and onto his page. Though in this case the "be" he asks for is only a part of the word "*be*cause," the progress he appears to be making is that the words he must write interfere less with the story he would tell, and it is no simple story he would tell:

> a goat was lazy   one day The goat
> went fishing he caught a bite
> The goat died be cause a heartattack
> by his Grandfather.

As in the discussion, the singing out of goat praise on the rug, the children, besides Allan and a few others, understand this writing to be a means of affirming desire and feeling—"I *like* therefore I am" is their Descartian argument to establish the existence of self:

> Sammy is soft
> he is nice
> and I like ham
> and I sad thank you to Tyler
> I like going out in the fresh

air and I like it I was glad to be
going for a walk and it was good
The End   (Karen)

The dady goat
I like the dady goat.
he was soft and he was
cute. I like sinbad.
And I like sammy too.
Because he is just nice.
The end.   (Ted)

The other alternative to this solipsism in the children's writing is to
borrow from the school's dominant literary form, the question:

sammy is soft
is he nice?
is he Bad?
is he curious?
aor is he good?
aor is he everything?   (Sherry)

is the goat powerful
is. the. goats. wild N   (Jim)

They continue their favorite games in print; they affirm the *primum
cognitum,* the first knowledge, of self-expression and they play at the
first professional role they've met, teaching.

Robin, sitting near to where I am making my notes, has not written
a word in the fifteen minutes the children have been at work. She has
drawn a house on the paper while Ruth has been busy at the board adding
new words and generally responding to the responsive ones.

The house is a triangle atop a square; Robin works in platonic ideals,
reducing all that she knows of houses to this gesture of seven lines on
the page. Drawing houses was certainly a possibility when Ruth handed
out the lined and blank paper, and Robin has chosen to stick to symbols
she is sure of. They are so much less arbitrary than letters; a triangle,
colored green, cues a *roof.*

When it is time to prepare for lunch, Ruth asks the students to put
their name on the paper and hand them in. Robin prints "Rodin" at the
top of her sheet and hands it in with the others.

[Ruth writes: "Robin! Robin! Robin! She refuses to take a literary leap. She has set up so many covers for her imperfections. She hides behind these constantly. She'll probably be a teacher when she grows up. *Robin I have failed you*. She knows I'll have nothing to do with her trite efforts; I can only stand, 'I like my bog' (dog) for five months, then that's it. Robin goes to Susan's room (a classroom with workbooks and readers) and flourishes—what can I say? Robin and I came together for a moment last week. We talked about how she found reading 'boring and difficult.' It was our first honest conversation without any lace. Maybe I can help her."]

I find in looking through the submitted pieces that nine of the eighteen students produced a sentence or more of text when confronted with a sheet of lined and blank paper, with near-invisible instructions, with fifteen minutes of writing time and a trip to one of the student's goat shed. After lunch Ruth picks it up again. Allan adds not a word to his work; Mitchell produces two solid pages of story set in columns as is his wont; Melanie covers all the bases:

> I like the sound of the rooster
> AND I liked the goats
> too AND I like sammy
> BEst Sammy is white
> Sinbad is black I would like
> too have one baby goat
> I think they are so cute
> AND I sill like the baby goats
> BESt.

What is there in these children's texts? Almost too much: seemingly, biblical reference in Karen's—"and it was good"—metaphysics in Sherry's "or is he everything?"—parenthetical clauses in Melanie's—"I think they are so cute." The sequence of their production was the *experience* of going down the road to Ted's, the sharing of *language* on the rug, and finally, the *writing* at their desks. Such field trip follow-ups are common enough in classrooms; they provide the educational excuse for leaving the classroom. But in Ruth's room the trips and writing are not a supplement anymore, but the main staple in a sequence which runs regularly from experience to language to writing. The motivation and the opportunity are what Ruth seeks to provide; they have become the heart of her instructional materials, her curriculum. She has, by degrees, given up what she had little patience with, and little sense of the worth of—workbooks full of sound-letter match-ups, readers with restricted stories and vocabularies—and she has, by degrees, begun to trust the act itself, as if writing produced writers, and literate activities, literacy.

But there are not always new-born kids to be visited. Ruth uses the simpler moments to provide a motive as well. There is "Sharing Time," a version of "Show and Tell," in the morning; there are the stories she reads to them; there are incidents in the playground, television programs or any number of small occurrences which will serve to provide a focus, a jumping off point. There barely needs to be reason at all, or at least a reason provided. For students come to school with enough to express, to give voice to; only one or two need prodding, or time left alone before they begin. The first assumption at work here is that expression is essential to all of us.

Thinking about this New Literacy

I realized during the process of making those field notes that Ruth's class presented both the promise of a new literacy and the troubling persistence of old problems which I now want to examine in some detail, problems of identity and gender stereotyping. But that is only the first part of this examination. When our efforts to document the development of Ruth's program left its first readers questioning the basis of our faith in the program and the claims we were content to make on its behalf, I tried a second, experimental approach complete with pre and posttests. Again I turned up what I felt were troubling results, limited by the scale of the study of six classes, but still troubles of the sort that I feel needed to be heard and explored by those interested in the New Literacy. This time, the results challenged the New Literacy on its very claim of improved attitude toward writing. The one study led directly out of the other, as I tried in the first instance to document the development of a New Literacy program, and finding a room full of doubters, attempted the second in which I moved away from qualitative research deliberately in search of the findings in decimalized numbers that speak louder, for some, than words. The results in both instances raise yet other challenges for the New Literacy that I want to introduce along with the issue of researching the new and different.

As I have been intimating, the New Literacy is underwritten by the Romantic project with expression. This guiding aesthetic creates an ideological link between art and education which dates back to Wordsworth and the cultural upheaval that arose at the end of the eighteenth century. However in exploring this association in my own research and teaching I have also come to appreciate the fact that Romanticism is by no means the natural ally of school. There appears to be a contradiction between these two phenomena, between the Romantic urge to self-expression and the Victorian desire to shape the student's soul, as advocated by Matthew Arnold in his role as School Inspector. This difference in spirit, in intention and temperament, can frustrate the educator drawn to Romanticism and its view of the child and learning which is the subject of Chapter 7. The example that I wish to present here from my work is of a troubling educational art, a Romantic paradox, of first- and second-grade children making the page over in their own image. This Romantic urge to expression in the New Literacy runs up against an equally progressive inclination to educate what is traditionally given in gender and identity.

Through a process of experimentation and gradual letting go of the basal reading program, Ruth seemed to discover the expressive and educational powers of the blank page in a child's hand. Over the course of a few months, Ruth found more and more of her school day given over to the marks the children were making on this blank paper. She didn't collect the readers from the students' desks; the students had soon buried them beneath the stacks of their own writings in their desks, some of it stapled into instant books, some of it floating loose.

While other teachers spent their time before class in the morning busily running off their worksheets in phonics, letter-formations, and math facts, Ruth simply picked up another stack of blank paper and went to her class, with her coffee in hand, to see what the children would bring to life there. In observing these students at work and looking over what they wrote, I was struck by the students' artful moments of discovery and risk, of false starts and sudden breakthroughs, sometimes in techniques, in spelling out new words and getting the story down, sentence by sentence, sometimes in what was said, as the students, pages in hand, moved quickly through the class with a "Come and hear this." Ruth and I did come to hear what they had written and could read; we were increasingly impressed.

Yet in trusting the children more and more, Ruth feared that she had left the great protector, the official curriculum and prescribed texts, behind; she needed something to support her venture against this sense of going her own way in what can be a lonely institution for adults and kids who go it alone. Even without having to face the judgement of standardized testing that so many teachers now face, this moment of creative intervention risked collapsing for want of sanction. The solution to this first obstacle was startlingly simple. She decided to write about it, to create the missing curricular sanctions out of the same blank paper the students were exploiting. What she gave to the students, she began to give to herself, as she gave expression to the accomplishments of her students and the manner in which she was learning.

The first thing she realized was that the usual order had been turned on its head. The students were beginning literacy with the book, and often their own books, rather than with the prepared worksheet; they leaped into awkward sentences that floated across the page rather than spending weeks on forging individual letters between the red and blue lines of the first-grade notebooks. She also realized that the test case for this books-*into*-literacy challenge was the child famous for not reading in the school, the problem child. Consider Allan, in the midst of repeating grade one, the least inclined of the children for the ordering concerns of the classroom; school, you might say, is something he would not sit still for.

When Ruth finally called in the students' "books" at the end of the term, Allan presented two bulging portfolios, both entitled "Pinnochio." That was a favorite book of his which he had eventually brought to Ruth to prove, I suspect, that he had a piece of the action and the icon which was so exciting the class. Each of his portfolios had in the area of a hundred sheets of paper, most of them covered in tracings from various books or free-hand attempts at sharks and tanks. These had been stapled into small booklets of five or six pages which Allan had proposed in earnest to sell as coloring books. He had solicited the help of two boys to do some printing in the books for him because he sensed that this would make them more commercially attractive. But this contracting of services hadn't panned out, and the books were wordless for the most part. Yet he had begun to realize himself as a producer of books, and no longer one failed by them.

He made progress, too, with the sentence as well as the book; among his more recent publications was a fully captioned illustrated series on the shark theme, running page after page:

> The Shark is a live
> Sharks is bloody
> The sharks chasing a sharks
> The sharks is going

Although his "sharks" is often only *a* lone shark, the structures of sentence and narrative are present, and he would seem to on be his way. More importantly for art, for the romance of expression, he told Ruth that "my books are going to last forever." There is no cry more Romantic than that, no more profound expression of the self found in art, than this wish realized in the first grade—*ars longa, vita brevis*—that his mark might outlive his life.

Yet a profound problem in this pursuit of art emerged out of the subject of expression, out of what the students chose to represent of themselves in their stories. Ruth was opening new realms of self-expression through literacy for the children, and thus she was able to bring into play interests which are not always welcomed in a grade one-two classroom.

She first grew distressed with the boys' obsessive literary violence, with story after story on sharks, *Star Wars* and monsters, until, it seemed, their pens dripped with blood and not an illustration passed without the tell-tale scar of the red marker. Here is a classic, the model for Allan's final piece, from the shark days that passed through the classroom:

> The shark is bombed. He is dying from the bullets and the
> bullets are murdering him and the shark doesn't give up.

In encouraging them to take the themes from their lives on the playground to the page and to spell out their vision, the boys increasingly spilled more than Ruth had planned on. She felt the extra responsibility of having unleashed this disturbing force with her new program. The boys were finding themselves on the page with an enthusiasm that they are notorious in the research for not displaying in the early years of school, and which I believe they would not have shown if she had kept their pencils to forming letters and matching pictures to sounds. The problem that she faced was that the spirit running through their work seemed to contradict what she wanted the children to be, now that they were finally free to be themselves.

Although it would be easy to dismiss this tendency to terror as the play of children, it seem to deserve serious consideration as this thinking had its place in the play of ideas and history. The aesthetic object of Romanticism, as helpfully identified by Edmund Burke in the eighteenth century, strikes a tone that these students seem attuned to: "whatever is in any sort terrible, or is conversant with terrible objects, or operates in a manner analogous to terror, is a source of the *sublime*" (1968, p. 39). In a sense, we might say that the boys had staged their own Romantic rebellion, in probing the uncivil struggle and terror that could give the page a new life for them. This glorification has a troubling history. The dangers inherent in this aesthetic sensibility are found in the way that the neo-Romanticism of the soil and the spirit became a source of this century's fascism (Rosenbaum, 1987). The terror the boys evoked is not far removed from the Futurists' fascination in the 1920s with the most fearsome of experiences, the technological rage of war, as Fillipo Marinetti's 1913 manifesto captured it in his response to the Ethiopian war:

War is beautiful because it initiates the dreamt-of metalization of the human body. War is beautiful because it enriches a flowering meadow with the fiery orchids of machine guns. War is beautiful because it combines the gunfire, the cannonades, the cease-fire, the scents, and the stench of putrefaction into a symphony. (cited in Benjamin, 1969, pp. 241–42)

The dreamt-of metalization of the body is these boys' very dream, the machine gun across the meadow of the page, their very manifesto of literacy. For Marinetti and the Futurists, Walter Benjamin may have been right when he identifies the Futurist manifestos as statements of extreme self-alienation (1969, p. 242). In a related fashion for the children, the initial realization of technology as a terrorist force pressing against life has become their vehicle into the world as it fascinates them and as they find themselves on the page through it. Yet alienation is not a term that comes to mind in seeing them work their stories about the classroom.

This allowance of their terrorizing art integrates them into the literate classroom. They play it out on the page and in the schoolyard without having to respect the traditional boundaries between these two sites. They play it out against its complacent denial by the genteel politeness of the school, and once played out in this fashion one hope may be to see it transformed rather than repressed as it had previously been. The students' reading series had always kept such Romantic morbidity at bay—the stories in the school readers had been scrubbed of violence

129

long before the current concerns with equality have mercifully, though only partially, scoured the books of ubiquitous Caucasian lads with their hapless sisters in tow.

The boys' attraction to the bloody struggle between life and death, to the metaphysical fascination with the idea of life spilling out, was matched in the girls' work in the classroom by an equally troubling, though far less sensational, absorption in a single arena of discourse. To continue the historical parallels in aesthetics, their work might be thought to partake of the classicism which eighteenth-century art historian Johann Winckelmann described as aimed "at a noble simplicity and a calm grandeur" (cited in Clark, 1973, p. 20). Yet this other classroom standard seemed to unfold with the same intensity, if only in another universe:

> One bright morning a little girl went outside and there was a beautiful garden. It was so beautiful that she ran into the house and told her mother and her mother was so excited, even when she was doing the dishes, she ran outside! And she started to pick the flowers too. The end.

In other instances, princesses wake up, dance with princes all the night long, and the woods laugh out loud. The telling of the story is tighter and an undeniable majesty hangs about their work. It contains a search for human connection in the disruption of domestic habits, between mother and daughter in this case, connections that the boys would tear asunder. Though in a different fashion than the boys, these works contain a form of breaking away, as mothers desert the kitchen sink and princesses call the tune. The girls are finding their own voice and writing their own stories. Yet the subtlety of the girls' break with the school tends to be overlooked as their garden scenes fit all too comfortably within the culture of the classroom. Feminist scholarship has made it apparent that the school contributes to the "cooling out" of girls through a tradition of downgraded expectations and distortions of self as these girls learn to, for example, read as boys in the books of boyish heroes which fill classroom and library bookshelves (Spender & Sarah, 1980; Weiner, 1985).

The cultural element showed up when Ruth found that she could proudly display the girls' work on the wall outside the classroom, while she had to brave the skeptical looks of her colleagues in posting the frenzied pages of the boys. The school would celebrate the quiet passivity of the girls' work, playing up its tidy expression of the world while failing to realize and encourage its subtle efforts at connection, and at breaking the domestic hold of dinner dishes on their lives. In another grade, to overstate it only somewhat, the boys' rough and tumble work will be paved over and turned into a parking lot of frustrated complicity with proper forms. Both the work of the girls and the boys, though deeply divided by gender, reveals an artful indulgence in expression which the school has traditionally failed to realize and which can become the way into a more powerful and meaningful literacy.

In observing this introduction to literacy, we felt the compulsion to educate, to intrude with lessons that would have them realize a perspective which is not so set in these artless stereotypes, so set in their realization of guns and gardens. Yet the further question of whether to challenge and educate, these typifications, these selves suddenly made out of blank paper, is at least one step removed from the matter of first fully allowing them to surface through the language and visual arts in the classroom. In this case, Ruth allowed the students' work to unfold as it would, but she did so troubled by this nagging sense of responsibility of addressing the question.

The gender stereotyping in Ruth's classroom was perpetuated in the students' writing and in the books they chose to read. Difference was important to them from the moment they walked into the room and went to the cloakroom where they maintained for themselves a boys' and girls' section for their winter coats and boots. They were left to find their own way in words and images, to create their own worlds upon the blank page. Rarely in this classroom was a student drawn across the gender line which they formed in the cloakroom and in the literary topics—between, say, dinosaurs and rabbits. In the vacuum of selection and direction that Ruth had initiated, the students held dearly to the one division of experience and sense of self which they had grown into since birth. Ruth was understandably disturbed by the contradiction which racked her best intentions; she would determinedly respect the children's self-expression, while wincing and wishing otherwise for the self that they sought to express.

The educator cannot easily step away from her charge to instruct. As an innovator, Ruth was in a state of heightened responsibility, having risked not just a curriculum with the New Literacy but herself. The classroom had taken on more of her style in its atmosphere, in the way that it moved through the day; it had grown into her own vehicle of expression. Yet in giving expression to her vision of the educational setting, she discovered that something still eluded her in the process.

She knew not whether to trust the direction it took. The nature of her responsibility haunted her, even as it excited her in working it up on the page herself. In promoting self-expression, she had relinquished an aspect of control over the children in exchange for a more engaging form of literacy.

This moment for Ruth would seem to expose the distance between Romanticism in art and education, even when they meet in a classroom set in the hills above a river. For the teacher, there is that initial daring of seeing what the page can hold and the child can tell, and the subsequent temptation to marshal the page into a lesson, not to let the opportunity to instruct pass. This allowing and encouraging of the child is one sort of educational moment, and this intervention in these students' expression is another. I did not know how to reconcile these two when we worked together on this project.

I now feel there is a need to challenge students' expressive inclinations. This begins with the teachers' response as a reader of the students' work. As part of this immediate community, there is room for this expression of the teacher's sense and understanding. What is expected from the students, must be allowed the teacher. To challenge students' habits of expression, when a teacher can see that they have much to learn by stepping outside the bounds they have set up for themselves, is to demonstrate what this expressive urge is about. Students can be asked to find new voices, to trade story lines to freshen their plotting, to write for new audiences, to mix genres to enrich their settings; teachers have them watch for the same patterns and for the twists in what they read. The issues come up in this literacy community because it is a concern. The teacher speaks out on this issue of gender in the classroom and beyond, finding new ways to be heard, and asks students to do the same, knowing that the work of these voices is not always or simply harmonious. Romanticism is full of troubled figures of speech, full of conflict and momentary stays against confusion.

Field notes from the New Literacy, part II

Finally, in June

> The Mistry horse
> one Dark and spuky
> Night RoBin Creped into

The Manchen and
a play gost poped
out from Behind
The Corner She
opened The Door
There stood horse
he was all black
she was So So So
So happy ThaT
She rode away
on The horse
and lived happily
aver after.
The End   (Sherry)

The students have learned to introduce into their work a greater elaboration of story more than anything else in the development of their writing. A year ago, in kindergarten, they wrote, or rather they dictated, single sentences to the teacher about their pictures—"Mr. Mugs is chasing Tiger" (Sherry). Now they seem able to write well enough to pique our curiosity with a title, to set the scene, to introduce the characters, to develop a plot with a twist and draw it to a conclusion, if only a cliched one. They have come to grasp the pattern of expectations and conventions in the written story.

the little pepermint with legs

one day a little
girl was runing down
town with a little
peppermint in her hand
fienly She got tiyred
So She lied down
And after a wile
She was fast asleep
and She was dreaming
about the peppermint she
she had in her hand
and she was dreaming
that the peppermint

had legs and when
she woke up in
the morning she
saw the little
peppermint and he did have legs
the End   (Melanie)

They also seem to have some idea of license and the possible play on conventions and imagination which permits and encourages reading, although they have yet to include all of the conventional elements. Their mastery of conventions in spelling and punctuation has not kept up with their urge to tell the whole story. This should not be surprising as their exposure to literary language has been through listening to stories and reading books; it is only natural that they have first to grasp these larger patterns of story making, the less-arbitrary conventions that seem to contribute to the meaning and enjoyment of the stories, before attending to an exactitude in spelling and punctuation.

What has been encouraged and allowed to develop in the course of the school year is a growing mastery of composition skills. The students have begun in their first year of writing to consider the elements of sequence and suspense, of cause and effect. They take up and play with the conventions in language which can charm, and hold the reader, making them over slightly in their own image. They understand the repertoire of options open to the writer—the dark and spooky night, the sudden scare, the dark horse, the dream fantasy. Our delight with their stories has always been a key element in the attractiveness of the New Literacy. It is partly in their imitation, in their clumsily dressing up in the classic forms. These forms, I would add, are assuredly literate, rather than visual and video. Television and the movies may provide heroes and villains, the settings and even the sensations they would create, but the conventions they are using are literate and print-bound—"one Dark and spuky Night"; "fienly she got tiyerd." The movie *Star Wars* may have driven the boys to the picture book, but it is the book which has influenced their writing to the point where George, using the accompanying cassette tape, has committed the opening pages to memory and proudly writes them out as if by some strange sort of magic—he has made *Star Wars* his. Long long ago, in a galaxy far far away . . . children used to learn favorite poems and stories by heart in a golden age of childhood literacy. The spirit has not been lost, and it moves, in this case, from the book through the cassette-reader to the blank page.

But beyond this skill in elaborating stories, their work with the word lists and with their stories, with Ruth as a group and as individuals, has led to an ability to read. Some are turning to the primers left over from the previous program but more are turning to library and classroom books. Paperback copies of the Clifford books by Norman Bridwell (*Clifford Gets a Job, Clifford Takes a Trip,* and so on) have been passing from hand to hand for months in the class. At one end of the scale, Allan has made the least progress in reading. He can read *The Book of ME!*— "My eyes see. My ears hear."—which is what he may need, but he remains a most reluctant reader. As a writer, though, he does somewhat better by June in both attitude and scope, which is again the direction that the other students have taken under Ruth's encouragement:

> The golden maps
>
> One day The
> pirate fond a
> golden Maps And
> he found The
> treasure A golden
> eagle flew out
> he name was
> PAUL   (Allan)

At the other end of the scale, Ted picks his way through *Old Yeller,* and Melanie reads selected passages from the *New Testament.* All of which is to say that there is the usual spread in abilities or, more accurately, in accomplishments in Ruth's class. Though, as mentioned before, these differences may have come to be exaggerated by the greater reach permitted students in their standard reading fare, from pre-primers to the good Book. Reading in this fashion, from books rather than readers, on one's own taste rather than as the class or reading group progresses, exposes the children to a much greater range of styles, formats, and subject matter; it again provides that immediacy. The children are not learning how stories are read through 'directed reading' led by the teacher, just as they are not being fed tidbits of stories to prepare them to make the right book choices later; they are reading now as readers read—for themselves.

The students have, in both their writing and their reading begun to show a mastery of the conventions of written language. On one level, there is nothing more to literacy than the adherence and attending to conventions. This is, in part, the psycholinguistic argument. The knowledge of conventions that they have acquired sets up the necessary expectations in the reader which make reading smoothly and with comprehension possible. Equally so with writing, the students apply their literary sense of how stories are told out of their knowledge of conventions— "One day . . . " But this reduction of literacy to a familiarity with a host of conventions is hardly adequate to convey what has transpired in Ruth's classroom and what the students have come up with in their writing.

The stress in her class has been on writing whole stories, individually set, though often arising out of a common experience, whether a goat trip, Easter assembly, or marbles season. Words have not been selected to be taught and learned, but called upon by the writer to tell the story. The writing has not been to fill in the blanks, match up the word to the picture, answer the guidebook questions, nor has it meant receiving the pages of check-marks, stars, scratch 'n sniff stickers. Writing has been directed toward meanings, to a degree unexpected, which might surprise, impress or delight Ruth and a reader or two a few desks away.

Through their collected works, the students find themselves in literacy. Their playground games and noon-hour play have all of the same marks of an adherence to convention, of participation in a common world of meanings. On these patterns they each make their mark and feel the sense of belonging, of existing within that closed and understood realm of ideas about the world in which the third strike means out and dirt pushed aside constitutes a road. In their written stories they have found another place to belong within a nearly closed set of meanings. It has provided a comfortable place to play, among the flowers, outside the castle walls or in with the sharks. The students' stories are recurrently marked by their understanding of what is of interest, fascination, and desire; they put on paper, as they put on in their play, the possibilities which intrigue them. Their hand can as easily be recognized in their writing as in their play. Earlier in this project I wrote of the banality in Sarah's writing; she was not in it. By June, however, she was willing to risk more of herself to the page. After a walk in the woods collecting this and that with the class, she writes:

> I'm a root. I
> have all differnt
> things on me and pieces

on me I have lots
of pink and black
stuf I thought
I was going to break
to pieces but I
didn't break
The Eng

Out of their writing, out of what they have found available in the shared meanings of language and literature they will make themselves on the page as they have in play. Gender proves to be a very strong part of that making; much of what they write is marked first by childhood interests divided by the conventional concerns of their sex. Their writing is a meeting of what they are interested in creating on the page for this hungry audience. Gender, so built up in the family setting, provides that point of belonging and identity in their play at school and now in their writing.

Writing, as this form of play, is doubly privileged in a way that gives it that extra value as an expressive activity for students. As a form of make-believe it has an unusual permanence. The castles they build are collapsed each day and the blocks returned to their boxes, while their papers and books gather in their desks and about the room to be rediscovered and reread weeks or months later. Their writing is also a prestigious form of play, where other sorts are beginning to fall into disrepute for seven-year-olds unless organized and socialized in the form of sports. It is valued in the school, touted as a skill, rewarded and reported on. They can see that Ruth is proud of what they can dream up, and she puts it on display about the halls of the school, as an artifact. These writers can see, as well, that writing is a part of a flourishing adult business— the book trade—which, if people they know don't make them, they understand that adults somewhere do.

The writing in Ruth's classroom has meant a continuance and elaboration of the expressive aspects of the children's play in educational activities, just as the approach has meant a greater continuance and elaboration of the expressive aspects of teaching for Ruth. Both the students and Ruth have been allowed to find much more of their own way in their work, and their work has become clearly theirs, as a personal statement that says something about literacy. Ruth would actually claim more than this for the prospering literacy in her room. She holds for it a larger mental development, a growing expansiveness of the mind and its conceptual abilities. There have been a number of such arguments put forward for the consequences of literacy. Yet the research into the effects of literacy discussed in Chapter 6 suggest that much of what has been noted has to do with schooling, while literacy provides little transfer to other intellectual abilities and remains an influence on a small number of reading and writing related skills, such as a sensitivity to grammatical corrections.

The claim for Ruth's approach to literacy will have to be more modest. The students wrote intriguing and entertaining pieces for a grade one-two class. They were engaged in work that counted for something outside of exercise and preparation. Literacy has not been trivialized on its introduction to the students nor removed from what they know or might want to use it for. Whether or not these students will later develop into what will become known as the Ruth Fletcher school of writers, or whether they become "effective communicators" in corporate positions, they will have known in their first experiences with literacy the pleasures of the writer, in creating something out of nothing, out of the blank page. That something in language is now a part of themselves as it is a part of Ruth, their teacher.

Testing the claims

One response to this work that we did with that grade one-two classroom in Goulais River was to ask if we really believed that this documentation was convincing. Was there proof that this way of teaching was better than what so many other teachers were doing? Of course, we found it convincing, but the point was that others wanted to see the claims we were making about this version of the New Literacy substantiated by a comparison with what other teachers were doing. The fact was that to depict the accomplishments of this program was to impugn the programs of others; we were implying that other teachers were not teaching students to write and to write in this imaginative, expressive fashion. This remains a large problem for the entire range of New Literacy programs. But exacerbating the resentment against the professed sense of superiority is that the New Literacy rarely goes about making its case with head-to-head comparisons against other programs. Providing elaborated field notes with moving instances from students' work, often photocopied to preserve their shaky handwriting, was not always considered sufficient evidence.

I, too, wondered if a greater degree of "proof" could be found. To that end, I designed a study which would compare the claims of both sorts of programs in the area of learning to write. Working on a fairly modest scale, I set out to ascertain the differences that a New Literacy introduction to literacy might make when compared to what students received in other classrooms. It seemed clear that there were a number of strong but often implicit claims made by those who advocate New Literacy programs, claims which might suggest measurable improvement. For example, in Great Britain the New Literacy had been motivated out of a concern for the limited functions to which a number of researchers had found writing was applied in the schools (Rosen & Rosen, 1973). Looking to M. A. K. Halliday's (1973) work on the development of a wide variety of language functions in the child, Harold Rosen and Connie Rosen found very few of these were being exercised in the classroom. The call was now for "functional richness" in the literacy program, as Don Holdaway put it (1979, p. 14). Thus the first claim I set out to measure was students' understanding of the function of writing after a New Literacy introduction to writing in the first grade.

The second was their attitude toward writing. Here the New Literacy drew on the shift of meaning to students' experience which I have described in the previous chapters. If, as the picture had been drawn, these students were freed from the labors of the worksheet and allowed to explore their own meanings, they should feel that writing was a greater thing for it. The third claim on behalf of the New Literacy was perhaps the boldest and that was an improvement of students' regard for themselves as writers and in a more general sense. This implicit call to self-enhancement is the real moral and psychological basis of the New Literacy. It traces back to the earlier Progressive Education movement's encouragement of expressive writing as a means of developing personality, self-confirmation, and personal dignity (Brand, 1980). To encapsulate the history of this stance, it begins with the sense that as the child wrote "the more a person he became" (Suffinsky, 1933); it then develops into a writing concerned with "the whole problem of individual identity and how it develops" (Holbrook, 1968, p. 1); finally, it is assumed that we were "writing to create ourselves" (Allen, 1982) and that "the child's marks say 'I am' " (Graves, 1983, p. 3). On a less existential note, it might be added that a positive self-concept has been found to be related to success in literacy and academic performance in general (Brookover et. al., 1964; Campbell, 1965). There is a good deal at stake on this claim.

On the skill-sequenced side of things, a greater sensitivity to the units of language in developing literacy has long been a part of reading readiness approaches (Evanckeko et al., 1973), and the worksheets are replete with the language of language—"Fill in the missing letters and use these words to complete these sentences." There were four claims all together which I planned to test over the course of a year using a pretest in October and post-test in May design. The test instrument included an interview schedule which asked students questions about 1) language function, 2) their attitude toward writing, 3) their sense of themselves, and 4) about the technical vocabulary of writing (see Table 5.1). Supplementing the questions on self-concept was a set of cartoons that were commissioned to represent youngsters in passive and active poses from which the students were asked to pick who they would be if they had to be someone in the picture.

The sample consisted of 109 students divided between three New Literacy first grade classrooms and three using a skill-sequenced program. The difference was established by collecting samples of what the classes produced, categorizing them as either skill-sequenced or expressive writing on the basis of the number of pages a week. While neither group provided a pure instance, the expressive-writing classroom wrote nearly four times as much in an expressive vein (defined as assignments asking for a sentence or more of the students' own making) while the skill-sequenced classroom did more than five times as much work on skills-sheets (defined as assignments asking for work in language at less than a sentence in length).

After a year of gathering the students' work and watching it develop in all of the class, the posttests in May produced some surprising, counter-intuitive results (Table 5.2). Of the four composite measures in writing function, writing attitude, self-concept, and technical vocabulary, only in the area of technical vocabulary was there a statistically significant gain, and that was by the expressive writing classes.[1] Students in both programs gained a greater sense of the function of writing, although the expressive-writing class was able to name a significantly larger number of meaningful answers to the question "What can be done with writing?" The skill-sequenced classes came up with fewer functions for writing in May than they had at the beginning of the school year in October.

Something similar happened with writing attitude in the expressive-

Table 5.1   Interview schedule

Writing Function
1. What are all the things you like to make stories about?
2. What can be done with writing?
3. Who do you know who writes?
4. Who do you write for (make stories for)?
5. What does an author or writer do?

Writing Attitude
6. What are all the good things about writing?
7. What are all the bad things about writing?
8. Is writing fun?
9. Do you make something with writing?
10. Is writing things down hard work?
11. Is writing a good way to say something?

Self-Concept
12. Who would you like to be in this picture? [seven pictures]
13. Are you a writer or a printer?
14. Are you a reader?
15. Who is interested in what you write (in your stories)?
16. Would you like to make books for others to read?

Technical Vocabulary
17. Is this a word? [say bicycle, er, friend, b]
18. How many words is this _____, one or two?
    [yellow; kangaroo; my friend; went swimming]
19. Does this card have one word on it, or more than one?
20. Can you find three sentences in this story?
21. Can you show me a period, a question mark, an exclamation mark, and
    quotation marks?
22. What things make up a story?

Table 5.2   *t*-tests of pretest to posttest gains on four composite measures

(N=109)	Skill-Sequence		Expressive Writing		(df=107)	
Item	Means	SD	Means	SD	t	p
Writing Function	.1105	5.771	1.2885	5.374	−1.10	.272
Writing Attitude	.1075	2.232	−.5962	2.107	1.47	.144
Self-Concept	10.5789	3.775	9.8269	2.988	1.15	.254
Writing Vocabulary	2.3508	4.042	5.0557	3.528	−3.71	.001

writing classes. After doing so much more writing over the year, these students gave fewer positive and more negative statements about writing after they had worked with it for a year! The decline was not great and the measure is crude, but this did raise the most interesting challenge of the study. When students were asked what they thought were "the bad things about writing," they gave the basics—"messy writing" and "scribbling"—and at least one offered a sense of the expressive writer's angst that I had also found in my work with high school students faced with similar writing tasks—"if you don't know what you are supposed to do." The good things about writing turned out to be such things as the fact that you "make pictures and write stories" and "learn about stuff," not to mention "exercise arms" which was thrown in to caution us over these interviews.

In coming to terms with these results, I think it important to point to the overall sense that both sets of students were off to a fair start in literacy and schooling. The self-concept gains were impressive among both groups. They saw themselves as writers and readers, and more students picked active characters over the passive ones in the cartoons presented to them after a year of being in school. The troublesome if slight decline in attitude toward writing among the expressive-writing students might have its explanation in their far greater familiarity with what's entailed in writing after a year of producing on average two and half pages of writing a week. The other classes faced three worksheets a week with each offering them a sense of correctness and accomplishment which they had every reason to believe was steady progress in writing.

It would seem that having students do considerably more meaningful writing, based on their own experience, does not ensure that they have either a better attitude toward writing or themselves as writers, at least in the first grade. Part of the reason, surely, is that they have no basis of comparison, as opposed to the teachers; they have no romantic notions of what writing might really be like. Yet they do encounter a good deal more of the difficulties with writing in a way reminiscent of Donald Graves's own experiences: "all of the writing in these years (1978–1982) was very painful to me" (1984, p. 5). No one said that writing would be easy in the New Literacy; the claim is that it will be worthwhile, that it will mean more in the writing and the reading. But then it also means as much to the students in the skill-sequenced program. The grounds are here for a more realistic appraisal of the romance of expression, for setting it up as one approach which draws teachers who are given to a certain vision of literacy and students, of teaching and working. More of this research will need to be conducted with more sophisticated instruments and larger samples of younger and older students. As I will argue in greater detail in the next chapter, there is room for this form of research within the New Literacy and the need for it as a means of helping educators make their own forms of sense out of the possibilities and challenges that it poses.

Field notes from the New Literacy, part III

Private acts in public places

After working on this documentation and reflection with Ruth for a few months, I have finally realized that our writing is no different than the flow of words we find on the children's pages. And this is disquieting. That we have begun to write now, when we are teachers, is somewhat absurd. The children, freed from filling in blanks—"add *ing* to *stop*"— are writing hard, if not fast, about this and that—"When It Was March" and "Killer Sharks." But they are not imitating adults. They are far from having seen an adult writer, as far as this school is from "town" where the odd poet, the one that Ruth and I know, scurries about the downtown streets with sheaths of paper in his leather pouch looking for a cafe in which to write away the morning. We are the misled in this vision of the children imitating adult writers, we, the teacher and the researcher, the teacher and the other teacher who lives down the hall; for we are imitating the children. We have fallen for our own line, taken the children's words too seriously and our own as well. Literacy matters, words count. Who are we kidding, when we are not kidding the kids?

It seems so obvious. No one else on staff is as foolish as to write— it is an unnatural act, this stringing together of word-beads on line after line, fussing about their order, restringing them, watching for the flow of colors, for the color of each other's face as the beads are read, said. Absurd. Foolish. Writing makes the others on staff a little uncomfortable. While eating my lunch in the staff room and scribbling down notes, I've been asked, twice, "What are you working on? A book?" I look up, apologetic, evasive. I was writing without apparent reason—no numbered sentences, no blanks, no ditto, not even a day-book page in three colors and clouds. Absurd, pretentious, so pretentious that they

143

have to ask, "A book?" How curious to sit in front of us all and carry on writing, line after line. What is there to say?

I watched Ruth writing like this one day close to the morning recess. I watched her where a window looks across a courtyard to a doorway. It was a strange sight and I stopped at the window. Ruth was leaning against the doorway, writing on a clipboard which she held at her waist. Her students were filing out beside her at a quick clip. She wrote with her head inclined down and the pen moved evenly, without hesitation across the page. She was not marking a child's paper, nor filling out the order form for next week's films. She did not look up to see how her children did after their leap out of the doorway; the snowbanks might have swallowed them whole. I half-expected furtive glances up as if she might be checking off her sheep, one by one. But she was just writing. Absurd. Just a step from a steady stream of hooting children in toques and snowsuits of so many toned-down colors whisking past as she was writing. A private act in a public school. Shirking vigilance; daringly anti-social. I felt it strongly enough to want to catch her eye, both to nod approval and to break the spell for her own good, as if her slip were showing, as if I wanted to approve that—"right, give them the slip"— but was worried too about what the teachers might be thinking of her. Writing?

(She thought for a moment it was so worthwhile, she did it herself.)

Before this, Ruth wrote poetry. She had written it in the school, in a special turquoise folder, that is not to be confused with a daybook, markbook, planbook or testbook. I now understand those poems as a kind of shorthand for private movements in a public place. There isn't time to write a full line, to write things out; there isn't space to compose.

> and the short sharp waves of the bay
> are left to say all.
>
> (Ruth Fletcher)

Another part to the story

There was an epilogue to this story of Ruth's classroom. The question that has been raised by teachers who have read up to this point is what happens to the children in the years to come. I've wondered about this too. Is this part of Ruth's responsibility to the children? They have responded to her changes, given them their own form of expression and meaning. They'll turn again, this way and that, through the course of the years and classrooms to come, some more adeptly than others, some more willingly. A few will remember Ruth, as grade one teachers tend to stay with you; fewer yet will recall the writing they did day after day, and it would seem to border on daydreaming to imagine an expressive seed planted somewhere inside them all, now dormant in one class, and perhaps re-rooted in another.

The question of a closer reading is rather what will happen to this teacher. With Ruth the change is not just a shift in the wind, it runs irrevocably through her way of seeing this profession as a profession of faith in the children and her time with them. The proof is perhaps in this epilogue which finds her only a few months after the year in Goulais River was completed, now in a one-room school, north by another hour from the rural school where she had first tried this way of teaching. Farther and farther, it seems to me, to be on her own; this time with a dozen children along with her two twin boys and her dog, Spike, who curls up on the square of rug in the classroom when the children aren't gathered there for a story or a lesson.

Ruth has posted her commercial cardboard cats which name the colors. She has brought little else that I can recognize from her old school room. The walls, though, and the bulletin boards and chalk boards bear the traces of the old program in a wide range of hands—pictures, poems, copies, and tracings; trees, geese, hockey games, and log skidders.

The 14 children run from grades one to seven; but they appear to run together. They have the approved texts for their assigned grade levels, but no grade-distinctiveness in their orientation that would set them apart by age. It would be too easy to eulogize my windy fall afternoon spent at Ruth's galvanized steel school that had been built by the power company among the swaying jack pines, with the big lake roaring on the other side of the highway, past the gas station and through the trees.

We walked with the class to the lake, down a narrow path through the underbrush until suddenly, there was the open water. We stood, buffeted by the wind, and watched the eight-foot breakers crash against the pebbles and push the driftwood to the very top of the beach. We went back to the school and worked up a series of plays based on scenes from the adventures of brave Odysseus. I saw that it was good in this two-room one-teacher school. She told me, too, that it was good.

I forgot for a while what a long way from town she had to go to make it so—miles and miles, years and years. Yet twice in the course of the afternoon she had used the phrase "my heart isn't in it," once to her son as she stirred a pot of spaghetti, and again to me as we planned out the direction the plays could take with the class. A strange phrase to use in paradise, as if the heart will always wander.

Ruth teaches in a one-room school now, I wrote in my notebook, and Melinda, one-half of her grade one class, writes in big letters on a sheet of paper the size of a poster:

> W hen I watch
> A wave it's like a
> V isit from someone
> E normous

Notes

1. To check the relationship among the four composites measures, a Pearson product moment correlation coefficient matrix between all of the pairs was calculated. The highest correlation was .26 between writing function and self-concept. Because gender has proven to be an important aspect of children's response to schooling, the results were also run for differences in the gains made by girls and boys with no statistically significant differences found. Finally, an analysis of variance was used to determine the interaction effect between program and gender; there was no significant interaction on the composite measures.

6
Putting Literacy to the Test

> The whole-language people speak of "emergent literacy" as if it
> comes from God. It doesn't.
>
> Jeanne Chall (Salmans, 1988, p. EDUC68)

Like all educational schemes, the New Literacy works from a dream
it holds for the young, the classroom, and the world. In this case,
the dream is of students working as young artists, exploring forms of
expression and self in studio-workshops with the teacher prompting,
facilitating, and promoting this artful and literate inquiry. This dream
of outspoken word-smiths artfully representing their own meanings implies an elevation in the level of public and personal discourse. The
world will be a noisier place. But such a vision needs to be tempered,
dreams being what they are, if it is to compete in the contest of pedagogies that determines the school curriculum. And to temper and strengthen
an educational dream in these times is to research it. This turns out to
be a particularly troubled area for the New Literacy.

Research, per se, is no problem; the New Literacy is awash in it. But
what is at stake for an innovative set of programs are specific forms of
research that hold its assumptions up to the light of existing studies
on literacy and schooling; that document its processes, products, and
implications; and that test its claims in head-to-head studies with other
methods. The New Literacy has undertaken bits and pieces of this
tempering process, primarily by offering a rich commentary on its classrooms practices illustrated with work from the students' own hands. We
should expect nothing less given that the New Literacy is about altering
the work of the classroom and the lives of teachers and students through
literacy. But also supporting my contention that specific gains in literacy

performance are secondary in this program to finding a new way of working literacy is the fact that researchers in the New Literacy have tended to step over the reading and writing research that deals with improving test scores and have shied away from direct comparison studies with such research.

It is time to rethink the research agenda of the New Literacy. Given the importance of the decision that educators face in selecting programs and an educational climate which makes it increasingly difficult for teachers to take up new programs, the New Literacy would seem to have a responsibility to research the questions that get asked. Teachers are rightly concerned that these innovations are backed by some form of assurance that they entail not only a new relationship to literacy and the classroom, but that they will prepare students for the inevitable rounds of testing to come, whether at the end of the term or in the grades ahead.

But it would be unfair to demand that New Literacy researchers completely capitulate to these pragmatic and political contexts. It is one thing to press for action that would remediate the deliberately unproven state of the New Literacy on standard measures in education; that much is necessary. But it is another thing to expand the entire discussion of literacy by situating these program within the context of historical and anthropological inquiries that speak to what can reasonably be expected from the cultural phenomenon known as literacy. To that end, this chapter follows up on close studies of literacy in schools that appeared earlier in this text while introducing others in the broader study of literacy. In something of a roller-coaster ride, if a little short on thrills, it wends its way through the cultural studies of literacy before moving entering the sociological and psychological investigations of literacy in educational settings. The chapter passes through half a dozen research areas in an effort to expand the horizons of this debate over literacy in the schools, stopping only long enough in each to confront New Literacy shortcomings or present the evidence in its favor, while making a few recommendations for improving its contribution to the great debate about literacy in the schools.

One obvious caution before getting underway is that the research on literacy is not the product of nonpartisan, third-party investigators who adjudicate over the claims of different classroom teaching strategies. Those who research also lead and advocate. Curricular ideas are advanced by the combined forces of researchers, professors, teachers, administrators, and publishers, among others. But among these parties, those who win the grants and conduct the research play a special role, as their work can come to carry the weight and authority of an established proof in mathematics or a precedent in law. All the educator who is confronted by a question about programs has to do is pluck out of the research literature the right study, preferably with the assistance of a computer search. But little in such a human affair as education is that simple. Certainly, the picture from inside this research community is less assuring as the field appears to be absorbed in constant fault-finding and undermining; no study stands unchallenged and each one has a place within its own camp. Educational researchers often get behind one program or another in their role as teacher educator and, on occasion, become heavily involved in lucrative publishing programs (Shannon, 1989).

For the educator approaching this question for the first time, the research on literacy must resemble a huge aquarium full of exotic fish. These fish swim in closely attuned schools happily breeding away and seemingly oblivious of the other schools except for the occasional public confrontation. In one sense, this chapter can only add to that frustration with the research industry as sought-after *answers* about literacy turn out to be only findings—limited, tenuous findings—in studies that are inevitably flawed in one manner or another. But setting hopes for conclusive evidence and definitive findings aside, it is instructive to observe the New Literacy within this tankful of propositions about the nature of reading and writing. The thrust of these lessons is that literacy's impact is limited by the contexts in which it is used. The powers of literacy are not unbounded. But if so, they are susceptible to certain forms of expansion and extension which bodes well for a program that is interested in the breaking down of traditional boundaries.

Literacy across the great divide

In the anthropological literature, literate societies such as our own have been set apart from others by striking a line between oral and literate cultures, as one might separate raw from cooked, savage from civilized. We might imagine that for the most part such divisions between peoples has gone the way of the Age of Imperialism. But this manner of thinking, like imperialism itself, has been transformed into less blatantly offensive, if nonetheless discriminating, forms. This fixing of a distinction between oral and literate cultures is certainly relevant to a school program which begins by reintroducing the integrity of students' oral discourse into a literate environment, as well as, welcoming the culture of the home into the school setting. Part of the New Literacy's liberalism, one might say, is to level the great divide between the languages of home and school, to diminish the sense of literacy as a civilizing mission that has governed schools and kept it apart from the lives of its charges.

The great divide between oral society and literate civilization was perhaps most clearly struck by Eric Havelock (1977) when he identified "the origin of western literacy" in the Greek introduction of vowels into the alphabet which took place about 700 B.C.E. He argued that with this graphic breakthrough of the phonetic alphabet, the spoken word could be transcribed and read directly for the first time. Writing didn't need to be nearly as predictable to be readable; it could take on an intellectual life of its own. And so equipped, the world began to turn into the sophisticated, masterly society that we know today, steeped in print, history, technology, and rationality (Olson, 1977). Although Havelock's impressive classical scholarship is hardly to be questioned in this context, I still think it wise to be cautious about breakthrough theories. Such theories are often haunted by precedents and precursors which tend to go ignored; they enshrine the breakthrough culture at the expense of others.[1]

My own modest challenge to this great divide theory of literacy has been to point out how traditional forms of oral discourse turn up at both ends of literate activity in a mutually supporting cycle of talk, writing, talk and so on (Willinsky, 1987a). The precedents for this public and oral sharing of the written word also have their roots in the glory that was Greece. Think of the ancient drama festivals and the Platonic dialogues that capture Socrates's street-talk; but precedents are also found in the less well known *midrash* tradition found in rabbinic literature with its evolving oral commentary on the Torah that has formed a model for the development of literary criticism (Hartman & Budick, 1986). Texts have always been the sites of highly social studies. The constant weaving of oral and literate practices continues through the medieval literacy of St. Augustine who found it remarkable that his master read without moving his lips, as if to keep to himself what he was reading instead of making a community event out of it. By the twelfth century, an age of literary revival in a manuscript culture, Europe was well on its way to becoming a civilization governed by a blend of oral and literate influences (Stock, 1984). And today, rather than suggesting a great divide between oral and literate cultural practices, our educational, political, legal, cultural institutions can be said to retain that mixture of the spoken and the written.

The New Literacy, especially in Great Britain, has taken this tradition to heart and strengthened the place of oral language in the classroom by treating it an exploratory tool of inquiry; talking things out becomes an important part of the intellectual and sociable processes of the classroom and a necessary element in the enhancement of literacy. The introduction of this element of an oral culture into the classroom is also intended to introduce a new, rich life to the curriculum by integrating the various lives of students. As Fred Inglis dramatically points out, this amounts to, in essence, an event of philosophical proportions:

> Where once the school had insisted on the absoluteness of the
> boundary between school and out-of-school, between street
> wisdom and book wisdom, between speaking properly and
> talking like a lout, an entirely new, irregular, but vigorous
> movement began to acknowledge the culture and experience
> which the children brought with them so inalienably in order to
> attach it to different forms of knowledge itself, and the
> purposes and actions which are the end, the telos of
> knowledge. (1985, pp. 126–27)

As part of the case that has been made for the efficacy of oral language in teaching, Douglas Barnes has tracked the manner in which students reorganize their thought orally across a number of subject areas through what he calls exploratory talk; he concludes that this use of language, in particular, is "necessary for hypothesis forming and testing" and thus an important part of the program (1975, p. 108).

As there is an historical tradition based on the great divide which would explain the development of Western rationality and culture, so the assumptions about literacy have also run with the development of individuals. Through education, literacy can be a breakthrough for the young as well as for cultures. After all, does the acquisition of literacy not constitute the first and necessary step on the path to a thoughtful and worldly success? The expression of faith in literacy and education that I am toying with here is not to be discounted, but only qualified. Literacy can be seen as other than the point of a great divide and that, rather, we have been living with what Harvey Graff (1979) has termed, "the literacy myth." The question is whether literacy offers a universal ticket to improved economic opportunities, as is generally assumed, and the historical and anthropological evidence suggests it does not in such cases as nineteenth-century working-class Canadians (Graff, 1979) or in twentieth-century Third World settings (Street, 1984).

There is also research indicating the degree to which literacy also leaves a people unchanged in their outlook, as Kenneth Lockridge notes with the growing literacy of colonial New England: "There is no evidence that literacy ever entailed new attitudes among men, even in the decades when male literacy was rapidly spreading toward universality, and there is positive evidence that the world view of literate New Englanders remained as traditional as that of their illiterate neighbors" (1974, p. 4). Yet literacy can also play a most subversive and divisive role, as it clearly did during the Reformation and other revolutionary times. Rather than depict literacy as a social force that will carry, of itself, the minds and fortunes of a people to some enlightened or enriched literate pre-destination, it is better seen as a cultural and economic vehicle that is always caught in the historical traffic of the times, whether at religious, economic, or national crossroads.[2] Exposing this literacy myth reiterates the importance of asking about the ends to which this or that literacy is turned. We expect too much from this technology of print, given the lessons of this history.

In trying to make sense of these lessons, Brian Street (1984) introduces an important distinction in his discussion of how literacy is treated by researchers. Some scholars give literacy an autonomous status, treating it as a free agent of change and development; literacy is the thing that will make a difference, whether moral, psychological, or economic, in a people. The obligation then is to improve literacy performance and test scores in order to improve the intellectual health and general prosperity of the nation. Others, in line with Street's own approach, see literacy as an embedded social practice that is fully implicated in the workings of economy and power. The New Literacy advocate may be tempted to treat literacy in this generalized, autonomous fashion. But it is clear that New Literacy programs place their emphasis on the way in which literacy is worked and the ends to which it is turned.

As part of the anthropological tradition which Street represents and on the side of literacy-in-context is the research of Sylvia Scribner and Michael Cole. Their work attempts to isolate the intellectual contribution of literacy. The problem has been to distinguish the impact of literacy from the influence of schooling, and their work with the Vai people of Liberia has permitted them to make such distinctions. In *The Psychology of Literacy* (1982), they report on the evidence they gathered from studies of the multi-lingual and -literate Vai which strongly suggests that literacy, as opposed to the general phenomenon of schooling, has limited and short-term transfer to other intellectual and logical capabilities besides those directly related to reading and writing. Literacy, of itself, did not seem to enhance mental abilities unless the exercise involved such related areas as an awareness of grammar, and yet in combination with schooling it did assist in school-like tests of ability. The fact that people with a schooled literacy out-performed those with an unschooled literacy is hardly surprising, of course, and the lesson is a simple one emphasizing the importance of the context of learning and performance. That is, the work to which literacy is put will determine the nature of the ability; it will not exist in a universal state equally applicable to all situations.

The point is that if you expect literacy to assist people in performing specific tasks, whether representing their own interests or in working out complex social problems, then it is appropriate to engage in those activities directly, rather than imagining that it is sufficient to give them what are seen as the basic skills for later application. As we have known about learning in general for some time, the transfer of skills to new situations is not always reliable.[3] Given that limitation, it becomes especially important to note that in school the lessons students are learning are not only teaching them how to be literate, but are also teaching them what literacy is good for. By virtue of the reading and writing activities they engage in, may you know the extent of their literacy. What also becomes apparent is that *if* literacy, of itself, is not the power and the glory, and *if* it cannot be expected to carry people forward by virtue of their fundamental mastery of it, then its potential influence lies in the dynamics of the supporting environment, the inspiring cultural context and conditions under which it is exercised.

These are, I hardly need to add, the central concerns of the New Literacy. As the New Literacy imagines it, literacy is not a series of subskills that are mastered and applied in isolated exercises; rather, judging from the contexts which it has established, students use literacy to solve problems through reading and writing within a course of study, problems that they have had some hand in selecting; they use literacy to discover, connect, respond, and confront. While they will still be using literacy in a limited number of situations, they are still in a better position to appreciate the way that it works and what it can offer. Scribner and Cole's debunking of literacy as something of a mental steroid suggests that the environmental realignment of the New Literacy should make a difference in students' facility with literacy.

A third area, after history and anthropology, that is rich in research on literacy and its intellectual impact is cognitive psychology. By studying student writers, through the analysis of think-aloud-protocols, video-tapes, and experimental testing, cognitive psychologists have made gains in charting the mental activities that constitute an effective writing process. Flower and Hayes (1981) have led in this area of composition research. They envision the writing process as a series of planning and evaluating activities involving generating and organizing ideas within a goal setting mental environment. Instead of seeking generalizable mental skills, this work focuses on the specific steps and strategies entailed in this literate behavior. Their research warrants the New Literacy claim that the use of the writing process ensures a higher level of mental activity in students than typical classroom writing situations, especially as students are encouraged to develop a facility in such highly complex areas of composition as revision (Flower et al., 1986). Although such research can often seem to be about adding another brick to a theory of the mind, I would offer one example which suggests how it might facilitate a more thoughtful form of literacy in the classroom.

In a study of grade 6 and 12 students, Marlene Scardamalia and Carl Bereiter have found that if a certain tension between *what to say* and *how to say it* is encouraged, there is some evidence of a "deepening of reflective thought" found in the resulting writing (Scardamalia & Bereiter, 1985, p. 327). Without this tension or dialectic between substantive and rhetorical issues, as Scardamalia and Bereiter describe it, literacy can easily enough slip into low-level processing of a mechanical and banal nature. Yet they also found that an increase in thoughtfulness did not always produce better writing in the study, as it could lead to work that was judged to "scatterbrained" and less than coherent in its constant taking up of new ideas. It seems that the closer research moves in on this phenomenon of literacy, the more intricate the picture gets. The balance is between production and reception, between trying to think it all out and then, having it out, to see it as it might be received and read by others. The sociability of literacy with the steady expectations of sharing the work with a varied audience is one way of keeping that tension alive for the student between private and public demands. Nothing comes of literacy itself, it seems clear, but what comes of the situations it is set in and what goals are set for that stimulating situation.

Another form of research that has suggested the appropriateness of

New Literacy programs has been the detailed assessment of how language and literacy are actually employed in the day-to-day flow of classes. Studies which have examined how much students are currently writing or speaking often point to a decided lack in the opportunities to engage in these activities as aids to learning and growth in literacy. In the United States, Arthur Applebee's (1981) study of writing in the schools has proven to be an influential statement about a need to expand the range of literacy activities in which students engage. He and his research team carefully recorded the amounts and sorts of writing which were being done in a sample of American high schools, not just in English classes but across the subject areas. His findings have an unmistakable shock value to them: "only some 3 percent of observed class time involved writing of at least paragraph length; even in English classes, the traditional center for writing instruction, only about 10 percent of class time was devoted to writing in this sense" (1981, p. 58). Applebee found that over half of the writing done in class was essentially "making notes." For written assignments done in class, students were given little prewriting time to sort out their thinking, while most of teacher's advice about writing took the form of comments and corrections that came after the work was finished.

Applebee paints a bleak picture of the chances students might have for becoming fluid writers in American high schools. Point by point, you can see how the New Literacy programs in writing speak to improving this inadequate situation. Applebee concludes the study with the results of the researchers' qualitative observations of 114 "good" to "best" classes; they identify such qualities as self-directed, connected, and integrated approaches to writing for students who were lucky enough to be part of the best lessons (pp. 104–5). While it does nothing to confirm the contribution that the New Literacy might make, this is the sort of research which lays the groundwork for its introduction into the classroom.

In Great Britain, a similarly dismal profile of writing in the schools had emerged from the Britton study that I introduced in the second chapter; his research team had found a high degree of rather uniform transactional, or expository, writing in the classrooms they visited with very little, at less than 6 percent, of the work falling into the valuable mode of expressive writing (Britton et al. 1975). There have also been studies of oral language in the schools which have revealed a similar potential for the New Literacy to improve the opportunities for learning. Gordon Wells (1981) in the Bristol Language Development Project followed a sample of 32 children making the transition from home to school and found that they suffered a decline in the amount of talk they conducted with adults regardless of the social class of the family: "In sum, compared to homes, schools provide a significantly reduced opportunity for children to learn through talk with an adult, and in the conversations that do occur, children find themselves forced into the respondent role, their contributions for the most part valued if they contribute to the teachers' predetermined line of thought" (Wells, 1986, p. 27). This challenge to the "linguistically rich environment" of the schools, recalling with some irony Bernstein's (1971) influential work on the "elaborated code" of the classroom, clearly speaks to the strengths of New Literacy programs which provide students with a greater role in the inquiry into and sharing of knowledge, that is where talk, if not always with adults, becomes an exploratory and expressive medium in the classroom.

In the first section of this research review, moving from Havelock and the Greek alphabet to Applebee and Wells, two points are worth reiterating. The first is that the legacy of the great divide theory is still with us. It resides in the untenable belief that the acquisition of literacy, by whatever means and in whatever educational setting, insures both cognitive and cultural advancement. Literacy, in this sense, might be thought of having the evocative powers of the church, something not easily defined and only loosely located in the architecture, yet in faith deeply felt as a force to rally around. The countervailing point to this magnification of literacy's powers is that it can more realistically be expected to conform to the contours of the specific contexts and task-environments in which it is deployed. That is to say, the uses to which students put reading and writing are going to have a profound and direct impact on the nature of the literacy that the schools are going to foster. This brings us to a second divide in the experience of literacy. If the New Literacy is going to expand the pedagogical possibilities of literacy then it may well have to take its examples from beyond the walls of the classroom.

The boundaries of the New Literacy

In an effort to offer a literacy which reaches beyond a series of isolated skills, the New Literacy crosses another divide, this time between the traditional schoolbook exercise in reading or writing and a literacy with its roots in the culture outside the classroom. This brings us to two studies that speak directly to how the New Literacy would undo the destructiveness and waste involved in the art of boundary maintenance between home and school. The premise about literacy underlying this approach to culture differs radically from Hirsch's (1987) position on cultural participation and literacy.[4] Here the assumption is that in order for literacy to be an effective part of the students' lives, it has to be integrated into their culture as a way of opening it to a wider world; literacy, in this sense, is defined not by learning the terms of cultural literacy, but by how it is lived from childhood into membership in the larger literate community.

No one has made a better case for this position than Shirley Brice Heath. In her *Ways with Words* (1983), she represented the ways in which literacy was a community and cultural practice that takes on the spirit and aspirations of those who live within it. Working and living within three nearby communities in the southern United States, Heath vividly captures the sociable forms of literacy that knits together each of them in different ways. She notes how community notions of literacy differ by social class and race, as well as between town and country, with those middle-class homes in town especially given to preparing children for future success in the schools. It was this community of "townspeople" alone that provided that glove-like fit with the literacy of schooling which the children in all of these communities face. Heath adds to the sense of the school's trade in a specialized language of literacy, by making apparent how adeptly these other forms of literacy fit the ways, the homes, and the times of the poor white and black rural communities in which she worked.

But Heath went a step further beyond recording the ways in which literacy functioned. In attempting to lend value to the different ways in which families and neighborhoods live their literacy, she takes that extra-curricular step for a researcher by working directly with the teachers and students in those communities to undertake their own studies of literacy in the neighborhoods and world outside of the school. This is nothing less than the promise of the New Literacy, as it offers more of literacy to those who may well have been denied twice, both in what they have brought to the school and in what they will acquire there. My concern is that this extra responsibility to those who have the most to gain is not taken up more often in the New Literacy. Heath concludes her study in rather marked political terms:

In any case, unless the boundaries between classrooms and communities can be broken, and the flow of cultural patterns between them encouraged, the schools will continue to legitimate and reproduce communities of townspeople who control and limit the potential progress of other communities and who themselves remain untouched by other values and ways of life. (1983, p. 369)

To slip back and forth across the border between home and school with these cultural forms extends the application of literacy in a crucial way to a thinking about how literacy operates in different settings. The point is not to deny the social reality of these various divides but to treat them as material for these students of language and literacy to investigate.

In a similar spirit, Harste, Woodward, and Burke have worked at undoing another sort of boundary set between the preschool child and the young student. In a study I briefly introduced in Chapter 2, their *Language Stories and Literacy Lessons* (1984) extends the boundaries of literacy not by looking at adults but by turning to children before they enter school. The 70 young children, from ages three to six, were not studied so much as treated as informants, and the result was that line between the child of the home and the student of literacy was undone. Harste, Woodward, and Burke recognized that students were living in literate environments and happily making sense of what was important to their lives. They demonstrated with their "environmental print" test drawn from the literate, colorful packaging of the child's day that three- and four-year-olds were in fact "reading" the advertising on the paper cup at Wendy's fast food restaurant, as well as the tube of toothpaste before bed.[5] Equally so, the authors discovered that at three years of age, children, working as they do with pencil and paper, appear to understand after a fashion that "writing serves a pragmatic function . . . that one can placehold thoughts with marks on paper . . . art and writing serve a semantic placeholding function, both are organized differently" (p. 38). Harste, Woodward, and Burke do not hesitate to declare that this child "has been a reader and a writer prior to this encounter" (p. 38).

Although they are not the first to make such a proposal, as Marie Clay (1975) had worked with the pre-instruction writing of the young some years before, it remains a radical designation which takes aim at those educators who belittle students' inherent competence in favor of their perceived and prescribed institutional need for instruction. More specifically, the attack is on the "reading readiness" programs used in kindergarten and the first grade which begin with the assumption that students entering school have not learned anything worthwhile about literacy. Harste, Woodward, and Burke do all in their power to suggest that the case is clearly otherwise and that we have much to learn from the children, although the children have been telling us as much for some time.

Finally, this untold degree of literacy among the young has political ramifications. Harste, Woodward, and Burke found that "the most salient home factor related to literacy learning is one we have termed 'availability and opportunity to engage in written language events' " (1984, p. 42). There were no observable differences on the basis of race, sex, and socioeconomic status, differences that they had been led to expect by the extensive literature in this field. Environmental sensitivity to literacy and initial competence in this literate world seemed to be equally distributed among different sectors of the population. However, the authors then conclude, mistakenly in my opinion, that the relative equality which they discovered supersedes the more common finding that literacy that is correlated with race, sex, and class (p. 48).[6] The National Assessment of Educational Progress provides evidence that the relative performance of "at-risk minority" students in reading and writing has improved in relation to the majority since 1971, the problem of black and Hispanic students falling "well behind" by grade 4 remains a major challenge to programs that would claim to make a difference (Applebee, Langer, & Mullis, 1987, p. 22). While the schools have made gains, common reading instruction strategies, such as the use of ability groups, can still be found to exacerbate differences in literacy and social class (Allington, 1983; Rist, 1970). Programs can make a difference, and the New Literacy has reason to believe that it could make a positive one in these settings.

The work of both Heath and Harste, Woodward, and Burke suggests a form of literacy that is more continuous with students' experience. To offer an alternative definition of literacy based on a level of meaning and engagement that is meant to bridge cultures would seem to promise a different pattern in students' achievement. The knowledge and language that students bring on the first day of school become primary resources for the New Literacy and, to wax idealistically, that potential stands to be renewed with each day, if this is truly a literacy that builds on the continuity of culture, language, and literacy in the student's life. As it promotes itself as an innovation in teaching, the New Literacy has a responsibility to plunge more fully into the great debate; this means finding a language that can be heard and situations that will test its mettle, situations that stand to greatly benefit by working in the New Literacy. While Calkins (1986) and Hansen (1987) have reported on an anecdotal basis their successes with "minority at-risk" students, the New Literacy has yet to conduct the sort of systematic documentation and assessment that would establish its potential in these schools; with so much in the balance, it is hard to imagine a greater challenge for the New Literacy. These themes of research, principles, and responsibility come to a head when New Literacy programs face the considerable majesty of the reading research enterprise.

Researching reading

For over a century, a dedicated community of professors of education and psychology, with a some help from anthropology, sociology, and linguistics, have isolated, measured, compared a myriad of physiological and psychological elements that go into sitting down and reading a book. This body of research is extensive and diverse, if not outright overwhelming, with more than a thousand articles a year written on aspects of the reading process (Dykstra, 1984, p. xix). From its beginnings in experimental psychology at the turn of the century, this research industry has moved between exploring all that can possibly be learned from a scientific investigation of reading and the more specific demands dictated by a desire to improve instruction in reading. Harry Singer (1985), in his "landmarks in reading research," begins with the tone-setting work on eye movement by Javal at the University of Paris, and what a fascinating nineteenth-century science of precision measurement it is:

> Javal (1879) showed that in reading, the eyes move across the printed page in jumps, which he called saccades. These are very rapid, ballistic-like movements that last about 20 milliseconds and bring the eye into the visual area of greatest discriminating power, the fovea centralis. The eyes then fixate on the print for 240 milliseconds. At the end of each line a sweep movement, lasting about 40 milliseconds returns the eye to the next line. (Singer, 1985, p. 9)[7]

The dissection of the reading act became the great research challenge for the new science of psychology. In a statement that is often quoted as a reminder to researchers, Edmund Huey laid out the scope of the challenge in 1908: "And so to completely analyze what we do when we read would almost be the acme of a psychologist's achievements for it would be to describe many of the most intricate workings of the human mind, as well as unravel the tangled story of the mostly remarkable specific performance that civilization has learned in all its history" (1968, p. 6). This quest was bound to inform and shape the manner in which reading is taught in the schools. While it is impossible to marshal in this brief statement the diversity of this research enterprise, it does seem fair to hazard a few generalizations about dominant trends that set it apart from the questions that the New Literacy would ask about reading. Dominic Massaro, for example, makes no bones about the mechanistic model guiding this scientific quest: "We seek to know not only the nature of reading behavior but, more importantly, the internal machinery guiding the observable behavior" (1984, p. 111). He identifies the basic contest as falling between psychological and physiological models which he would integrate with a cybernetic analogy: "A psychological model is analogous to a model of a computer's software programs rather than its physical hardware" (p. 113).

In assessing the progress that reading research has made over this century, two of the current leading figures, Richard Anderson and David Pearson (1984) claim that Huey would be delighted with the gains made, although they concede that "there is still much work to be done in order to build THE definitive model of basic processes in reading comprehension" (p. 285). There is something about THIS ambition that resembles the passion of a Thomas Edison. Not only does it imply that reading and instruction are mechanical processes, which in no small measure they are, but that the best approach, to draw on the Edison analogy, is to experiment with different filaments in different environments until that electric bulb lights up and unfailingly glows for a reasonable length of time. If only it were that simple; if only we taught in a vacuum. Marshall McLuhan once had the opportunity to tell the General Electric Company that, of course— which is how he always put his oddest assertions—the light bulb was not about illumination but about information, pure information (wonderfully recounted in Wolfe, 1980, pp. 389–90). In this case, the glow of information captured in this allegory illuminates a literacy that has only an *on* and *off* stage, one that operates at the throw of switch, that exists within a vacuum free of social purpose and individual intentionality.

The model of reading driven by this research tradition bears the marks of a curriculum movement which Raymond Callahan (1962) has described as the "cult of efficiency." It was a spirit which he found dominated educational administration during the first half of this century with its industrial-military complex of intent and language. Although certainly removed from the time-motion studies which represented Taylorism at its worst, the research and development work on reading instruction has also pursued a pedagogy of proficiency. The historical reviews and the state of the art statements in reading research specify the same goal in their concluding phrases—significant advances in instruction (Venezky, 1984, p. 29; Kamil, 1984, p. 54). More recently, this same way of thinking has developed into the research on effective teaching which has become a field with its own interests in effective reading instruction (Hoffman, 1986). The student demonstrates the efficacy of instruction by responding to a set of questions about a text rather than responding to the text itself. The text is processed; the answers retrieved. To teach reading is to take students through those procedures which improve text processing. Frank Smith, for one, makes an eloquent New Literacy plea on behalf of something more to reading and writing:

> But if just one aspect of reading and writing must be
> highlighted then perhaps it should be the *creation and sharing
> of experience*—the generation of possibilities of knowing and
> feeling. Authors create landscapes of ideas and experiences
> through which they and their readers may travel and explore.
> Reading and writing are creative enterprises, not the shunting
> of information. (1988, p. 97, original emphasis)

But even with Smith's attractive depiction of literacy, it still seems peevish to begrudge this research its success with students' test scores and reading levels by implying that this approach to research and instruction is too narrowly concerned with instructional efficiency and individual psychological processes. This is a debate that is over principles and tone in working literacy within the classroom. And what the New Literacy appears willing to risk in pursuing that alternative conception of teacher, student, literacy, and culture is brought to the fore by Jeanne Chall's (1983) assessment of the literature on reading instruction.

Chall has pursued the "great debate" in reading instruction through a systematic review of the research that spans this century. She sets this debate as falling principally between "code- versus meaning-emphasis" in reading instruction (1983, p. 3). The emphasis on decoding skills falls principally on direct instruction in phonics while the meaning programs include Look-Say, Whole Word, and Language Experience programs. In her initial review of the literature, published in 1967, she found that the decoding programs produced better results through grade 3 at which point the evidence stopped. As she reports in the second edition of her book (1983), the emphasis on phonics has increased in U.S. reading programs. And in her subsequent review of the studies which have documented the development of reading skills in the early grades, the evidence in favor of decoding has grown stronger in her estimation with some support for direct instruction in letter-sounds and blending (p. 43). Chall is hardly alone in reaching these conclusions (Flesch, 1981; Williams, 1985); moreover, she accentuating the importance of pursuing this instruction course has been her call for giving a decoding advantage to at-risk minority children in their early years of schooling (Chall & Jacobs, 1983). In sum, she has elevated the stakes in this debate over reading by holding out the possibility to advocates of the New Literacy that they may be further disadvantaging the disadvantaged by leading them down the Whole Language path.

However, while the evidence is in favor of phonic-first, it may not be against the New Literacy. The great debate in U.S. schools, at least, is actually among the basal reading series that dominate the primary classroom, with estimates that 90 percent of classrooms use them for 90 percent of the instructional time (Shannon, 1989, p. 43). At one time not too long ago, 85 percent of these series favored a sight-word approach over phonics-first (Flesch, 1981, p. 1). Language Experience and Whole Language programs, as New Literacy variants, have been dragged into the debate on the side of meaning-emphasis which appear to be dominated by basal reading programs based on sight vocabulary. Certainly, while providing more of a meaning-emphasis than a strict decoding approach, basal reading programs remain decidedly short, in New Literacy terms, on the rich context of meaning and story that fosters reading. In fact, former basal-author and current New Literacy champion, Kenneth Goodman (1986b) has accused basal readers of being part of the problem rather than the solution for fostering literacy in the schools. Not only does Chall's assessment fail to offer a true measure of such New Literacy programs as Whole Language, Shared Big Books, Choose-Your-Own-Books, but the side she declares the loser in the great debate is one with which the New Literacy has clearly distanced itself.

However, this does not relieve the New Literacy of a responsibility to enter this debate. Studies in the New Literacy are being conducted that use standard measures, but they are still few in number and suffer a deficiency of scale.[8] One of the obstacles amounts to a clash in world views. Advocates of the New Literacy have bravely chosen to carve out a research path that is congruent with their understanding of literacy, tending to favor qualitative, collaborative, and case studies which turn to students as informants, rather than subjects. This philosophical congruence between vision of literacy and research method is no less the case for those doing massive quantitative studies of basal reading programs, as they *encode* the data in studies that move from the *parts to the whole*. Yet the New Literacy finds that even the limited case it makes on its own behalf is dismissed, not because it claims are unfounded, but for failing to use the measures currently governing education. The predominant discourse of quantitative studies and standardized measures makes it difficult for New Literacy programs to gain a national hearing. The tendency to discount New Literacy studies is exacerbated by the lack of publishers' extensive promotional support for basal reading programs of both the phonics and look-say camps. By dominating the form, as well as the substance of educational discourse, this reading tradition, in effect, suppresses the spread of new programs seeking to overstep the governing cartel in reading of researchers, professional associations, and publishers which Patrick Shannon has described in some detail (1989, pp. 28–40).

To consider one instance of the New Literacy approach, Judith Newman in a Whole Language discussion of research and the reading process offers a "miscue analysis" of ten-year-old Hugh's oral reading of "The Fisherman and the Mermaid" (1985, pp. 21–22). She offers a record of the errors in Hugh's oral reading and with a certain adeptness demonstrates how they were made in an effort to sustain the meaningfulness of the story for Hugh. Although Dr. Newman was once my Whole Language teacher, and an excellent teacher she is, I feel compelled to point out that she goes that extra step in her discussion of the research, suggesting that this work supports the contention that in reading "more is brought to the page that is received from it," from which she concludes that reading instruction "frequently overemphasizes the graphophonic aspects of reading at the expense of meaning" and that "many nonfluent readers read the way they do because of the instruction they receive" (pp. 21–23). These are serious charges indeed, charges that Goodman, Smith and others have made in their exasperation over current methods of instruction, methods that appear to frustrate the child's urge to meaning. Yet not only are the charges unsubstantiated, they cry out for the very research methods and measures these educators have rejected because of the failure of philosophical fit.

However, as I have pointed out in the first chapter, New Literacy programs have made considerable inroads into the teaching of English and language arts through the force of its own rhetoric and research. It will continue to do so. But to eschew quantitative studies not only denies a fair basis of comparison to the educator trying to assess both sides of the debate, it leaves educators who have embarked on a New Literacy course stranded, adding considerably to their test-anxiety. They can not be sure how this attractive method of working with Big Books or the writing process will affect the test results that often come back to haunt the teacher. To call for New Literacy engagement in the great debate resembles its own concern to assist students who have not been heard for reasons of the propriety of their expression. To ignore this issue of evaluation seems unfair and unrealistic, while a benefit of changing its tactics in this area is the opportunity to bring change to the process of evaluation. Under such influence, the province of Alberta has incorporated components of the writing process and expressive writing into its high school diploma exams and Britain has accepted at certain levels the use of writing folders for certification. But equally important and innovative would be an extension of the New Literacy's collaborative spirit to encompass researchers working the other side of the street, that is, to have researchers from both camps set up joint studies of decoding- and meaning-emphasis programs with a variety of techniques and methods agreed upon.

The dynamics of curriculum demand that a case for these innovations be built out of existing resources even as it works to set in place an alternative conception of literacy and research into it. This work is needed to support those who have taken the leap into the New Literacy and for those who are still toying with the idea. For above all else, the curriculum is not an idle field and those on the side of decoding are not silent or shy about this contest: "If we do not continue to beat the drums of good decoding instruction, the gains we have made in this area will not be maintained" (Williams, 1985, p. 212). If the New Literacy marches to the beat of a different drummer, it has to learn to find rhythms that carry above the din of the crowd.

Lessons from the New Literacy in action

Up to this point in reviewing the research on literacy, the anthropological and historical work has emphasized the ends to which literacy is turned; the sociological observations of language in use in U.S. and British schools confirms that schools are failing to utilize literacy to expand learning opportunities; and the psychological research on reading has confronted the New Literacy with a need to establish itself against what have become common measures of achievement and competence in literacy. In this final section, I examine two studies that have captured the New Literacy in context, as it is worked in English classes in British high schools and as it stands up to other methods of writing in a huge meta-study of composition research in the United States. The results are suggestive of refinements and realities that might better inform the New Literacy projects.

Working with a similar approach to Britton's study of a decade before, Douglas and Dorothy Barnes (1984) examined the "versions of English" at work in 18 British secondary school classes and were able to find the influence of the London School over the course of a decade. Concentrating on the English classes, Barnes and Barnes do offer a profile of the different sorts of writing and reading activities in the classroom. What is interesting in this case is not the urgency of numbers, as it was with the Applebee (1981) writing study, but the combination of classroom observations and student interviews. Although the study covers the entire program of studies in secondary English, I want to focus on their findings with personal writing in the curriculum and the use of a reader-response approach to literature.

As I reported in Chapter 1, Barnes and Barnes found that by the early 1980s "personal writing" was used in 16 percent of the academic classes and 35 percent of non-academic English classes, figures that suggest that the New Literacy, or at least the London School, has had its impact on the English curriculum in Britain. While personal writing is a small, but critical, component in the New Literacy approach to writing and literature, it does distinguish this method of teaching from other programs and is thus likely to be used in assessing its achievement in the classroom. Barnes and Barnes found the sort of contradiction in students' responses to personal writing that makes this work interesting, dispelling as it does any complacency over what makes a good literacy program for students. When asked what they liked to write, the genre of choice for these students was the story, which was hardly surprising. The important finding was the number of students who were less than enamoured with the requests from their eager teachers for personal writing, for compositions along the lines of "my earliest memories" or "the pains and pleasures of teenage life" (1984, p. 81). In putting a number to this dislike of personal writing, an equal number of boys and girls, amounting to about a third of the 157 students interviewed, spoke out against personal writing, while only about a fifth of the students (22 girls and 10 boys) openly supported it (p. 133).

The problem with personal writing for these students was divided between an inadequacy in understanding how to find a topic from within oneself ("I can't think what to write") and the invasion of privacy that this could constitute ("I prefer to keep my feelings to myself"; pp. 133, 92). At the heart of this disaffection for personal writing were questions on the part of students about the issue of integrity:

> I'm scared of it. I don't know what to write, whether I'm being vain or whether I'm being dishonest or whether I'm being too honest. . . . You always try to picture yourself something that you aren't, always try to grade yourself above everybody else. Everybody does; it's nature. But if you put it on paper, people who are reading it will think that's not you. (p. 133)

Confronting this unknowingness of the self is a brave piece of personal expression in itself, as I hope to make apparent in Chapter 8 by probing the of self in contemporary theories of subjectivity. Their very anthem might well be "We cannot picture ourselves." This act of reflection on the student's part is telling in his grasp of what is at stake in this discourse and the naive demands that teachers can place on students when they ask for this writing out of the self.[9] We might turn this student's autobiographical plea into three specific suggestions: 1) if "picturing yourself" seems near to impossible, educators can make it more accessible by treating it as a meeting of history and fiction; 2) if the difficulty is compounded by a lack of purpose, educators can use personal writing as a starting point, not simply for forays in autobiography, but for reader-response topics in literature and beyond; and 3) as writers are rightfully concerned about the "people who are reading" their work, they can turn to collective projects, from magazines to reports, that give the work an initial audience and sense of purpose before reaching beyond the classroom with their work.

Students in the Barnes and Barnes' study went on to provide the basis for other improvements in this approach. For those students who wish to avoid getting personal, the solution was often "to use fiction as a way of dealing with first-hand experience, since it freed them from the danger of giving too much away or of adopting an unacceptable persona" (1984, p. 134). This turning to artfulness is yet another way to understand the personal nature of literacy, as it can construct its own truths about life more telling than the array of authentic facts. This artfulness is another way of understanding subjectivity in school as the negotiations of a private self in a public setting. Students turning their first-hand experience into fiction are not cheating the personal writing assignment, but gaining, as writers do, a distance on what they have learned.

I think it important to note that Barnes and Barnes did find that students who most easily took up the personal writing were from "professional homes"; these students "most easily moved into a persona that allowed them to deal with personal experience without feeling at risk" (1984, p. 153). But then Barnes and Barnes allowed in this impressionistic fashion that the middle-class students were also better prepared to write in the "public-impersonal," "fictional," and "belles lettres" modes as well. The irony in this finding is that the personalizing of the curriculum was much stronger in the non-academic classes, with fewer students from professional homes, while the academic classes were exam-driven in impersonal directions. For the non-academic students, this greater reliance on personal writing in the curriculum marks a considerable improvement over "watered-down" academic programs which have formed their common fare. Yet it still has to be asked to what ends is the teacher to stage these acts of engagement to avoid suggesting that there is nothing else more profitable to be done with the time, especially compared to other classes doing *Macbeth* in preparation for college. If the division of classes into such streams is not to be dislodged, the teacher can still structure projects that can build out of a personal response, that can engage and develop their literate interests. By way of example, Chris Searle's *World in a Classroom* (1977), is a collection of works by his early adolescent students who wrote out the nature of their own world and soon moved on to the nature of the larger world, which they came to realize was very much tied to their experiences, to the way people were treating each other in their inner-London neighborhood. *Letter to a Teacher* by the Schoolboys of Barbiana (1970) is another project that grew out of response that began in the classroom and that is clearly instructive for writer and reader in the nature of a personal and a critical literacy.

In their investigation into the teaching of literature, Barnes and Barnes divided up what they witnessed into two methods which they characterized as *transmission* and *initiation*. The transmission model hinged on the teacher's and the examination's authority which demanded that students seek and adopt validated positions on the works; the initiation model is similar to the reader-response theory I featured in Chapter 4 as it encourages an expression of students' sense of the text. Barnes and Barnes found that the transmission model clearly dominates British schools, and for that reason they are drawn to speak of a paradox in the "public representation of a private world" in literature study (1984, p. 231), amounting to "paraphrase and commentary on the local meaning of texts along with stylised account of theme and character" (p. 244) transmitted from teacher to student and then back again. Evidently, the New Literacy approach had not made the same inroads in literature as it has in writing. Yet, again in the manner of the Applebee, Britton, and Wells studies, Barnes and Barnes have set up this disparity of an impersonal treatment of what is so clearly personal in such a way as to open the door for a New Literacy approach.

In assessing the effectiveness of the two literary methods on common examination results, they compared "six roughly comparable 'top' classes." As it turns out, reader-response classes scored somewhat better: 77 percent of students in the initiation classes scored a C grade or better, while only 58 percent of those in transmission settings did (p. 227). It appears that the level of engagement may have made a difference in at least getting students over a basic pass. However, in the highest level classes they observed, students played the least part in the interpretive process, looking as they were for the most authoritative analysis on which to build their academic careers at that point: "they had surrendered their autonomy as readers" (p. 395). Barnes and Barnes venture that "unless the learner has some opportunity to 'own' the texts, the study of discourse, however well taught, amounts to no more than the induction of the learner into a closed system, not initiation into a framework for critical thinking" (p. 395). Although it remains a conclusion that is more hopeful than borne out by their findings, I need hardly add that calling for a form of literary possession among students speaks to the spirit of the New Literacy.

For a final look at New Literacy in action, we leave aside the close observation of students in classrooms to enter the statistical palace of the meta-study. Hillocks's *Research on Written Composition* (1986) attempts to build a comprehensive structure out of the results of 2,000 studies of writing published between 1963 and 1982. The book is a mine of information on various aspects of the composing process, but for our purposes I wish to extract a lesson from the ranking of teaching methods. When it came down to the crucial question of comparing the results across different methods of teaching students how to write, Hillocks ended up with 60 studies that included 75 experimental treatments principally between grades 6 to 13, which included New Literacy programs. He grouped the treatments by "modes of instruction" into four groups— presentational, natural process, environmental, and individualized—and the "focus of instruction" into six groups—grammar, sentence combining, models, scales, free writing, inquiry. He then proceeded to calculate the cumulative levels of success in improving writing scores by focus and by mode. I find the distinctions more clear-cut and thus more helpful with the focus of instruction.

Let me start, for the sake of drama, with the least promising of the six. Hillocks found that, as has been established since the turn of the century, that the teaching of grammar is not a profitable path to proficiency in writing. The use of models in the teaching of writing, while better than grammar, is still not very productive, especially for want of focus for students: here is a model from which to write—but what, the student asks, is it precisely that I am to model and where do I begin this modeling. At worst, it lacks a sense of process, based as it is on working from the product. Also superior to grammar but not to the other methods he examined is "free writing" in which "students write freely about whatever interests them" (p. 249). Although free writing is only one part of the writing process, when this notion was expanded to encompass peer editing and revision, it still did not prove as effective as other methods. The problem in the writing process, Hillocks declares, is captured by Bereiter and Scardamalia's identification of a "what next" syndrome among free writers which inhibits organizational concerns and the focus of an overall plan or project with the work (pp. 221–232). It is worth adding that the 13 studies measuring the effects of revision did not produce evidence of its assistance to students (p. 219).

On the more promising side of teaching methods for composition was sentence combining, which has been subject to a good deal of experimental work; it "proved twice as effective as free writing as a means of enhancing the quality of student writing" (p. 249). The use of scales, criteria, and specific questions also proved twice as effective as free writing. The secret here, again drawing on the research of Bereiter and Scardamalia, is that instead of a "what-next" approach, there was a guiding "means-ends" strategy with a designated goal. Finally, what Hillocks identifies as the inquiry method proved the best of the methods examined. It turned out to be four times the effectiveness of free writing (which seems to be the common measure for Hillocks) and two-and-a-half times more effective than using models. The inquiry method offered the student elements of a writing process, direction in terms of a goal, criteria for assessing the development of the writing, as students set out to examine data in search of generalizations or search for solutions to problems that have been posed.

The lesson from Hillocks's ratings is clearly twofold. In terms of pedagogy, I think that the New Literacy is well-advised to incorporate more explicit elements of both the criteria and inquiry model which are certainly in accord with its intentions (leaving aside sentence combining as contrary to the program in a way that the other two are not). In terms of meta-studies, I reiterate once more the need for the New Literacy to experiment with the adaptation of research methodologies that reach outside its own circle. If Graves claims that experimental designs "have contributed least to the classroom teacher" (1984, p. 96), Hillocks chastens the New Hampshire School for confusing observations with findings. The essence of Graves's charge—that teachers "have been unable to transfer faceless data to the alive, inquiring faces of the children they teach each morning" (1984, pp. 96–97)—is met by publishing interests who have proven more than happy to assist in this transfer from research to textbook and back to research. Hillocks, for his part, suggests that the sort of observational studies favored by New Literacy advocates be "improved" by defining what counts as valid data and recording this data systematically. For my part, I have already proposed that collaborative studies be conducted with researchers from other paradigms.

Yet while advocates of the New Literacy need to take up the challenge thrown down by Hillocks and others, I do not think that they should capitulate before it. If Donald Graves provides a record of how students handle a problem with revision to their own satisfaction, or Margaret Meek offers an anecdote about a student's absorption in a book, or David Bleich relates a student's complex and personal response to a short story, they are undoubtedly documenting both the value of literacy and the sort of knowing that these programs would encourage. The insularity of this approach to the research question is part of its integrity. In exploring the meaning of these programs on their own terms, these professors of New Literacy are up to what they would have students do and find in the language. But as they are students of literacy, they must also come to appreciate the ways in which it operates in a contested area such as curriculum.

In the epigraph for this chapter, Jeanne Chall quips that Whole Language people speak of emergent literacy as if it came from God. And she is right, it neither comes from on high nor have Whole Language advocates been as secular about it as they might. Literacy is constructed by a very human process; it is driven by a dream, perhaps, but it requires the rhetoric of research to get a fair hearing. The New Literacy has raced ahead with programs in reading, writing, and literature, while building on what it has learned from the close observation of students at work in these different contexts for literacy. But it has yet to marshall the arguments in research necessary for the great public debate; it has yet to take on the measures through modification and accommodation that would give it a greater public and educational hearing. In yet another form of research, the next chapter turns to the historical and literary sources of that dream to demonstrate that the ways in which it draws from prominent, if sometimes subversive, cultural forms. This inquiry, too, adds to the tempering and earthily rooting of the New Literacy, and in another fashion puts our ideas about literacy to the test.

Notes

1. In the case of Ancient Greece, for example, Martin Bernal (1987) has begun to document how modern historians have prejudicially set aside the Afroasiatic roots of Classical Civilization.
2. It might be fair to say that the turning point for literacy on a broad scale was not so much the invention of Greek alphabet but Gutenberg's moveable type and the explosive proliferation of broadsides, pamphlets, and books through this new public broadcasting system of the printing press. Here, the historical research strongly points to the sense of social purpose that underlies the promotion and growth of literacy among the populace (Resnick, 1983; Graff, 1981). If the Reformation was a battle fought in print as well as with the pike, literacy was one of the winners with the effects of Lutheranism in creating a literate Sweden (Johansson, 1987) and Calvinism success in Scotland (Houston, 1987). These effective literacy campaigns of the early sixteenth to the nineteenth centuries were blends of religious and national fervor that were meant to enhance the solidarity of the community.

But if literacy served Protestantism, it was quick to serve many other masters. In not a totally naive hope, government and church attempted to incorporate the people into the commonwealth through literacy; but this was nothing less than Rousseau, Paine, and Marx hoped and to some degree realized through this congenial and disruptive medium.

3. At the turn of the century, Thorndyke and Woodworth (1901) established that learning was not readily transferable to new contexts; Thorndyke who set the psychological tone for the development of American reading programs, found in this proposition the basis for a skill and drill approach that worked systematically through the behaviors required for reading (Shannon, 1989, pp. 16–27). The pivotal idea is to identify the nature of the literacy that we would have of the students and design the contexts in which they work with this literacy.

4. E. D. Hirsch attacks the school's vacuous practice of teaching literacy skills in isolation and free of specific cultural content, an attack that the New Literacy supports. He has advanced a concept of "cultural literacy" for the schools that is rich in the arts and sciences (1987). However, in practice his concept has been reduced to the mastery of a list of "what every American should know" and our expectations for a literacy based on mastering terms should not be too high (Estes, Gutman, & Estes, 1989).

5. Lea McGee, Richard Lomax, and Martha Head (1988) make similar claims in their study of 81 children, three to six years old, of which 75 percent were able to "read" or identify in a "meaningful" way such items as the phone book (with responses such as "phone numbers"), the newspaper ("*State Times*"), and a grocery list ("tomato"). They are clearly pushing back the meaning of reading—as taking sense from print—but this change in perception, in meaning, is what innovations in programs often entail.

6. This finding both in its challenge to the literature on the relationship between class and literacy, as well as in the importance that it places on home literacy events is supported by the far more extensive and longitudinal Bristol Language Development Project (Wells, 1981) discussed in the first section of this chapter. My alternate reading of the significance of these findings stands with both pieces of research.

7. Javal's approach did receive its amplification in Philip Gough's (1972) famous dissection of "one second of reading" into 100 millisecond intervals. Yet it is worth noting that Gough, who had broken the process down to the level of letter identification, later tempered his claims with the frank acknowledgment (1985) that "this model is wrong": "The claim that we read words, letter by letter from left to right is . . . almost certainly wrong" (p. 687). Yet in his defense he still challenges the field to establish a more accurate model, with presumably the same degree of scientific precision, based on a physiological examination of the reading process as a matter of the eye moving across marks on the page.

8. Setting aside for the moment the observational studies of Graves and the New Hampshire School, there is still research in the New Literacy's favor which use both specific measures and at-risk students, as the following brief synopsis of three such studies would attest: 1) Trachtenburg and Ferrugia (1988) found that 14 students who had been judged unready for grade one

were nearly doubled their scores on tests of basic skills when they had the opportunity to collaborate in the making of shared Big Books over the course of a year; 2) Schweinhart and Weikart (1988) found in a study of 123 pre-schoolers, "living in poverty," that settings which offered child-initiated learning produced similar academic achievement results as teacher-directed instruction, while fostering in these children greater social development; 3) Church and Newman (1985) in a case study found that a grade-nine student who suffered "an instructionally induced reading problem" brought on, in their estimation, by remedial work with decoding skills was able to raise his standardized test scores from 2.6 to 4.6 (a gain of two years in nine months) by being introduced to such devices as diagramming information which concentrated on moving from the whole to the parts of a text.

9. "Personal response" has become a component on the Alberta high school diploma examination in English with interesting ramifications. Within a year or two of the exam's introduction and ostensibly in response to student anxiety of preparing for these examinations, English teachers who had been involved in the marking of the examinations had begun to coach their students on the nature of a well-received "personal" response as teacher-markers were likely to judge it (Bobie & Willinsky, 1986). They understood it to be another variation on the educational game, although one that presented new problems in figuring out what was expected.

7
Popular Literacy and Romanticism

The only knowledge which is of any service to the working people is that which makes them more dissatisfied and makes them worse slaves. This is the knowledge we shall give them.
Bronterre O'Brien, *Poor Man's Guardian,* 1830
(Hollis, 1970, p. 20)

Prophets of Nature, we to them will speak
A lasting inspiration, sanctified
By reason, blest by faith: what we have loved,
Others will love, and we will teach them how;
William Wordsworth, *The Prelude,* 1850
(XIV, 444–47)

As Ruth Fletcher's grade one and two students were busily filling blank pages with their new-found literacy, I suspected that these dramatic acts must have a historical precedent. To root her program in a larger perspective, I decided to look beyond education, where it often seems that all has been tried before, to the annals of social and literary history. I soon found two historical phenomena that bode well for what the New Literacy was up to, the one leaning toward its public aspects, as popular literacy took its own hold on people with the rapid spread of the printing press, and the other tending toward its personal predilections, with the organic powers of the imagination and self made famous by the Romanticism of Wordsworth and Coleridge. If the New Literacy has yet to fully take up the great research debate, it is still well-equipped to match intentions with other programs by delving into historical precedents and its intellectual heritage. This two-sided history, of matters literate and literary, sets the challenge of the New Literacy to other instructional paradigms on a grander scale, reminding us of curriculum's place in the clash of politics and philosophies, a clash that educators do not leave behind, even after shutting the classroom door.

As I have already pointed out in this book, the New Literacy draws heavily from the earlier efforts of the Progressive Education Association. Many of the populist and Romantic conceptions have been picked up and shot ahead by progressive educators from the turn of this century to today. But in this chapter, I leap over the more immediate precedents to find these ideas in their original setting. The New Literacy aspires to reach beyond the school for its models, and I do as much by bringing it face to face with its sources. It can then test and refine its assumptions without having to work through a thick swarm of intermediary pedagogical texts. As Wordsworth imagines learning directly from nature—"my mind hath looked / upon the speaking face of heaven and earth / as her prime teacher"—so it can be on occasion with the history of ideas.

This chapter commences with a three-part discussion of popular literacy which finds in its energy and sociability its parallel in the hum of New Literacy classroom workshops. The second part of this chapter takes up the relevant themes in Romanticism that inform the New Literacy. Among these are the guiding metaphors for talking about learning and mind, as well as a resistance to a certain bookishness and, in the spirit of popular literacy, a reaffirmation of the vernacular language as an expressive medium. This look at the history and ideas animating the New Literacy not only offers a sense of intellectual heritage, itself a handy defense weapon in today's educational debates, but raises its own questions about what these new programs would have from literacy. This is yet another means for understanding what is at stake in the New Literacy's challenge to school, teacher, and student.

Part I

The popular roots of the New Literacy

Popular literacy provides another way of understanding this technology of culture found in the ways of literacy. This phenomenon of a populist-print-for-the-people roughly dates back to the fifteenth century and the invention of moveable type and a suitable ink allegedly by the modest goldsmith, Johann Gutenberg, in the German city of Meinz. This made the printing press a viable commercial enterprise and turned a sudden flood of printed materials into a public broadcasting system and entertainment industry. As printing shops spread throughout Europe, the printers quickly realized the limits of Latin manuscripts and their highly restricted readership, and they began to look to the much larger market that might be created in the European vernacular languages. In turn, this sudden wealth of printing in these native tongues gave rise to something of a self-taught literacy among the people, a literacy in many of the overlapping dialects and languages that held across the continent. This was a popular literacy in the oral discourse of everyday talk and storytelling; it was a literacy beyond the reach of the dominant clerical form, in both a religious and bureaucratic sense. This literacy was a political and social force; it was a vehicle of sect and nation, as well as a constant bit player in revolution. But more often than that, it was the source of story, ballad, tract and sermon, and it brought to the people a new source of hope, dismay, laughter, and tears.

My conception of popular literacy is taken in part from Thomas Laqueur's article "The Cultural Origins of Popular Literacy in England 1500–1850" (1976) in which he colorfully sets the field in his opening sentence: "For all its maypoles and rough music, its bear baitings and St. Monday drunks, its ancient feasts and more ancient folkways, the popular culture of seventeenth and eighteenth century England was fundamentally literate" (1976, p. 255). The New Literacy has taken up aspects of this popular literacy, as it was used to challenge, if not subvert, the realm of convention in ways that are connected to the spirit of Romanticism as well as Laqueur's sense of carnival. This popular literacy ignited interests in the literature of public dispute and profane entertainment. By the seventeenth century, even the humble yeoman was being drawn into an energetic print culture. As Margaret Spufford notes in her history of popular fiction from the period, "the seventeenth-century parishioner . . . was, if he could read, as over a tenth of agricultural laborers could, exposed to a steady hail of printed pamphlets of news, political and religious propaganda, astrological prediction and advice, songs, sensation, sex and fantasy" (1981, p. xviii). This popular literacy in an everyday language, which predates the emergence of systematic schooling, was accomplished by an unsung class of school-dames, as well as the proverbial village schoolmaster (Spufford, 1981, pp. 19–44).

This history has a special salience given the criticism that the New Literacy has garnered from both the left of the political spectrum, for

177

ignoring the pressing social issues of the day, and from the right for not keeping alive the cultural heritage that literacy has fed and sustained. The New Literacy programs are populist at heart; they make a writer of every student, a self-published one at that, as well as an active contributor to literary meaning. In the first part of this chapter I wish to explore three parallels between popular literacy and New Literacy: a) the sociability of the literary enterprise which both of them encourage in the sharing and performance; b) the non-standardized origins of English literature and popular writing which roughly corresponds to the current approach of putting expression ahead of correctness in the New Literacy; c) the political nature of this popular urge to expression which is concerned, not only with nurturing the cognitive skills of individuals, but empowering them as active participants in the shaping of the community and state. Looking back over the historical development of popular literacy strongly suggests that reading and writing tend to reverberate soundly through the body politic. A consideration of these parallels brings to the fore the overlooked political and social implications—of what it means to have an active popular literacy—and raises the fundamental question of why we would have so many take up the pen.

A sociable literacy

The first parallel I wish to draw is between a new sociability and spirit of cooperation in the modern writing classroom and the historical and ongoing blend of oral and literate cultures that this sense draws on. The years of that quiet time set aside for weekly writing and recopying have passed in the innovative classroom. The enforced privacy of literacy, made painful in full classrooms of friends who were not to share their creative excitement, has given way to a spontaneous comingling and testing of what has been found and created. In the previous chapter, I introduced the great divide between oral and literate cultures which prove to be both a false dichotomy in our culture and which, among educational programs, the New Literacy transcends. Literacy serves the sociability of language in a manner that has engaged a larger public in sociable settings.

Well before the printing press and for some time afterward, "literary compositions were 'published' by being read aloud; even 'book' learning was governed by reliance on the spoken word" (Eisenstein, 1979, p.

11). It only took one or two accomplished readers in every village and town to share the latest published ballads and tales. During the Reformation, Martin Luther is reported to have been repeatedly surprised in his travels at how fast and how far his tracts traveled. The ballad soon became a bestseller. The Oxford bookseller John Dorne recorded selling up to 190 "ballats" a day at a halfpenny each in the 1520s, and for those who couldn't afford that, ballads were available, free for the memorizing, on posted broadsides; at feasts, wakes, and fairs, folk plays were performed that carried on an old oral tradition with found bits of print woven into them (Spufford, 1981, pp. 12–14). In France, not long after the invention of printing, it began to become clear that the common people were "active users and interpreters of the printed books they heard and read, and even helped to give these books form"; as historian Natalie Davis summed it up, "oral culture and popular social organizations were strong enough to resist mere correction and standardization from above" (1965, p. 225).

Toward the end of the eighteenth century, the London Corresponding Society was formed and soon became a model for a "poor man's society" in which men could regularly meet to discuss political works, as well as publish and distribute tracts, manifestos, handbills, pamphlets and the ever-popular ballad (Lankshear, 1987, pp. 84–99). At the same time, pubs, coffee shops, and reading rooms were becoming welcome places to read what one could not afford to purchase, as well as providing a chance to discuss the issues with others over a pint at these "penny universities" (Stallybass & White, 1986, p. 98). The written word was meant to be shared and often read aloud, an approach that held until the latter part of the nineteenth century; "reading" in McGuffey's popular *Eclectic Readers* meant a training for public speaking, and authors, perhaps most notably Charles Dickens, travelled the countryside and continents filling meeting halls and theatres with public readings of their work (Ong, 1980).

In New Literacy classrooms now, children are to be heard acting out or chanting from books which play on the patterns in language; they are then encouraged to create their own variations on these themes (McCracken & McCracken, 1979). In the older grades, the spoken and dramatized word includes the sharing of drafts, the staging of interviews, impromptu skits, and the accompanied celebration of students' work (Burgess, 1984). If the historical parallels are sometimes lost to sight, teachers of the new writing also seem to overlook the potential to be found in that contemporary blend of literate and oral cultures known as "the media." Teachers working with New Literacy programs could tap the central place of the media *script* in our lives which haunts us from the McDonald's commercial to the six o'clock news, from "Masterpiece Theatre" to the music video. These scripts provide interesting instances of work in a constant state of revision up to the final moment of production and of writing with a place for collaboration and multiple contributions. Like the broadside and chapbook, here lies another artifact of a popular literacy, a contemporary one this time, that lends itself to classroom and student production. This one has the added bonus of being a highly lucrative field adding a vocational aspect to the program.

In spite of this spirited advocacy on my part, I am not blind to the intellectual cost of explicitly taking up aspects of oral popular culture. The price has been most perceptively calculated by Walter Ong (1980) in his deliberations on the differences between orality and literacy. He describes how oral cultures, whether Homeric or adolescent, have as their cultural thrust the effort to be "with it," to "get into the act," to participate and take up the celebration of the heroes and wisdom held in common. Ong points out how Plato was among the first to realize that an oral culture had little place for analysis or for the sort of critical questioning he encourages in the pursuit of the good; to ensure a conversion to such a reflective state in his republic Plato banned the (oral) work of the poet. Popular literacy and culture have been equally disparaged as too taken up with the sentimentality and sensationalism of bad taste dressed up in bad form. While in our modern, blended approach to writing instruction, the temptation is to simply get "with it," to simply have students "get into the act," the possibility remains of encouraging a move to getting "at it" in a critical way in unpacking the grammar of its appeal either through exposition or parody.

An ungoverned language and literacy

The second parallel I wish to point out is a historical tendency among English writers to resist a standardization and regulation of the language, a tendency which was gradually overcome by concerns with correctness and propriety in language. The public school system in its traditional efforts at fostering literacy has been notorious for, though not notoriously efficient at, holding with propriety before all else. New Literacy programs have been challenging these convention-bound ways, though not for the first time. The tale begins with the Renaissance and the early days of the printing press in Europe which was a period of invented spellings and creative grammar finding its way into publication, setting a certain principle of recapitulation for the New Literacy that takes students through a similar development.

When Gutenberg cast his first set of type, he set in motion a revolution in literacy that affected many areas of European life. Hand in hand with the Reformation, it brought the Bible before the people in their native language, and generally gave a literate respectability to the European vernacular languages that had been overshadowed by a clerical Latin (Kahane & Kahane, 1979). The introduction of affordable texts created a wide market for sacred texts, beginning with the Bible as well as those troubling indulgences. But the printers soon realized that an even bigger market lay before them in the area of secular and profane publications, and these were soon finding their way about the countryside in what often became an illicit book trade. As reading was a public and sociable enterprise, these works had a distribution and influence far beyond the extent of the fully literate citizens.

Yet for our purposes, it is well to remember that the vernacular languages, unlike Latin, had neither a governing grammar or consistency of spelling. Literacy and mass publication simply raced ahead of the standardization of the European languages. Ivan Illich (1979) has described the situation in fifteenth-century Spain as one in which people were soon reading in a dozen dialects as the book trade flourished across the Iberian Peninsula. The spread of this "wild untaught vernacular literacy," as he terms it, demonstrated that printing does not necessarily require either a standardized composition, a schooled mother tongue. or a silent and private literacy (p. 61). Officials of the government were soon complaining that the people had begun to "waste their time on novels and stories full of lies" (cited in Illich, 1979, p. 38). Illich discusses the gradual taming of this unlicensed literacy in Spain by Queen Isabella's adoption of a governed and official Castilian, replete with a Latin-based grammar textbook to guide it. A national language was intended to exercise linguistic control; it was presented to the Queen as a "consort of empire" (cited by Illich, 1979, p. 35). The idea was that with such a language in place the people could understand the messages of officialdom, even if they could not use it to return their sentiments. Illich has described this move to standardize the language in political terms: it "established the notion of ordinary language that itself is suffi-cient to place each man in his assigned place on the pyramid that

181

education in a mother tongue necessarily constructs" (p. 45). This is an issue addressed by today's writing programs which attempt to lessen the sole focus on mastery of the standard language—as the threshold point of communication—even as they promote editing strategies to ease students into its use. The new programs tend in this way to shake up, though not topple, Illich's pyramid.

The story with the English language has a slightly different twist to it. A similar historical move to take hold of English and create a standard was resisted in England, first by the Elizabethans who chose to raise the status of their language, in relation to the prestige tongues of Latin and French, through eloquence rather than subscribing to a prescriptive grammar modeled on that of Latin. A strong example of the Elizabethan position is found in Philip Sidney's *An Apology for Poetry*, where he made a proud claim for English over Latin:

> Nay truly, it hath that praise that it wanteth not grammar: for grammar it might have, but it need it not; being so easy of itself, and so void of those cumbersome differences of cases, genders, modes and tenses, which I think was a piece of the Tower of Babylon's curse, that a man should be put to school to learn his mother tongue. (Sidney, [1595] 1970, p. 85)

The Elizabethan writers, without benefit of an apparent grammar or systematic spellings, found "a short cut to literature without caring whether the language was ruled or not," as R. F. Jones describes this blossoming of English literature in his *Triumph of the English Language* as (1953, p. 215). In those days when Shakespeare was playing for the groundlings and literature in the English language came into its own, a corresponding increase in the spread of popular literacy occurred. This growth in literacy among the common people was accomplished for the most part on an informal basis within families and communities; as a result the level of literacy reached as high as 60 percent among men in the larger towns of southern England by the seventeenth century (Laqueur, 1976).

The spirited resistance to formalized grammar in English, which Sidney expressed, was eventually to take the form of political opposition to the proposals for an official language academy in England comparable to the *Accademi della Crusca* established in Italy in 1582 and the *Acadèmie Français* established in France in 1659. The effort in England, beginning in the late seventeenth century, to establish a language academy was supported by the likes of Daniel Defoe and Jonathan Swift: "The Work of the Society shou'd be to encourage Polite learning . . . and advance the so much neglected Faculty of Correct Language, to establish Purity and Propriety of Stile" (Defoe, [1702] 1961, p. 59). But the proposal failed in England, as it did later in the early days of the United States where it was raised by John Adams and others (Baron, 1982).

Though the movement for an academy faltered, the fight continued for a regulated language. Those who felt that an ungrammared English was a danger and disgrace pressed ahead with prescriptions for improving the language. These grammarians based their claims on the model of the classical languages, on both national and male chauvinism, and on principles of consistency in the language. By the end of the eighteenth century, they had succeeded in setting unofficially in place what Sterling Leonard (1962) has identified as "a doctrine of correctness in English usage." English had effectively, if not legislatively, acquired the system of grammar and the basis of instruction Sidney had once disparaged. The doctrine was based on a prescriptive grammar, developed for the most part by retired schoolmasters and clergymen; it was intended "to enable us to judge of every phrase and form of construction, whether it be right or not," in the words of Robert Lowth, a leading grammarian of the day (Lowth [1762] 1959, p. viii).

I have dealt with these historical developments, if only sketchily, to raise this decisive split in language attitudes, favoring either a natural development or a prescribed conservation for the English language, which continues to be played out in the schools and in the press. My concern here is with the public schools which have since their inception taken up, with few exceptions, the doctrine of correctness as their very mandate. The curse that Sidney foresaw of children being schooled in their mother tongue became a daily practice regarded as both intellectually and morally uplifting. One can still find it defended today after a half-century of research demonstrating that the teaching of grammar does not facilitate better writing.[1]

The historical split which I have been describing over the regulation of the language had been between educated parties, the one citing Horace ("usage is both the rule and norm of speaking") in favor of following naturalized patterns in the language, and the other taking Horace's Latin as the very model of the well-governed tongue. While the side of resistance to regulation had its populist roots, there has also been a long literary tradition, encompassing such notables as Lawrence Sterne and

Gertrude Stein, whose writings have fully and delightfully played against these doctrines and standards, as if art could best flourish in the cracks and disruptions of convention. But insofar as I am arguing that the New Literacy is borrowing heavily from traditions of popular culture rather than a strictly literary one, I will introduce another sort of resistance to convention in the development of literacy which also holds a lesson for the current movement toward a broader participation in literacy. Here we begin to consider the encouragement of publication and a public voice which has become a major concern of the new pedagogies in writing. In an unrecognized alliance of interests, popular literacy was in some ways carrying on its own class action against prescription and formality across Europe. However, this promising growth area in literacy was met with less than unbridled enthusiasm among the educated classes; popular literacy seemed to smack of a subversive interest in knowing and being able to publically say so.

The dangers of a popular literacy

In England, the rush into print also took an explicitly political turn as the pamphlet and the broadside became the broadcasting vehicles of choice. In the heady year of 1642, for example, on the eve of the English revolution, 2,000 pamphlets were published (Stone, 1969, p. 99). Efforts to control this provocative trade had already been set into place in 1637 as books and papers were required to be licensed and registered, and in 1712 publications began to be taxed. Cobbett's *Register,* founded in 1802 for the "interests of the otherwise unrepresented people," ran this taxing gambit. The stamp tax raised the price to over a shilling and workmen grouped together to buy the paper gathering in pubs to read it; the publicans' licenses were threatened as this resembled a "seditious meeting." Cobbett then went to unfolded sheets diving through a loophole in the stamp tax and was soon selling 44,000 copies a month at twopence only to lose the battle to more restrictive taxes in the 1820s (Lankshear, 1987, p. 96). It was a literate contest of ideas and economies.

This outspokenness in the political domain seemed destined to disturb the sleep of the genteel classes as the news of this urgent if incomplete literacy arrived with their morning mail. E. P. Thompson in his cele-

brated history of the working class has recorded a number of improprie-
tous letters from the early part of the nineteenth century:

> I Ham going to inform you that there is Six Thousand men
> coming to you in Apral and then We Wil go Blow Parlement
> house up and Blow up afour hus/labring Peple Cant Stand it No
> longer/dam all Such Roges as England governes but Never
> mind Ned lud when general nody and his Harmey Comes We
> Will soon bring about the greate Revelution then all those
> greate mens heads gose of. (Thompson, 1963, p. 784)

Thus it is understandable that widespread reading and writing skills
were not always welcomed by those in positions of power or comfort.
This new literacy repeatedly gave voice to an independence of spirit and
thought, within a class which many of their betters thought had no
apparent need for these disrupting elements. The British instances of
suppression range from an act of 1543 forbidding women and men under
the rank of yeoman to read the English Bible, to the use of the stamp
acts in the eighteenth century to constrict the press (Williams, 1961;
Innis, 1951). Stallybass and White (1986), in their study of "the politics
and poetics of transgression," report that after the Ketts Rebellion of
1549 "there was a proclamation banning all plays 'in the English tongue'
since 'most contain matter tending to sedition and contempnying of
sundry good orders and laws' " (p. 61). Lawrence Stone has described
"the terrible spectre of a literate, politically minded working class" which
faced the respectable classes: "Should a Horse know as much as a man,
I should not like to be his rider," Bernard Manville quipped in his *Fable
of the Bees* (1726, cited by Stone, 1969, p. 85). The schooling of the
working class from 1780 to 1850 has been described by Richard Johnson
(1976) in terms of a crisis in hegemony over who controls the education
of workers' families. Literacy on a popular basis sent shivers among the
propertied classes; in the nineteenth century this literacy produced the
Poor Man's Guardian, the Unstamped Press, the Chartist Movement,
and countless anonymous ballads all with a similar thrust—the ability
to write is the ability to name, to sing out against, inequity and inequality
(Hampton, 1984).

Johnson has concluded that the institution of philanthropic schooling
for the working class was initiated, not as a measure against widespread
illiteracy among their children, but against their control of their own
education through private, Chartist, and Owenite schools (1976, pp. 50–

51). The ruling classes found other means of countering this ungoverned literacy. During the nineteenth century, as an instance of literacy's intended part in pacification, the Mechanics' Institutes, of which there were 500 established by 1850, introduced lectures on literature: "Literature was included in the instruction, on the grounds that its study would protect the young workers against the corrupting effects of seditious political material and the sensational products of the cheap press" (Mathieson, 1975, p. 17).

This struggle between a popular literacy that disruptively entertains and a governing concern with civilizing that very populace may seem the distant and unenlightened past. We may take for granted that in these liberal times, the freedom of expression is an entrenched right which cannot be restricted and that the power of the written word is open and encouraged for all. However, counter instances abound and at the very least must be considered as a contested issue on almost a daily basis. During the weekend that I write this, I find Germaine Greer explaining in Saturday's newspaper that she refused to sign at least one petition protesting Ayatollah Komaini's death sentence against novelist Salman Rushdie for writing *The Satanic Verses* because the petition assumed the superiority of our freedom of expression: "Basing an argument on the supposition that we have free media and other people don't just is hokum to my mind. . . . You have to understand the inequity of access to print media (Kirchoff, 1989, p. C2). The inequity of access to print and literacy too, I might add, given such cases as the British Arts Council denial of grants to a adult literacy project on the grounds, as a Brian Street has reported, "that the work produced in this way was not 'literature,' and complaints by at least one Member of Parliament that the content of students' own materials was too politically radical" (Street, 1984, p. 15). In Sunday's paper, I read that the Corcoran Gallery of Art in Washington has cancelled an exhibition of Robert Mapplethorpe's photography and Senator Jesse Helms has taken legislative action to prevent government support for such works marred, in the Senator's opinion, by "a homosexual theme" (Russell, 1989, p. H31).

The power and the politics of representation has not been fully realized by those New Literacy advocates heavily engaged in exploring the writing process. The question of the subversive and outspoken as a part of the history of popular literacy has been sidestepped by the advocates of the New Literacy even as they provide students with many of the same vehicles—pamphlets and broadsides—which on more than one occasion carried disturbing messages. Publication is the principal post-writing activity for the serious writing program; it is intended to demonstrate a regard for students' work, treating their word as if it counted in the world. Most importantly, the new approaches to writing turn around the school's typical denial of a student's mother tongue which is other than the standard and help in that way for more students to gain a stronger sense of their own voice and how it might be expanded.[2]

There is undoubtedly a romantic bent to my reading of both the history of literacy and the potential of this new wave of writing. But it bears a hearing in the face of the more isolated concerns with writing expressed by New Literacy advocates who see their goal in abstract terms of the "expansion of learning" (Haley-James, 1981; Donovan & McClelland, 1980). In surveying this field, Miles Myers, for one, has expressed a fear that writing instruction risks becoming "a hodgepodge of gimmicks without a foundation in theory" (1983, p. 3). He sees the resolution of this shallowness in the pursuit of instructional paradigms grounded in a psychology of learning. The missing question for this foundation in theory, it strikes me, is whether the encouragement of the written organization of thought and feeling simply constitutes a cognitive capacity without context or moral imperative—a rhetoric without commitment. The New Literacy is encouraging the young to take up the pen and yet at the same moment they seem oblivious to the historical implications of this act. This rooting about in the past is meant to do no more than to frame the question of the ends to which a popular literacy is turned in the future.

Part II

The romantic roots of the New Literacy

A second method for getting at the heart of this project in reading and writing is to realize the marked parallels between Romanticism and the New Literacy. It is yet another way of grappling with the thinking behind the teaching, as educators find their best ideas played out historically and sometimes in what seems embarrassing innocence. After all, Wordsworth turns with reverence to the musings of the child-philosopher only to be mocked by Coleridge. And Coleridge's own paeans to the powers of the imagination, which also have their echo in the New Literacy, were realized on occasion through a certain chemical enhancement. All that seems naive and dated can be disavowed, refined, and redefined, but to appreciate the current accomplishment with this approach to the world requires a searching out of those earlier voices and the music that is being replayed and reworked.

The European literary movement of Romanticism emerged out of the age of revolution in its own fiery glow during the final years of the eighteenth century only to fade well before the middle of the nineteenth. During that period in England, first Blake, Wordsworth and Coleridge, and then Shelley, Keats, and Byron, set poetry, and indeed all of literature, in a new direction; they moved through a series of different literary paths which, taken together, gave form and substance to this movement now known as Romanticism. The term is used widely and freely, especially as it continues to influence the arts, in part because defining Romanticism or even pinning down the cast of original members remains a formidable task.[3] Although it is clearly foolish to try to offer its essence in a single phrase, in light of the project at hand, I am tempted to at least begin with Wordsworth's famous Romantic manifesto which declared that good poetry derives from "the spontaneous overflow of powerful feelings" (Wordsworth, 1968, p. 43). This effusive phrase sets the theme, the sense of ideal experience if not actual practice, for what might be termed the Romantic urge in writing a new literature that was intended to represent spontaneity and power. Further to this sense of what Romanticism has come to stand for, Morse Peckham (1970, p. 8) has identified three dominant patterns of thought: Romanticism favors organic metaphors rather than mechanical ones, becoming rather than being, and relationships rather entities. That much stated, it should begin to be apparent that over the course of the last two centuries, the once-radical literary movement of Romanticism has taken on the forcefulness of common sense, turning almost invisible in the process of becoming the most sensible way of imagining what children should be doing with language in their reading and writing.

I have been arguing that the appeal or impetus to implementation is a sense of philosophic affinity among educators—as if to say, "this is how I would see the world, the child, the mind, and the nature of literacy; after that let the research follow." In order to fill out the details and basis of this affinity and to describe what Romanticism and the New Literacy have both struggled to set into place, I take up three areas of shared concern: first, the primary metaphors of the mind, second, questioning authority and undoing of the book, and third, a common language for an uncommon literature. Such a comparison of the two movements brings to the fore not only the terms of affinity but those of disparagement toward the New Literacy, terms which mark its boldly Romantic reconceptualization of the student and the teacher, as well as the curriculum field.

The primary metaphors of the mind: the machine and the garden

Those writers associated with Romanticism initiated a subversive struggle of ideas about art and life toward the end of the eighteenth century, only to succeed during the first half of the nineteenth in becoming the dominant intellectual force. In England, beginning with Blake's poetry of innocence and experience, the work of the Romantics must be seen in its heroic challenge to the Age of Enlightenment. The Romantics were disheartened by the very achievements of the Enlightenment which seemed to go hand in hand with industrialization. Toward the end of the seventeenth century, Locke had constructed a philosophy of the mind through the metaphor of a tabula rasa, an appropriate enough choice for a chalk-dusted teacher intent on filling that blank slate with all manner of necessary facts or, in our case, steps to literacy. In a similar manner, Descartes had built a conception of the world in the grip of a mechanical determinism, while Newton had begun to uncover a number of the operating principles in a Nature forged by the Grand Engineer. By the eighteenth century, to overgeneralize the governing sensibility only slightly, the world was perceived to be unfolding as it should within a clockwork universe.

In the area of literature, the Enlightenment disposition was championed by the poet Alexander Pope who found countless ways to turn his decasyllabic couplets to "what was oft thought, but ne'er so well expressed." His work amounted to an eloquent and often biting satire of the human condition after the Augustan or Classical tradition. Half a century later, a new generation of writers were not as amused and began to turn their backs on this somewhat detached objectification of the world; in walking away from the Enlightenment project, the Romantics created more than a new wave, more than a variation on this Enlightenment theme. Though James Engell (1981) has built a convincing case for that important Romantic conception of the imagination being continuous with and built upon the Enlightenment notion, a

189

fundamental distinction did crystalize between the two periods in the Romantic rejection of an Enlightened search for the precise machinations of the mind and the heavenly spheres.

The Romantics feared that what was lost in that search outweighs what was found, as Mary Shelley made clear in her Romantic fable, *Frankenstein*. This was a battle with classical origins, but for the first time with the instance of Romanticism, it took on literary significance. The great contemporary critic of the Romantics, M. H. Abrams (1953, p. 168), has identified how the Romantics succeeded in dislodging the conception of art from its mimetic function, from its ability to *mirror* the world, to a state in which the apt metaphor for creativity becomes the *fountain* and the *lamp,* as art becomes an important and original source of meaning. This fundamental distinction in the function of the creative moment is clearly one that sets apart the New Literacy's regard for the child from the traditional conception.

If the mechanical view looks to the domain of the well-tuned machine or flow-chart for its model of thought, the organic theory turns to the garden, to fields of living, growing things, in which the self-evolved interdependence of parts is the secret of life, as Abrams (1953, p. 175) has described it. (It is perhaps worth noting, parenthetically at least, that one of the epithets the New Literacy classroom has earned from its critics is "bloom-room.")[4] Abrams's choice of "secret" is apt for its suggested reverence of the process, a reverence which is not driven like the Enlightenment by a need to uncover the gearing of its mechanism and the logic of the engineering. While Locke might speak of the mind as a mirror which captures and fixes images from the outside, Coleridge spoke of the imagination as a living faculty of "blending, fusing power" (cited in Abrams, 1953, p. 169).

The very language used by the Romantics to speak of thought created, in effect, a tamperproof seal around their discourse; it precluded a breakdown of the process for purposes of refining (or in our case, teaching) the individual elements. Not surprisingly, this revered imaginative power took on a spiritual sensibility for the Romantics and encouraging its expression became a moral imperative. The imagination became both the aesthetic and moral center, or as Shelley described it, "the great instrument of moral good" (cited in Harris, 1969, p. 20). Coleridge also spoke of it in markedly religious terms: "The primary IMAGINATION I hold to be the living Power and prime Agent of all human Perception . . . in the infinite I AM" ([1817] 1983, p. 304). Now while New Literacy advocates of the imagination dare not indulge in such homiletic expression, they are at least as concerned with mobilizing the children's imaginative powers as the means to enriching their creative and cognitive claim on the world.

Ann Berthoff (1983) is one advocate of the New Literacy who draws directly on Coleridge as "our best guide" to the imaginative powers of the organically conceived mind. She makes the reasoning of this return remarkably lucid: we are in danger of losing ourselves to the new science so lacking in imagination. She openly engages in a paradigm battle with what she claims is the narrowness of positivism—"positivists believe that empirical tests yield true facts and that's that" (p. 191). She reclaims the imagination "as a way of knowing or a means of making meaning" (p. 193), rescuing it from its relegation to the affective domain, as opposed to the cognitive realm, by positivists who are, after all, the inheritors of the Enlightenment (p. 193). Her attack is against a positivism in psychology and education that lacks a proper regard for language and she mounts this attack with the help of I. A. Richards, a literary critic from the early part of this century who has done much to bring Romanticism and psychology into alignment. At one point, she cites Richards's (Romantic) attack on this heartless positivist: "He thinks of it [language] as a code and has not yet learned that it is an organ— the supreme organ of the mind's self ordering growth" (p. 192). This reification of language and mind into organ and body is the mark of Romanticism's uncritical reverence for the powers of expression, though it cannot help but appear as self-congratulatory reverence on the part of the writer.

Or consider the organicism of another New Literacy advocate, Frank Smith. He opts for the loftiest of metaphors in making his case for rejecting a mechanistic model of the world and the mind. He creates in the process something of a small morality play with the artist-creator set against the shifty dealer: "My metaphor pictures the brain as an artist, a creator of experience for itself and for others, rather than as a dealer in information" (1985, p. 197). He treats the phonics approach to reading with an organicist's disdain; it is an educational act of "decomposition," which for the child become "the fundamentally incomprehensible aspects of reading instruction." His challenge to the decades during which the teaching of phonic's dominated reading instruction in the school remains the defiant claim that "the essential skills of reading—namely the efficient use of non-visual information—cannot be taught" (Smith, 1978, p. 179).

The secret for the teacher of the New Literacy is to resist the urge to instruct through the breakdown of processes into discrete stages; though it may seem strangely archaic, the answer seems to be to stay true to a Romantic and organic conception of the imagination. One reason for faithfulness to this particular metaphor, Frank Smith has pointed out, is a matter of intention and an intention of serious consequence:

> The relative value of metaphors cannot be assessed
> "objectively." There is no statistical test that will decide which
> is "correct." The question is which metaphor is the most
> productive, and the answer will depend on what one's intention
> is in the first place—to measure and control human behavior or
> to understand it. (1985, p. 212)

Smith dares here to name the politics of positivism. Its side of his dichotomy—to measure and control—certainly has a nasty ring to it and a seriousness that may convince many teachers of the urgency and rightness of the organic metaphor. I only caution that we put a good deal of faith in the medical profession's measurement and control of the machinery of the body in hopes of the most benign effect, and that in my efforts here to "understand" the phenomenon of the New Literacy, I wish to temper these most forceful and rhetorical statements of principle.

The classroom experiences fostered by the teacher's embrace of organic metaphors over mechanistic models is intended to provide for students more than blissful, surprising acts of creation. The literature of the New Literacy also claims that it can nurture a self-reliant and improved level of thinking among students. There will be a flowering of thought "at the point of utterance," to use James Britton's phrase (1980). If their own writing is thus thought-provoking, then children can be said to be responsible, by this act of writing, for their own intellectual stimulation. Simply put, the New Literacy has begun to shift the educational authority from without, from the experience and knowledge of the teacher, to within, to those qualities in the student. Britton stresses the importance of student using their own experience as touchstone by citing the philosopher Ernst Cassirer: "If I put out the light of my own personal experience I cannot see and I cannot judge the experience of others" (Britton, 1972, p. 154). Wordsworth, too, repeatedly reflected on the primacy of his own experience and the inspirational power of time spent reflectively alone, without a teacher except Nature, as for example in "Tintern Abbey":

In Nature and the language of sense,
The anchor of my purest thoughts, the nurse
The guide, the guardian of my heart, and soul
Of all my moral being.

Trusting the experience of children and the natural power of their minds to find their own way was an idea which was no more than incipient in Romanticism. The Romantics did not move from the idealization of their own childhoods into encouraging the publication of the poetry of children, even from their own children or their own childhood. They celebrated the particular genius of the accomplished poet, to the special qualities of mind which the poet alone demonstrated, which Wordsworth, for example, went on about at some length in his preface to *Lyrical Ballads*. Looking to the New Literacy, it might seem a great advance to extend and democratize our concept of the mind's powers until it has become the right of every child to lay claim to a kind of unconscious genius which requires only a writerly opportunity to bring it into play.

Not only is writing to come that much easier and more powerfully for Romanticism and the New Literacy by turning to the organic metaphor, this writing will serve to awaken and advance the mind. Shelley speaks glowingly of this cognitive agitation in his "Defence of Poetry": "For the mind in creation is a fading coal, which some invisible influence, like a constant wind, awakens to transitory brightness" ([1821] 1965, p. 135). On behalf of the New Literacy, a similarly salutary effect has been noted by Frank Smith, who states more prosaically, that "by writing we find out what we know, what we think" (1982, p. 33). The rhetoric of the New Literacy, in its Romanticism and psycholinguistics, promotes a blend of mental growth and self-development in a mixture of literacy activities which, while seeming to look back, is nonetheless sensitive to our current anxieties with functional skills and cognitive achievement.

Questioning authorities and undoing the book

Among the paradoxes that Romanticism happily embraces is a theory of literature which rejects a certain sense of bookishness. Wordsworth, in his long autobiographical poem, *The Prelude*, speaks of attending to a voice more profound than written language—"the voice / Of mountain

193

torrents"—a voice which could foster thought that was not the prisoner of books. That Wordsworth's concern was directly addressed to education is made clear in the fifth book of *The Prelude* ([1805] 1971) which takes as its subject the influence of books on the young:

> they who have the art
> To manage books, and things, and make them
> work
> Gently on infant minds, as does the sun
> Upon a flower; the Tutors of our Youth . . .
> Sages, who in their prescience would control
> All accidents, and to the very road
> Which they have fashion'd would confine us down,
> like engines . . .
>
> (V, 373–83)

The danger of teaching by the book, as Wordsworth foresaw it, was a metaphorical reduction of the child from a flower to an engine, all for want of the accidental and spontaneous. For tutors and teachers, having learned how to manage the book, there was the temptation to use it to control and confine those they instruct. In the spirit of Rousseau's model pupil, Emile, who was to be kept from books until after he was twelve, Wordsworth feared the fate of the child stuffed with learning. He held the more natural path to wisdom to be an independent process of comingling with experience, which in the case of his young poet was underway by the age of "twice five summers:"

> I held unconscious intercourse with beauty
> Old as creation, drinking in a pure
> Organic pleasure from the silver wreaths
> Of curling mist, or from the level plain
> Of waters coloured by impending clouds.
>
> (IV, 559–66)

In a similar vein, Romantic essayist Thomas de Quincey warned against the "language of books" and the "contagion of bookishness" which implied writing in something less than a natural voice (cited by Jacobus, 1984, p. 219). He was attacking the language of classicism as it was bound up in an imitation of the past. Yet de Quincey was careful to treat the matter of a writer's style—a point of deserved pride on his

194

part—as an organic instance of thought in its most subtle manifestation. He took particular issue with "inkhorn" or formalist concerns over grammar which took a mechanistic approach to language. Echoes of de Quincey's attack on the classicist theories of rhetoric and grammar are found today in such works as Knoblauch and Brannon's (1984) argument against the persistence of the old rhetoric. Both Romantics and neo-Romantics take issue with composition instruction by the book, that is, through the naming of the parts, whether they be the colors of rhetoric as they were once known in medieval times—repetito, conversio, complexio, etcetera (Geoffery of Vinsauf, [1200] 1967)—or through the new classicism of the generative rhetoric of the sentence (Christensen, 1978). Taxonomies and techniques are eschewed in favor of a more natural (organic) approach in which students close the book on composition techniques and rhetorical tricks in order to find their own authentic way and meaning.

In the New Literacy, the attack on the authority of the book is, as with Romanticism, a focused assault. As we saw in Chapter 3, along with a shared distaste for the grammar text, the New Literacy has the basal reader as its other prime target. These engineered storybooks of controlled vocabulary and authorless, anemic selections suggest a horrific initiation into literacy for the advocates of the New Literacy. Opposed to the banality of the basal is the more lively and organic state of children's literature. Without threatening the integrity and authority of the children, these books are envisioned as part of the student's world-building. As Margaret Meek describes it, the experience of literature is as necessary to the child as to the adult: "The virtual experience of the sequence and salience of literature, language 'in the spectator role,' however defined, extends and confirms the inner fiction which is our way of interpreting the world" (Spencer, 1984, p. 93). Another target of this focused assault on the traditional classroom is the primacy of reading instruction among the language arts in the schools. As we have seen, advocates of the New Literacy move writing and the other expressive arts in language into a collaborative if not leading role in literacy education, just as their intention is that the expressive powers of language are about to play a more integrative (organic) role throughout the curriculum.

This anti-instructional temperament is a central paradox of the New Literacy: it would teach what cannot be taught in a course essentially without content. It demands of teachers a willingness to relinquish their claim on the special knowledge which the child needs to read and succeed. Harste, Woodward and Burke caution that "teachers must be particularly careful of not taking ownership of the process from children" (1984, p. 206). The New Literacy offers a different way to be with children; these ideas have the power, not only to encourage a new form of reading and writing, but to alter what it means to be a teacher and a student.[5]

However, to so vigorously challenge this living tradition of texts and teachings is to invite a vehement counterattack, which in this case has amounted to charges of vanity and academic dissolution. I have yet to deal with the question of anti-intellectualism in the New Literacy as an educational program which proposes that the students be their own best teachers. This seems like an appropriate setting to raise the issue as it has been raised before with the Romantics, and the two are linked in this point of challenging bookish authority as much as on any idea that they can be said to share.

To return to the earlier precedent, the original questioning of authority in Romanticism was fostered by Rousseau's call to let nature rather than convention be our guide which came to a rather daring, if ghastly, head in the French Revolution. However, the initial British enthusiasm for Rousseau and the French Revolution was tempered by the eloquent and powerful voice of Edmund Burke, even before the Revolution seemed to betray its own cause. Burke's attack on Rousseau during the Revolution is relevant to both Wordsworth's and the New Literacy's debt to this influential French thinker. The instance of Burke's attack was the French National Assembly attempt in 1791 to implement an educational scheme inspired by Rousseau in order to advance the Revolution. Burke took this opportunity to accuse Rousseau of being "the great professor and founder of the philosophy of vanity" (cited in Chandler, 1984, p. 115). He chided both Rousseau and the members of the Assembly for turning their backs on what Burke felt was a natural social order made up of such matters as "plain duty." Burke attacked them for their shear self-absorption, which Rousseau had seemed to advocate in education through his encouragement of a skeptical and solipsistic posture. Burke's charges against Rousseau could stand a hearing in current educational discussions of the New Literacy. Consider the typical young student of the New Literacy: published by the age of seven, nurtured by supportive coaching and editorial assistance, celebrated and excerpted in educational studies. The child-author may well emerge with something less than a natural humility. Nonetheless, against this fostered vanity, it seems likely that the student's actual regard for books will have been improved from having been less schooled in them. The book is a compatriot and all authors are now fellow-authors and colleagues.

However, Burke's charge of vanity is part of a more serious allegation of anti-intellectualism which has been leveled at both Rousseau's Romantic educational visions (Chandler, 1984, p. 112) and the Progressive Education Association in general (Hofstadter, 1962). Rousseau, for his part, virtually begs such an attack in *Emile:* "Reading is the plague of childhood"; "I hate books. They only teach one to talk about what one doesn't know" (1979, pp. 116, 184). In his "Intimations Ode," Wordsworth unrestrainedly celebrates the Platonic glory of the child-philosopher:

> Thou, whose exterior semblance doth belie
> Thy Soul's immensity;
> Thou best Philosopher, who yet dost keep
> Thy heritage, thou Eye among the blind,
> That, deaf and silent, read'st the eternal deep,
> Haunted for ever by the eternal mind
> > Mighty Prophet! Seer blest!
> On whom those truths doth rest

Yet this was too much for Coleridge, who was more than a little intellectually inclined himself if in a rather undisciplined way. In his *Biographia Literaria,* Coleridge saw fit to call the jig and demand of Wordsworth an explanation of the ways and means of this immense and prophetic insight on the part of the mere child:

> In what sense is a child of that age a *philosopher?* In what
> sense does he *read* "the eternal deep"? . . . By reflection? by
> knowledge? by conscious intuition? or by *any* form or
> modification of consciousness? . . . Children of this age give
> us no such information of themselves. ([1817] 1983, p. 138,
> original emphasis).

It has been left up to the research teams of the New Literacy, through ethnographic research and think-aloud protocols, to encourage children of this age to offer us such information of themselves. Whether this encouragement inspired by Wordsworth's sentiments has produced a blessed reading of the eternal deep or something less prophetic suggests the need for a continuing comparison of the claims made for children and what they do produce on behalf of the New Literacy.[6] One of the more sensible solutions to this dilemma in Romanticism's vision of the child that I have stumbled across is in the unlikely source, *Science of Logic* (1831), by the German philosopher Hegel: "Childlike innocence no doubt has in it something fascinating and attractive; but only because it reminds us of what the spirit must win for itself. The harmoniousness of childhood is a gift from the hands of nature; the second harmony must spring from the labour and culture of the spirit" (cited in Newsome, 1984, p. 29). And in a sense, that second harmony in the culture of writing and reading is the very thing that the New Literacy classroom labors toward.

The allegation of anti-intellectualism is also part of the New Literacy's more immediate inheritance from the Progressive Education movement. The questions that American historian Richard Hofstadter (l962, p. 368) raises in his attack on the already fading Progressive Education movement were focused on the difficulty of maintaining a sound line between "respect" for the child and "a kind of bathetic reverence." He is distressed by a certain aimlessness in the encouragement of the child's potential: "The child's impulses should be guided 'forward'—but in what direction?" he pointedly asks, citing Dewey's simplistic prescription (1962, p. 375). In the New Literacy, with the act of so much writing intent on moving the student forward, the question of what they will reach at the end of this labor, besides the bottom of the page, can hang in the air unanswered for the duration of the program. It is often assumed that the point of writing is to facilitate yet more and better writing in some vague sense, which I suppose is not at all foreign to the nature of skill development in other school subjects. From among those who have grappled directly with the question of function, the goal of a greater facility in writing appears to be divided among such concerns as cognitive activity (Hays et al., 1983), knowledge assimilation (Britton, 1972), and, somewhat bathetically perhaps, self-development (Medway, 1980). This immensity of cogitation, assimilation, and self-development describes the directions in which this education runs. True to the emerging ethos of this decade, the New Literacy points to a psychological blossoming of individual potential, thoroughly free of content and context concerns about what might amount to the proper ends of education.

From the British side, Peter Abbs is another whose doubts about progressive education seem relevant to the vulnerabilities of the New Literacy: "I think it just to say that they possessed an effusive concept of the child, at once intolerably vague and hugely indulgent. In their minds, the poet and the child become synonymous; yet the poet expresses and extends his own culture in a way *no* child can possibly do" (1982, p. 11, original emphasis). What is at stake in these various charges of anti-intellectualism is the assumed responsibility of education to both culture, in the narrower and higher sense, and discipline, as an academic training of the mind. Progressivism turns to the student and asks the student to look inward, to explore personal truths and interests. In so doing, it undoubtedly misses out on the sort of academic rigor reflected in the quip of headmaster George Bradley from the last century: "If once you interest boys in the work, you lose half its disciplinary profit" (cited in Murray, 1977, p. 114), and it seems as well to miss out on insisting that the student take hold of the surrounding culture.

Yet the New Literacy has moved beyond the progressive education movement in ways which tend to meet at least some of these charges. For example, consider that the New Literacy turns to literature and away from the textbook for its reading and inspiration, that it introduces the student into the community of writers, and that it strikes a bridge to that idea of literary culture which education is often asked to impart to the young. As it repeatedly turns to writing to promote cognitive growth across the curriculum—promoting "first drafts for first thinking" (Martin, 1983, p. 11)—it has not forsaken intellectual goals in the disciplined pursuit of new knowledge. It might be said that students at least begin to constitute a more literate community as they write and read more willingly and deeply. Equally so, the artifacts created in the classroom might be said to extend students' participation in their own culture, if that is not too wildly effusive and indulgent a speculation. For my part, I have already recommended a plunge into pressing research questions, and in the next chapter I will promote a New Literacy engagement with poststructural theories of language and self. Still, the charge of anti-intellectualism will always have a toehold on a movement which challenges the authority of the book. Advocates of the New Literacy are obliged both to recognize and address the direction that education is going to take under their spell.

A common language for an uncommon literature

Both Romanticism and the New Literacy have set about in a similar way to make a place for themselves by denouncing the old texts and declaring the unrealized potential of a commonplace language for their new works as poets and teachers. In reclaiming poetry to personal and organic purposes two centuries ago, the Romantics had to rewrite the literary language of their time. In the eighteenth century, the Classical model served as the supreme literary authority. With imitation as the method— as art was the mirror—there had emerged in literature what the critic Irving Babbit has described as the twin doctrines of probability and decorum. Though there were lively exceptions among authors of the Augustan age, it is clear to Babbit that this neo-classicism "tended to narrow the scope of human spirit": "Correctness thus became a sort of tyranny" ([1919] 1977, pp. 33, 25). Romanticism's attack on these limits began with Wordsworth's realignment of poetry with the vernacular and indigenous language of the people, moving it away from the Classical standards. Wordsworth issued notice of this revolution with his celebrated statement on the proper diction and subject for poetry in the preface to the *Lyrical Ballads* in 1798. These poems were to relate "incidents and situations from common life . . . in a language really used by men," and this was enough to suggest that poetry had entered a new age (1968, p. 26). As it was, the "romance" had originally been a vernacular form of popular literature which dated back to medieval times, but here a common language was being turned to a more serious and ambitious project (Babbit, [1919] 1977, p. 36).

Now of course, Wordsworth's claim for "a language really used" was somewhat bolder than poetry could stand at that time, and his actual diction, as can be seen from the lines cited above, may still strike us as archly poetic. Yet his objective of bringing the vernacular to serious verse has become the stuff of poetry since and the certain mark of modern verse. Equally so, this insurgent movement in Romanticism has opened the way for the schoolyard talk of children to become the poetry and prose of the classroom publishing house. It has become clear to the advocates of the New Literacy that students' language expresses a certain truth and integrity even before it becomes fully the standard, just as for Wordsworth the common language "arising out of repeated experience and regular feelings is a more permanent and a far more philosophical language than that which is frequently substituted for it by the Poets" (1968, p. 27).

This usurpation of traditional standards in language and literature was extended by Romanticism to the subject matter of the creative act. As part of the naturalization of poetry and the new creative importance of the poet, the writer became the natural hero of the literary quest (Frye,

1968, p. 37). Wordsworth, for example, felt justified spending the fourteen books of *The Prelude* to trace his development as a poet. His declaration of independence in the poem—"no Helper hast thou here" (XIII, 102)—lent to this sense of heroics, as well as signaling a break in the long association of religion with poetry (Jay, 1984).[7] In the place of this religious quest, the pursuit was for an "active self-realizedness," to use Hegel's phrase from the period. This nineteenth-century soul-searching initiated something of a new theology of literature, a regard for its works as a spiritual and textual home, which continues to this day to console many. In *The Prelude,* Wordsworth also advanced autobiography into a self-conscious literary form; the critic, Paul Jay, has described the scene of writing in this poem as a theater, "a site where the language of imagination struggles with the perception of fact" (1984, p. 94). In the New Literacy, the privileged self-expression of the child—the very voice Wordsworth venerated ("The things which I have seen I now can see no more")—is the source of inspiration in the classroom. The self-text is the point of dramatic focus in this writing theater. Graves, for example, instructs the interested teacher with student-teacher writing conference scripts. The writing classroom becomes the students' vehicle to self-realization, as they use it both to discover their own meaning on the page, as well as to take their own story as the one worth telling. In its own way, this encouragement of the children's writing indicates a similarly significant break in the classroom with conventional proprieties of expression and topic.[8]

Another distinction that Romanticism introduced into this reconsideration of language was a division between the emotional and the rational, a distinction that Wordsworth declared the "philosophical one of Poetry and Science" (Wordsworth, 1968, p. 33). Alexander Smith (1968), in an anonymous essay published in 1835, attempted to formalize this dichotomy as one between poetry and prose. Smith struck these rhetorical divisions in a manner which seems to foreshadow Britton's distinctions between transactional and poetic discourse, between participant and spectator roles. Britton reserved the term "expressive," which Smith actually used to cover poetry, for the personal work of the student-writer trying out ideas before going public with them. But at the heart of the expressive/poetic mode for both Smith and Britton is a form of emotional self-absorption, individualism, and something approaching analytic indifference, though more rigidly so for Smith: "prose is the language of *intelligence,* poetry of *emotion*" (1968, p. 176, original emphasis).

Both Smith's and Britton's divisions were created to make room for forms of discourse which seemed to have been unduly excluded from serious consideration in society and education. For the Romantics, poetry had to find a way to scale new heights, beyond such works of intelligence and wit as Pope's "Essay on Man," and against such treatises in verse they chose the expressive and the personal, the seemingly spontaneous and fragmentary. In our day, Britton has posited a legitimate alternative to predominance of the student essay and other prosaic forms in the curriculum. Through his categorical distinctions he has opened a space for expressive writing and created a pedagogical continuum with the poetic and transactional modes. However, Romanticism also warns against the divisiveness of taxonomies; recall Richard's claim that language is "the supreme organ" and once divided is bound to falter. In the case of Alexander Smith, the fixing of distinctions came some years after the heyday of Romanticism and had little impact. But Britton's division—between poetic and transactional, spectator and participant roles—has taken a central place in a number of versions of the New Literacy and not without taxonomic complications which I point out in Chapter 2 (n. 10). The difficulty in Britton's assignment of literature to the spectator role is highlighted by Shelley's "Defence of Poetry" with the famous final declaration that "poets are the unacknowledged legislators of the world" (1965, p. 140). Poets will not sit by in the stands; they would affect the world with language. The argument of this chapter is nothing less than Shelley's point: the writers discussed here were not spectators when they first broke the ground which this New Literacy is now ploughing.

Between the flurry of seventeenth-century pamphlets filling the streets of London and the quietude of Wordsworth's Lake District excursions, it may seem a long way to the contemporary school classroom. Yet if only through Romantically tinged lenses, the battle of popular ballads and broadsides, metaphors and mock-books can give a certain focus to the New Literacy attack on the mechanisms of the well-planned basal reader, step-by-step composition book, and false-logic grammar text. The New Literacy attempts to replace these unnatural texts with the authenticities of a popular literature; it speaks against undue regulation of expression. It remakes students and teachers into co-conspirators in this popular and Romantic vision of literacy. However, these parallels are not all exoneration and exhilaration. The other advantage of this historical vision is the catalogue of criticisms that it offers this related project of the New Literacy—charges of politicizing education along with accusations of vanity and anti-intellectualism. In preparing to meet these criticisms, the New Literacy is under no obligation to stay true to O'Brien's *Poor Man's Guardian* or Wordsworth's *Prelude*. Instead of an allegiance to founders, I have argued for thinking through the language and ideas underlying these contemporary curricular events.

This examination of popular and Romantic precedents has been something of an experiment, to use a favorite term of the Romantics, in understanding the roots of curriculum. I am by no means the first, especially in revisiting Romanticism in search of a guide for school practices as Alfred North Whitehead (1967) and Kieran Egan (in press) ably demonstrate. In this case, however, it has given me a chance to set out on a much larger scale the elements of a public and personal literacy that are at work in the New Literacy. It allows us to catch these ideas in action as they arise from and work upon a culture. Popular literacy played an instrumental part in broadening the extent of political enfranchisement among the people; Romanticism, especially for Wordsworth, took its first fire from the French Revolution, while eventually making its own peace with the Burkean, conservative reaction against it. Turning to history in this way allows us to catch sight of the driving ideas of the curriculum in different landscapes, where we can watch how these ideas have worked themselves out in the lives of the people. Having gained a historical sense of the precedents and consequences of the New Literacy, we now ready to ask in the chapter ahead how the classroom versions of these ideas relate to the tenor of the times, giving some thought to where our new literates might be headed with their new-found powers.

Notes

1. Baron (1982) reviews the moral imperative of grammar in the last century; Davis (1984) demonstrates that the case is not closed by providing a contemporary defense of grammar if for somewhat different reasons, and Lyman's (1929) work gives an indication of how long the unsuccessful debunking of grammar teaching has been going on. In Bourdieu's analysis of the schooling of verbal manners, "the whole trick of pedagogic reason lies precisely in the way it extorts the essential while seeming to demand the insignificant . . . the concessions of *politeness* always contain *political* concessions" (1977, p. 95).
2. English teachers' recognitions of this issue has been most cogently put in "The Students' Right to Their Own Language" (1974) which was a position paper adopted by the Conference on College Composition and Communica-

tion, an affiliate member of the NCTE. That this acceptance is still a controversial position among English teachers is indicated by Sledd (1983).

3. Nobody provides a clearer indication of the sheer mass of confusing and contradictory claims made for this movement since its inception than Arthur Lovejoy (1960) in his essay "On the Discriminations of Romanticisms," even as the Romanticism of writers such as Jane Austen continues to be contested (McGann, 1983, pp. 18–19). In light of this problem, I have stuck to mainstream figures and easily substantiated contentions which can be safely labeled the Romanticism of early nineteenth-century British poetry.

4. Mary Bryson gave me this gem in exchange for a shared cab ride to an airport some years ago.

5. As you may recall, the teacher has the opportunity to become a writer among a class of child-writers (Graves, 1984); a shop steward for her writing workshop (Parker, 1982); a coach and a cheerleader (Pearson, 1985); and finally the teacher becomes a student of the child-informant (Harste, Woodward, & Burke, 1984). Support for the attractiveness to teachers of this letup in the disciplinary role and its somewhat illusory nature is found in Rachel Sharp and Michael Green (1975). It should also be noted in this matter of instructional practice that Bereiter (1984) has attempted to draw a fence of limitations around the interpretive and seemingly instructionally passive Frank Smith, faulting him for being more given to exhortative metaphors than to practical measures. Yet while Bereiter and Scardamalia (1987) argue for systematic instruction in cognitive independence as the only path to "high literacy," they still refer to the teacher's role as an exemplar and coach.

6. Among the progressive educators from earlier in this century, Marjourie Hourd gave a pedagogical hearing to the child as one who "read'st the eternal deep" in *Educating the Poetic Spirit* (1949), as did W. S. Tomkinson before her as he spoke of the connection between child and poet: "The child strives after the expression of himself and does it in the same way as the poet—by creative work" (1921, p. 81).

7. But, of course, he still did not go it as alone as he often portrayed. In another place I have explored the considerable and complex role which William Wordsworth's sister, Dorothy, played as his Helper which brings into focus the domestic scene of his creative activity which offers yet another lesson for the New Literacy (Willinsky, 1989).

8. Jay also develops the connection between Wordsworth's and Freud's dependence on what he terms the recuperative method (1984, pp. 74–82). Both would return to the past, to the memory, for its restorative and therapeutic powers. The connection of this tendency with the New Literacy can be traced through the Freudian aspects of Progressive Education (Cremin, 1961, pp. 209–15) or more directly through the common use of the student journal or writer's notebook as a teacher's means of tapping the "salutary" power, as Britton refers to it, of experience reworked in writing (1972, p. 253).

8
Meaning,
Literature, and Self

> I have come increasingly to recognize that most learning in
> most settings is a communal activity, a sharing of culture. It is
> not just that the child must make his knowledge his own, but
> that he must make it his own in a community of those who
> share his sense of belonging to a culture.
>
> Jerome Bruner, *Actual Minds, Possible Worlds* (1986, p. 127)

Jerome Bruner's work on the psychology of learning has exercised a
formidable influence on the New Literacy over the last two decades. As
he has investigated the nature of learning through language and introduced the work of Soviet psychologists Lev Vygotsky (1978) and A. R.
Luria (1976) to the West, the New Literacy has been happy to follow,
finding applications or these ideas in the classroom. But in *Actual Minds,
Possible Worlds*, Bruner declares a shift in his regard for learning, a
shift that I wish to encourage the New Literacy to pursue in a number
of directions. In essence, Bruner has found that *learning* is a far more
"communal activity" than has traditionally been credited. This view of
the social construction of learning and literacy provides a strong basis
for the New Literacy plan to work reading, writing, and literature in a
new way. "Bruner's shift," as I might term it, offers an initial move
away from treating literacy as the isolated acts of individuals and toward
its greater part in the social universe. New Literacy rhetoric is full of
the individuality and personal integrity of meaning, while at the same
time it extols the intersubjectivity of response, the supportive environment of the workshop, and the public reach of writing. If, as I have
argued, a restructuring of the classroom is a foremost concern of the
New Literacy, the social basis of learning, language, and literacy are

crucial elements in the development of these programs. The spirit of individualism that finds expression in the New Literacy is the product of at least three central concepts—meaning, literature, and self—that can be rethought in light of Bruner's shift. It no longer makes sense for New Literacy programs to strive toward a literate community in the classroom while continuing to speak of literacy principally in personal and individual terms of self-realization.

Yet rather than divert the New Literacy from this pursuit of individual self-realization, I want to suggest that 1) it can no longer carry on the quest visor down and blind to how this goal is itself a cultural artifact of literacy, and 2) it can discover new lessons in literacy lurking in this shift to a sociable view of learning. The social formation of meaning, literature, and self seem likely topics for a classroom that is going about the reorganization of its own social formation. Bruner's shift is a first step toward these new lessons, but I also recommend a return for a moment to his earlier work in which he posits that "the curriculum of a subject should be determined by the most fundamental understanding that can be achieved of the underlying principles that give structure to that subject" (1960, p. 31). Although we have something broader in literacy than the academic disciplines Bruner has in mind, it remains a primary topic for the classroom. In what follows, I am going after what can be taken as the poststructuralist principles of literacy, principles that I feel should inform the New Literacy and the case that it is making for new programs in reading and writing. In this discussion it should become apparent that the scope of the New Literacy project may well be much larger and more encompassing than its most far-seeing advocates have realized.

Meaning

As part of Bruner's shift to a constructivist position, he has come to consider *meaning* as a cultural process rather than the solitary invention of the individual: "culture is as much a *forum* for negotiating and renegotiating meaning" (1986, p. 123, original emphasis). The implications of this reconception clearly support a New Literacy approach to language and literacy, for "if it is going to prepare the young for life as it is lived, it should also partake of the spirit of a forum, of negotiation, of the recreation of meaning" (1986, p. 123). But while I applaud the shift here to the social situation of language, I also worry about a certain idealism in this serene image of the cultural scene. If we are talking about "life as it is lived," then, as students already know, there are few forums where all voices are either heard or treated as equal members of the bargaining unit in this language-wide negotiation of meaning. The social construction of meaning that Bruner is drawing our attention to brings students to the crossroads of history and power out of which whole bodies of meaning, in gender, race, and social class, have already been forged for them.

But if Bruner tends to avoid that busy corner of meaning, Mikhail Bakhtin finds in it the crux of culturally formed meaning. Bakhtin, a compatriot of Vygotsky and Luria, has stressed the uneven balance of power in this negotiation of meaning. This clash is set in motion by "the social organization of the participants and also by the immediate conditions of their interaction" (writing as Volosinov, 1973, p. 21). For Bakhtin, language is "dialogic" or rooted in exchange and use, that is, rooted in the social relations of use. The dialogic quality and organization of language is profoundly affected, in Bahktin's analysis, by the dynamics of social class, but given the discussion in this book thus far, his conception can easily be expanded to include the play of race and gender. Many meanings are established in the very intersection of these interests, in the play of differences that sets the meaning of one term in relation to another. One need only think of how meaning works with primary social categories: man/woman, Christian/Jew, white/black, conservative/liberal, or to take up a few from this book, decoding/meaning, personal/public, and oral/literate. The differences are established as one group writes the equation that defines their meaning in relation to each other with a privileging of one term over the other in a manner that is soon taken for granted. The schoolyard forms a microcosm of this process; the name-calling of the powerful articulates their rightful place at the top. When the bully is called names by the others, speaking under their breath or out of range, it only accentuates the bully's control of the discursive field of schoolyard banter.

Bakhtin also recognizes that meaning is still fluid, although the important point for students of literacy and meaning is that the dominant are more than a little reluctant to allow the negotiated flow of meaning to break free of their control. Nonetheless, meaning in many instances is openly contested. The campaign against sexist language is an excellent example, and the pattern of support and opposition by women and men makes an excellent instance to study the process in a more explicit fashion than it normally takes. But all of this is to say to Bruner that to suggest that meaning is negotiated in an open forum resounds of a golden age of democracy that doesn't wash on the streets of our conurbations, if it ever did in ancient Athens.

Yet if Bruner seems a little naive about this meaningful process, he still strikes me as heading in the right direction by stressing this shift to a more communal understanding of the learning process. But why this need for a shift; what is my complaint here? The New Literacy has invested heavily in the rhetoric of individual expression and voice. It has happily taken the personal and the public aspects of literacy to consist of a one-way street; the individual finds a vehicle in writing for those deep and hidden thoughts at the core of the self and goes increasingly public with them. In the writing process, those holding to the importance of revision claim it is a clarification of those thoughts while those, like Britton, speaking in favor of "shaping at the point of utterance" see a more direct expression of "the moment by moment interpretive process by which we make sense of what is happening around us" (Britton, 1980, p. 63). But in both cases, the individual can easily be misunderstood as this isolated source and starting point of meaning.

For the New Literacy, the danger is in turning the individual into the unit of meaning as both a guiding psychological and moral principle to guide classroom practices. John Dewey turned this principle into a touchstone of progressive education or the "newer school of education" as he called it: "the beginning of instruction shall be made with the experience learners already have" (1938, p. 74). One of the more radical instances of that guiding proposition for the New Literacy is that the child has already begun to take meaning from print before arriving at school. They arrive on that first tremulous day with a knowledge and experience of literacy, as the previously discussed work of Harste, Woodward, and Burke (1984) has demonstrated, but also a knowledge and experience of the world that becomes the basis of their expression in language and literacy. To further students' introduction into literacy means, then, facilitating this personal process of creating meaning. For too long children have had to park a good deal of what they already know about such things as literacy outside the classroom with their muddy boots and winter coats. The literacy they encounter in the class-room is removed from the world of print which they have run into before, based as this classroom work is on breaking down language into less than meaningful units in order to teach students the constituent parts of literacy. It fails to build on what is already meaningful to the child. The new opportunities provided by the classroom are those of a community driven by the meaningfulness of print and a faith in the fact that students will ultimately find their own way to meaning. This valuing of the learner's experiences needs to be seen in its moral dimension which can be stated rather directly: *To diminish the potential for individual meaningfulness in students' work is a denial of their basic humanity.*[1]

Once again, the New Literacy can seem to strike just the right note with this call to meaningfulness. Who could be so hard-hearted as to deny a meaningful time to the child? Only a Mr. Gradgrind? The issue at stake here is not simply an educational one but is related to the question of work. Not long after the grinding school-lessons of Dickens's *Hard Times,* William Morris had set in place the moral principle of meaningfulness in work by creating workshops for artisans and design schools as opportunities for ennobling work against the transformation of craft into a form of meaningless labor through industrial processes (Stansky, 1988); Morris' work, as I suggested in Chapter 2, provides something of a model for the writing workshops of the New Literacy. In this century, Hannah Arendt (1959) sets the distinction between *live work* and *dead labor,* between work that is satisfying in its accomplishment, and a labor that is seeks only completion. But note that the meaning of work in these formulations can still seem to be isolated in terms of individual dignity, even as the workshop is a highly sociable and cooperative setting. I have turned in this book to the metaphor of work for the classroom to draw attention to the social relations entailed for teacher and students, along with a sense of transforming resources (in the language) into goods for the consumption of others which forms a model for the New Literacy.[2]

But the New Literacy tendency to root meaning in the individual is only one problem that they have with this crucial concept. Another is the exclusivity of their claims to it. In building the case for Whole Language on meaning, Kenneth Goodman lambastes the decoding school for "uninteresting, non-meaningful, irrelevant lessons" which he sees as a direct result of their approach to literacy: "When schools break language into bits and pieces, sense becomes nonsense, and its always hard for kids to make sense out of nonsense" (1986a, pp. 8–9). However, to imagine that in a classroom the meaning of a text is a private affair between the reader and the author shortsighted and, shall we say, somewhat *self*-righteous. Not only does the decoding approach "teach" students to read with considerable regularity, but the lessons taught in the process, including those worksheets of broken-down language, are enriched by the institutional context. It begins with that immediate sense of accomplishment that a worksheet affords; the sticker and gold-star approach to literacy seems no deterrent to students' attitudes toward literacy as my research indicated in Chapter 5. But as well, we might recall from Chapter 3 how the phonics lesson exists within the realm of ceremony, as Madeleine Grumet evokes it in the sounding and sing-song chanting of rules echoes the sense that "touch and the voice are the sensual passages between parent and child": "speech sings the world, phonics provides a choral grasp of meaning that brings social and emotional resonance to the meaning of texts" (1988, pp. 141–42).

However, Grumet qualifies her support for this resonant moment of phonics; it is soon lost to workbooks and other silences. Yet this initial and communal pursuit of reading richly sounded out, if it does exist in the phonics classroom, is indeed the ritual unification, syllable by syllable, often without the meaning of the text getting in the way. Meaning lies in the shared act, which is a part of the page. In that silence which Grumet notes eventually overcomes this sounding out, there resides another form of meaning negotiated between student and classroom. Many students do learn that disembodied meaning is the very language of schooling and that not only is attending to such meaning the way to get ahead, it works in its own way to reduce the personal risk of not doing well. For language exercises, made up of questions one to ten, students rarely risk any show of commitment. This is a schooling that dares to leave the privacy of meaning aside, apart from perhaps passing judgement on the unfortunate language and attitude brought from home. As we saw with the Barnes and Barnes' (1984) research on personal writing in Chapter 6, to ask students to draw on the stories that lie within, is to ask for what does not seem as natural as is supposed. Many prefer to keep the substance of schooling apart from the meaningful in their lives—the education-as-small-change school of thought.

It is as if the New Literacy is attempting to dismantle the schooling that everyone has learned, and students are bound to remain suspicious about the motives. Is it a cheap trick to make school seem more sensitive? Is it worth this retooling for the new classroom? The advocates of the New Literacy have clearly succeeded in convincing many students that there is another way of doing classtime, and that there is a writing and reading with a meaning that runs beyond the end-of-class bell. But the New Literacy needs to also consider why some students and teachers will continue to resist this appeal to engagement; is there room for an open discussion of the limits on what the New Literacy offers these

students and teachers, in return for this opening up, this act of commitment to the project of writing and reading? This resistance to the New
Literacy, most often in its expressive guises, is one indication of the
need for a balance, as dialogue or dialectic, between personal meaning
and public display.

The individuality of meaning can be found running under a good deal
of New Literacy rhetoric. Less often is anything made of the social
construction of meaning. Berthoff and Britton are instructive exceptions
with ears for the two poles of personal and public meaning. The distinction receives particularly lucid treatment in the musings of Ann Berthoff
(1981). She has gone further than anyone in bringing a philosophical
perspective to composition with its roots beginning in the Romanticism
of Coleridge and the very individualism of imagination as the formative
power in the "infinite I AM." In that private act of making sense, the
mind acts independently and apart from the world with the mind like a
vacuum cleaner that picks up and balls together what it finds; so Berthoff
advises teachers, "Begin where they are as language animals with the
form-finding and form-creating powers of mind and language" (p. 9).
But at another point in *The Making of Meaning* (1981), under influence
of Freire and Vygotsky this time, Berthoff rejects the idea that we begin
with thoughts that we then communicate in language; she advances
instead a tenet from the social construction of meaning: "It is in dialogue
that meanings are created and discovered and shaped" (p. 111). The
New Literacy carries these two tendencies, between the individual and
the social group as the units of meaning.

James Britton has also swung away from this emphasis on the individual, as the unit of meaning to a more social conception of meaning,
but not without complications. In *Language and Learning* (1972), he
suggests that the child begins with a "language which embodies powers
of organization he cannot achieve in thought," until gradually the child's
mature "powers of organization in thought come to exceed his powers of
organization in speech" (1972, p. 205). As Britton lays it out, children's
thinking is initially led by the ways of language, until they eventually
overtake the intellectual resources of the language and think for themselves as it were. The problem with this later stage is that it suggests a
form of disembodied thought, a thought that takes no form, whether in
language, dance, or tricks on a bicycle. Britton is all too ready to separate
thought from language: "Thus we see language and thought as two
forms of behavior, powerfully interacting but distinct in origin and with
different forms of development" (1972, p. 206). The idea of thought as

an independent behavior removes it from the social sphere, from language or other shared forms of meaning.

Ludwig Wittgenstein, for one, has offered a few clever philosophical objections to this rift between thought and language, including the anecdote of a French politician who "once wrote that it was a peculiarity of the French language that in it words occur in the order in which one thinks them" (1953, p. 108e). He also points out how Augustine mistakenly viewed children learning to speak as if they might be strangers recently arrived from another country, that is, as if they already had a language in which they were thinking (1958, p. 16e). This is obviously not the case, Wittgenstein is stressing, for the child is born into a language, into a *form of life* which becomes a way of thinking through language, and which the child animates and works to different ends.[3]

This form of life in the language, I am suggesting, can be greatly enhanced through a project such as the New Literacy, especially as it realizes the determined sociability of meaning. It offers students both opportunity and motive to work the language, to participate in the cultural formation of meanings, new and old. It encourages students to work these cultural meanings actively with others in moving toward a greater articulation of the form of life. This is clearly a New Literacy pedagogy of reflection through language. My objection to Britton at this point is to this seeming isolation of thought from the influence of social discourse and making thought seem prior to language. This misrepresents the social nature of thought awash in the varied resources that a culture affords. Students can then realize and reflect on the nature of their participation in this social realm that pervades their thinking and the form-finding and form-creating powers of mind.[4]

Fortunately, Britton concludes *Language and Learning* by toppling the division between language and thought in his celebration of the child-artist who is able to think through the medium of expression: "an artist may find that he has articulated ideas he had not conceived before his work presented them to him" (1972, p. 219). You might recall from Chapter 2 how Peter Elbow (1972) was moved at about the same time as this to consider "writing without teachers" when he found students stymied by this thought-language two-step: first the student is to think out the ideas and then find the words that effectively convey this thought. The New Literacy, I am recommending, would rest easier and more securely on a foundation of language as a social enterprise to be worked relentlessly as a form of thinking in itself.

But before leaving Britton, I must point out how he misses another opportunity to realize the integrity of meaning within the social realm of discourse. In his description of the hierarchical relationships among words, he points out how we find it useful to speak of the cod falling within the fish family which forms part of the animal kingdom. This web of meanings governed by subordination and superordination is an integral part of learning any discipline, not just zoology. Yet in a way that Britton does not explore, it speaks rather eloquently to the manner in which the social organization of language structures the world of thought. It is assumed that these categorical distinctions reflect the ways of the natural world, as water might be said to read the landscape in finding its way down a valley. But the first point to raise is that through these distinctions, language overwhelms thinking and it does so under the influence of culture rather than nature. An immensely clever parody of our natural taxonomic logic is the often cited tale of a "certain Chinese encyclopedia" by the novelist Jorge Luis Borges which serves as the starting point of Michel Foucault's book, *The Order of Things:*

> The passage quotes a "certain Chinese encyclopedia" in which it is written that "animals are divided into: (a) belonging to the Emperor, (b) embalmed, (c) tame, (d) sucking pigs, (e) sirens, (f) fabulous, (g) stray dogs, (h) included in the present classification, (i) frenzied, (j) innumerable, (k) drawn with a fine camelhair brush, (l) *et cetera,* (m) having just broken the water pitcher, (n) that from a long way off look like flies."
> (cited by Foucault, 1970, p. vx)

Out of the charm of these defiant categories, Foucault explains how he began to realize how order is brought to mind by the language and its embodiment of culture. That Borges makes it a Chinese book points to the ethnocentrism of our own "natural" divisions of knowledge in the order of things. It brings into question the categories by which we live.

Britton's appreciation of dialogue as the site of meaning construction in language was to come, as it was for Bruner, from the work of Vygotsky. In *Language and Learning* (1972), he uses Vygotsky, as well as Bruner, to address the individual development of the child through language. In his later work, Britton arrives at the importance that Vygotsky places in the social underpinnings of meaning: "It is Vygotsky's view that human consciousness is achieved as the individual internalises the forms of shared social behavior: the nature of those communities in which the child spends his formative years must be absolutely crucial to his development and to the development of society" (Britton, 1985, p. 5). He concludes that "true community comes from communion" (p. 5) which is to have traveled some distance from a concentration on language and learning.

I might add that Vygotsky did acknowledge forms of "intelligent action" in infants which occurred prior to and independent of language, but as part of the child's intellectual development language became increasingly instrumental in thinking. This development began with the child's increasing participation in the social realm of language; the child then learns that not only is talking to others a creative and productive way of ordering the world but that talking to oneself is equally helpful in the same way: "The history of the process of *internalization of social speech* is also the history of the socialization of the children's practical intellect" (Vygotsky, 1978, p. 27, original emphasis). This practical intellect was also greatly enhanced by ending the child's isolation in working on problems; working with another for assistance and the chance to imitate actions was found to greatly boost the intellectual reach of the child (1962, pp. 103–5). He referred to this reach as the "zone of proximal development" which was to form a fundamental pedagogical principle for Vygotsky, with obvious connections to Bruner's shift and the efforts of the New Literacy to end the isolation of literacy tasks.

Vygotsky posited a fascinating reversal of both the Romantic sequence—as Rousseau imagined the individual corrupted by society—and the traditional classroom paradigm—as the child is to be alone in learning. He describes the ways in which meaning for the individual develops out of social experiences especially in language and is then internalized and made to seem private; this understanding of the world is extended by working with others. This flow of meaning and understanding from the public to the personal seems a relevant lesson for literacy in the classroom. In a sense we might say that the child is able to go it alone with the page because of this familiarity with, and ability to project, its social implications. One indication of the social influence on mental processes is found in the work of Vygotsky's student, A. R. Luria. Luria's investigations of Russian agricultural workers involved in the transition to "collectivized forms of labor and cultural revolution, showed that, as the basic forms of activity changed, as literacy is mastered, and a new stage of social and historical practice is reached, major shifts occur in human mental activity" (Luria, 1976, p. 161). However far the New Literacy classroom is from post-revolutionary

Russian steppes, it needs to be seen, I am emphasizing in this chapter, as a new stage of *social practice* in education.

Literary individualism

Another major obstacle the New Literacy faces in affecting a Bruner's shift is the special place awarded to literature in fostering literacy and the creation of meaning. Literature might well be thought of as a font for anointing our individuality; it evokes the most vivid and moving expressions of the unique place each of us occupies. Bruner, much to his credit as a cognitive psychologist, draws our attention to the narrative as an equally valid expression of knowing, equal to expository prose as a powerful mode of thought (1986, pp. 11–34). Yet he fails to take into account the special place that literature holds in the formation of the self. Literature can easily be seen as staunch holdout for the individual uniqueness of meaning. Yet in spite of a literary tradition that celebrates that individuality, the public formation of meaning is necessarily there at every turn in literature. Let me work from a few recent literary examples that ostensibly celebrate and inevitably undermine this quality of independence of meaning. Here is novelist Ursala Le Guin speaking of a writer's needs in an essay she has written to dispel "the books-or-babies myth" as a choice that women writers have too often had to confront:

> The one thing a writer has to have is a pencil and some paper.
> That's enough, so long as she knows that she and she alone is
> in charge of that pencil, and responsible, she and she alone, for
> what it writes on the paper. In other words, that she's free. Not
> wholly free. Never wholly free. Maybe very partially. Maybe
> only in this one act, this sitting for a snatched moment being a
> woman writing, fishing in the mind's lake. But in this,
> responsible; in this, autonomous; in this, free. (Le Guin, 1989,
> p. 37)

The illuminating irony in this piece is that as Le Guin argues for the free space that writing affords as a kind of private act, she rightly attacks those who wish to "push mothers back into 'private life,' a mythological space invented by the patriarchy," (p. 37). She sets writing up as itself a "private life," as a form of privacy and piracy against other demands, even as she speaks against having women pushed backed into a private life. The conflicting sense here is of literacy as a private act, when, in fact, it is that very public and political connection to the world that Le Guin will not have denied. Our literary tradition of authorship encourages this sense of the literary as a time of "she and she alone," although less often in that gender. In reading a book or in writing with pencil and paper, we are apart from the others around us. In what we select to read and the sense of experience that we have with the book also sets us apart, not just for that moment of reading but after we walk away from the text. In the writing, it seems that we grow autonomous, asserting of ourselves on the page. In this solitary literary act, we find ourselves on the page. So it is to be in the New Literacy classroom; but with Bruner's shift, I want to keep to the fore the initial sociability of experience, especially as language gives it meaning, which later permits this time alone, away, on the page.

To take another example, John Updike offers the ineffable moment of literary self-realization with delicacy and yet frankness in the concluding lines to his short story "Here I Am":

> In this low-ceilinged room the light is antique, preserved and
> brought from the Shillington house, my first tender, childish
> winters in it, with their evergreen secret of Christmas. The
> light holds my first inklings of celebration, of reindeer tracks
> on the roof, of an embowering wide world arranged for my
> mystification and entertainment. It has the eggshell tint, the
> chilly thrilling taste, of my self. (1989, p. 37)

This story in which he visits his mother on the farm near Shillington, Pennsylvania, is transparently autobiographical, and yet he seems to more clearly find himself in the fictional space of the page rather than the actual farm. This *shared* meaning of self, as writer and reader realize themselves in those fictional lines, is a lesson in literary understanding. From the first grade and first page for the student, the New Literacy is in a position to encourage a search for this "chilling, thrilling taste, of my self" and other inventive literary qualities that are realized in the sharing. "Lightness" is one such quality that Italo Calvino highly recommends as "everything can be transformed into something else, and knowledge of the world means dissolving the solidity of the world" or as it can be found in "the search for lightness as a reaction to the weight of living" (1988, pp. 9, 26). The sense of control over the medium and the mind ultimately makes this lightness of being more than bearable, and which might allow the student writer-reader to enter the embowering wide world arranged for our mystification and entertainment.

But to undermine this literary self-interest is not to deny Le Guin's point that the self may seem more wholly free, in a busy household, an old homestead, or a classroom, during this one act of literacy that has become the symbol of private reflection—fishing the mind's lake—in what is clearly a public forum. But writing might also be romanticized as a profound reaching out to imagined and real audiences, just as reading can be cast as a form of sublime connection with an author, a character, a period. This constant dialectic between the private and social in our conception of literary reading begins to find itself spoken by Fay Weldon in her *Letters to Alice:*

> Of course one dreads it: of course it is overwhelming: one both
> anticipates and fears the kind of swooning, almost erotic
> pleasure that a good passage in a good book gives; as
> something nameless *happens*. I don't know what it is that
> happens: is it the pleasure of mind meeting mind, untrammelled
> by flesh? (1984, p. 13, original emphasis)

This otherworldly eros is a pleasure of intimacy, of deep personal meaning that Weldon suggests can be found in the meeting of minds. She is, in this case, heavily recommending Jane Austen to her punk-rock niece Alice, in itself a search for meaning in connection. Weldon's literacy moves beyond the schooling of literature which can come between the reader and the text, between "mind meeting mind untrammelled by flesh." She offers that double ideal of both losing and finding yourself as the intimate moment of text. The New Literacy has within it this very suggestion of self-engagement in literacy that has students becoming something more, if nameless, in reading and writing. It proposes that we are what we read and write, and that we can become more by pursuing these acts of self-assertion. Students find their voice and define their knowing on the page; they bring themselves to the text integrating their own meaning and sense with the story or argument that they find there.

Yet this intimate casting of the reading act is still too narrowly conceived. Reading Jane Austen cannot be that simple. Beyond, or perhaps

as part of, that pleasure is the public construction of authority in literature. It begins with the additional fact that Austen only came up for
Alice, this radical niece with the green spiky hair, because of an English
literature course she is taking. Literature often has great trouble today
escaping the institutional cover story—"Well, I read it for a course
once." Weldon tries to free it by offering up this deeply personal praise
to the drunken pleasures that subvert the schooling of literature. But ask
a class of literature students how many times it happens in the run of an
English course? Such readers of Austen spend their energy on figuring
out the sense which they are to make of the novel for their class. The
New Literacy also tries to spare reading from this sense of constraint to
allow for forms of intimacy with the text through reader-response theory,
but it also needs to bring to mind the nature of response as a larger
social question of producing literature, as prize-winners, best-sellers,
suppressed-books, rediscovered-texts.

Literature first earned its place in the school curriculum as a form of
"moral technology," to use Terry Eagleton's phrase (1985/86). In 1880,
Matthew Arnold, in his guise as Her Majesty's Inspector of Schools,
successfully promoted poetry by promising that "Good poetry does
undoubtedly tend to form the soul and character; it tends to beget a love
of beauty and of truth in alliance together, it suggests however indirectly
noble principles of action" (1908, p. 142). The New Literacy has added
an additional moral dimension, which Arnold had only begun to consider, that of engagement in response—only connect. In encouraging
students to respond to the literary work by reaching within themselves,
the New Literacy deploys literature to form the soul in the form of a
self, just as it would provide the moment of its realization in the writerly
response to the text. That has been the literary project of literacy in our
culture, not just since the period of Romanticism, but certainly boosted
by its introverted absorption. Literary critic Raymond Williams describes
this Romantic legacy in which the individual is "abstracted and defined
as 'creative subjectivity,' the starting point of meaning" (1961, p. 31).
Peter Hohendahl takes literature's social role even further by identifying
the role which literature has played in the development of the middle
class: "Literature served the emancipation movement of the middle class
as an instrument to gain self-esteem and to articulate its human demands
against an absolutist state and a hierarchical society" (1982, p. 52). It
continues to play something of this liberating role, as we find self-esteem
and articulation in reading literature, and yet as Bill Green (1988) among
others have argued, it can serve in classrooms and examinations to

reinforce class distinctions by sorting students even as it defines the boundaries of the literary canon.

In introducing literature to students, teachers are bringing to the classroom a complex phenomenon in language, one that has about it a long history of subversive, emancipatory, and institutional elements. The formulations of Le Guin, Updike, and Weldon are a part of the literary heritage of the individual. This fishing of the mind's lake to which they draw attention can seem a pure act of creative subjectivity, both in writing out the self and in responding to it as we read others. I do not mean to walk away from, even if I thought that I could, the experience of this voice being mine and of being something that I fashion apart from myself, of being able to fashion an outspoken or very subtle self on the page; nor would I want to deny the strong and true experience of finding that startling connection in the work of another. There are many expressions of literature's vastness, but perhaps none more suggestive of its intellectual range and intrigue, between the true and the imaginary work of literature, than this singular sentence by the philosopher Maurice Merleau-Ponty:

> The paradox of the true and the imaginary, truer than true—of intentions and achievement, often unexpected and always *other*—of speech and silence, in which expression remains indirect—of the subjective and objective, in which the writer's deepest secret, still barely articulated inside him, surrenders itself in all clarity to a public which his work creates for itself, which he possesses most consciously remains by contrast a dead letter—finally, the paradox of the author and the man, where it is evident that it is the man's lived experience which provides the substance of his work and yet, in order *to become* true, needs an elaboration that is the very thing that cuts the writer off from the living community; in other words, all these surprises and traps force literature to see itself as a problem and drive the writer to ask "What is Literature?" thus raising questions not only about his practice but even more about his theory of language. (1963, p. 81)

The starting point for understanding what can be fairly asked of literacy begins with these questions of the barely articulated, the need for elaboration, the meaning that falls between a theory of language and that practice known as literature. To ask that the social formation of this literary sensibility be kept present in these educational programs means also thinking about and introducing into the literature lesson the constructed, negotiated, and shared aspects of self-expression.

The self in literacy

The realization and connection of self through literacy forms a theme that runs deeply through the work of Britton, Smith, Goodman, Meek, and other advocates of the New Literacy. To have it stated clearly, Robert Probst's *Response and Analysis* (1988) presents an excellent example of a program that is conceived in terms of the self; students' responses to literature become, in part, a process of "self-definition":

> Thus, exchange with the text can become for the reader a process of self-creation. The entire process—responding, correcting errors, searching for the sources of the response, speculating about the author's intent, and weighing the author's values and ideas against one's own—culminates in a sharpened, heightened sense of self. . . . [The student] needs the opportunity to see, judge, and reshape those responses, consulting his own heart and mind as he does so, since he is the one ultimately responsible for what he becomes. (1988, pp. 21–22)

While Probst makes each student ultimately responsible for this self, we have to face the fact that the self, as that pure and singular essence of our being, is no longer a reliable figure in the psychological or literary landscape. Under current scrutiny, the *self* has begun to shimmer like a figure in the distance, seeming more like a mirage the harder we try to reach it or even keep it in focus. The conception of the self in question here is the product of a humanism that developed during the Enlightenment: the human subject is the source of meaning, knowledge, and action; it exists as an autonomous subjectivity, an ahistorical universal and rational soul, which forms the foundation of society and the basis of human rights and emancipation. Foucault (1970) and other poststructuralists have examined how this humanism brought about a shift to a bureaucratic/medical model for normalizing discipline and power, rather than the promised emancipation of reason and light. In a much more modest tone, I am proposing that this Cartesian experience of self—I think (therefore) I am—needs to be tempered by Bruner's shift as the self, too, is learned in "a communal activity, a sharing of culture" which deeply implicates the role of language in our seemingly individual makeup. The self takes its meaning from what is said about it; we constitute ourselves out of what we overhear in the language and imagery of our culture, as our identity is wrested from the symbolic value of such elements as gender, color, ethnicity, vocation, and the words that have become common to this symbolization.[5]

I raise the specter of a less-than-certain self exposed by a fascinating array of poststructuralist fashions, direct from Paris for the most part, because the New Literacy rest on this second pillar to meaning—a developed and realized self achieved through language and literacy. Current work on the "theory of the subject" has a good deal to do with the nature of language and literacy. In a sense, the New Literacy has taken as its unacknowledged project the literary enhancement of the subject. I only ask that this project not naively rush into a celebration of self-expression, while nearby some of the most exciting intellectual work of our times struggles with the theoretical underpinnings of self and representation. To find ourselves in this manner, I take "the process of self-creation," as Probst casts it, through two related analyses: the first is with the presence of voice and self on the page, and the second moves into literature and the self-in-process.[6]

This rethinking of the self might well begin with the student's *voice* which the New Literacy is quick to prize. What becomes valued in the program and the student is this realization of one's self in speech and writing, whether in response to someone else's work or in telling one's own story. As it turns out, this idea is in good company. This elevation of voice in writing is nothing less than the grand project of Western literacy, at least according to French philosopher Jacques Derrida (1976) who has constructed his science of writing, "grammatology," around the question. He speaks of a *logocentrism* in philosophy by which the word is privileged as a means to the truth, as able to reflect our essence; writing, in this way, aspires to that authentic self-presence found in speech. This is the very faith in language that deeply motivates the New Literacy's search for the child's voice in writing. In his famous excoriating fashion, Derrida "deconstructs" this writerly desire for presence in the text as it aspires to convey the core of our essence and being. As we saw with Wittgenstein, there is reason to doubt our access to the thinking behind language, and in this case, Derrida cast doubts on the "being" that lies behind language. Could our work in language be simply creating a self as an artifact of writing, an artifact that through the use of special effects can seem to have been brought from the murky depths into the eggshell tint of light, as per Updike?

Derrida is interested in understanding the ways in which writing can project a true and certain essence. It might well seem that as we read we look through the surface tension and social formation of the writing as if to peer into the very soul of the writer or perhaps our own. Yet Derrida's point is that we cannot trust the very surface of the page to reveal what lies beneath for it shimmers as part of a meaning system that is fabricated in the most shaky manner out of a thousand texts and voices. Derrida succeeds in deconstructing this once-privileged haven for the voice and presence of self by pointing out the ways in which meaning is always open to variations in interpretation and internal contradictions in its own project. The text is taken over by the worldliness of language and meaning, by the ways in which language is more than *I* can control in its reach into the world of writing. This may seem needlessly destructive, but after taking down the singular presence of the self, there is room to build on the multifarious meanings from within the discourse of texts. In the work of this philosopher and the critics that follow in this chapter lies an expanded project for meaning, literature, and self. The world is far more textual, always ready to be rewritten, always bearing traces of the already-written; meanings are far more open to writers and readers. This reconsideration of reading and writing is at the forefront of knowing the structure of our subject area, to recall Bruner's point on forming a basis for curriculum.

Among those exploring theories of subjectivity, Julia Kristeva has had an important role in connecting the self in language and literature. If she unsettles our notion of the self, it is not to demean it to the status of a psychological convenience that grows habitual with time, like acting the same role in a play over the course of a three-month run. The self is at once more dynamic, more given to flux, as we carry on in language, signifying or enunciating ourselves. Kristeva is given to speak of "the questionable *subject-in-process*" which is worked upon by the unconscious through language (1980, p. 135, original emphasis). This thinking is not as removed from the progressive educational scene as it might first seem. The French avant garde meets the American pragmatist John Dewey on just such points. After all, Dewey said as much in his work on ethics in the 1930s: "Our personal identity is found in the thread of continuous development which binds together these changes. In the strictest sense, it is impossible for the self to stand still; it is becoming, and becoming for the better or the worse" (1932, p. 340). Subjectivity, in this Franco-American sense, can be thought of running through its own process of prewriting, revision, and publication as we work on our stories and find them well received or sent back for further editing. We all have days and encounters that are like that.

There is also a greater lesson about the function of literacy in this than the analogy between processes. Against the indeterminacy of self, Kristeva places the integrating forces of literature. The literary work continues to offer a form of assuredness to buffer the uncertainty of self. She speaks of literature in pursuit of "an effect of *singular truth* . . . against the ascendence of theoretical reason" (1980, pp. 146–7). This is literature's claim on language and meaning. With the form of literacy under discussion in this book, students are encouraged to turn in on themselves in search of that singular truth, that unitary self, which is taken as the true expression of themselves. But their resistance to this expression in their own writing and its elusiveness when they are reading the works of others suggests that they are ready for the idea that this authentic moment of expression is an *effect* rather than an actuality. There seems little need to mistake the fiction of literature—"an effect of singular truth"—for what is more accurately seen as a process of signifying on the part of students, of finding the signs of themselves-in-process on the page. The unity of self in the text is a piece of work, labored at in its coherence. It may be worth recalling that in *Hamlet,* with its subject of a wavering self, Shakespeare gives the line, "to thine own self be true," to a foolish, platitudinous Polonius, destined to meet his fate while eavesdropping on behalf of the king. And yet by virtue of this "play," we are afforded, even in its indeterminacy, the in-process nature of this presence known as Hamlet.[7] Literature, as it declares itself made-up, takes on a renewed realism and persuasiveness as Kristeva, Derrida, and company undermine the claims of nonfiction to represent the truth of the world.

The crucial threads in this tangled web fall between self and language for the New Literacy. Language is not to be celebrated for transparently reflecting students' thinking, their different states of mind, or their best selves. Literacy is not simply polishing the mirror of language; its power is far more generative. And that power, as Kristeva describes it, arises out of the play of significance: "What we call *significance,* then, is precisely the unlimited and unbounded generating process, this unceasing operation of the drives toward, in, and through language; toward, in, and through the exchange system and its protagonists—the subject and his institutions (1984, p. 17, original emphasis). She identifies "drives" rather than "thoughts" as the impetus behind the language and between "the subject and his institutions" (and it is worth adding that these "institutions" are very often *his*). Gender, for example, is a question of identity generated toward, in, and through language. The girl is signified and finds herself and her significance in a language that speaks of her differently that it does of boys. To work, as teachers must, with not only language and literacy, but the generating processes of these young subjects-in-process is very close to the heart of Kristeva's "unceasing operation" of signification.

But surely to make this process of signification in gender, to explore how we are formed in the language, will bring the walls of the school tumbling down. If we were to form it into a topic, type it up as an assignment due Monday, then what next? It's a question that Luce Irigaray, yet another Parisan, elaborates in all of its ramifications as this society rests on a gendered system of speaking subjects:

> For, without the exploitation of the body-matter of women, what would become of the symbolic process that governs society? What modification would this process, this society, undergo, if women, who have been only objects of consumption or exchange, necessarily aphasic, were to become "speaking subjects" as well? Not, of course, in compliance with the masculine, or more precisely the phallocentric, "model."
>
> That would not fail to challenge the discourse that lays down the law today, that legislates on everything, including sexual difference, to such an extent that the existence of another sex, of an other, that would be woman, still seems, in its terms, unimaginable. (1985, p. 85)[8]

For the New Literacy, the symbolic processes that govern the classroom, as a society are rewritten and a new legislative regime instituted based on speaking subjects. And if another sort of student is still somewhat unimaginable in this case, too, at least the possibilities are there to be worked through in language and literacy. The New Literacy could easily take on this responsibility in its formative project of examining the ways in which language sustains and transcends differences; recall the responses to literature informed by questions of gender introduced in Chapter 4. Literature comes into it, for Kristeva, in articulating "the outer *boundaries* of the subject and society" (1984, p. 17). The New Literacy, in its own way, has taken on the boundary question between the subject and her institutions in renegotiating the nature of learning and literacy. This book asks that advocates of this educational program look to the limitations in their conceptions of language and self. As they refit the classroom, they could also confront "the exchange system" that forms the students within the significance of gender, race and class; these would be the lessons in literacy that travel beyond moments of self-realization to the larger fabric of subjectivity afforded by language and literature; such is the material out of which we fashion ourselves.

In considering how it is that we put ourselves together, Foucault might complete our Parisian quartet with his historical research on the construction of the self. He has examined the various apparatuses or practices that can be thought to form or reform the self, such as prisons, insane asylums, and clinics, but of particular interest here is his work on writing as a "technology of the self" (1988). He has found that at least since the Hellenistic Age, writing has facilitated a cultivation of the self as the writer attends to the details of life in letters and journals (1988, pp. 27–28). In a similar spirit, Teresa de Lauretis (1987) has described film and fiction as technologies of gender. We employ these technologies of identity to make something of ourselves; they are only able to "victimize" us out of our desire to trade in meanings.[9] Movies do not, in de Lauretis's view, simply teach the viewer the nature of sexual difference, the difference between what is masculine and feminine; they become the substance, the cultural manifestation of that difference which "ends up being in the last instance a difference (of woman) from man" (1987, p. 1). She holds that *gender is a representation,* and we make ourselves out of such acts of re-presentation. Students, too, as they write are re-presenting gender and contributing to its construction in themselves and their readers. Again, this perspective both challenges the unassuming naturalness of the New Literacy project in its naive pursuit of an authentic voice and setting for learning and working, and brings into view overlooked powers in the work of literacy and literature. Literature and film, advertising and music videos, are the machinery of imagery in our day; they generate the meaning of gender and other systems of difference out of which selves are made.

One consequence of this theory of the subject is to undermine the privilege of the personal in literacy and language and shift our attention to their public aspects. I spoke freely in the first chapter of my own

225

personal moments with books and public times with literacy, the distinction is so rooted in my experience that I cannot speak of undoing it or of theorizing my way completely out it. Yet I can recognize that, although we are tempted to think so because of this cultural tradition, no aspect of language or literacy is completely removed from the public realm; no aspect is the sole privilege of a private experience. One strength of the New Literacy in what I find to be its best practices is its repeated reinforcement of the social enterprise of literacy. Its thinking about literacy has not kept up. This theory of the subject, as something constituted in language, should make New Literacy advocates wary of leaning too heavily on the personal nature of literacy and the individual as the unit of meaning. It can lead to educators defending the privacy and privilege of students reading and writing as sacrosanct, rather than understanding its growth out of a public sphere of available and contested meanings, from young adult romances to Jane Austen. It is not enough to have the students find and express themselves, to elaborate their responses. For they are being articulated in the process, and that question of what they might become needs to be opened and wondered at as part of the response and the writing, just as the school's changing role in this formation needs to be examined as a restructuring of literacy. The *self* is tenuously formed, multiple and in-process, around both experience and reflection, and that process may be affected, to a degree not yet appreciated, by the new forms of work in language and literacy offered by the New Literacy classroom.

Notes

1. The direct expression of this moral sense in the New Literacy is found in Britton's use of the theologian Martin Buber to describe the way a teacher serves a student as a buffer against the chaotic absence of meaning: "Because this human being exists, meaninglessness, however hard pressed you are by it, cannot be the real truth" (cited by Britton, 1972, p. 185).
2. Ferruccio Rossi-Landi (1983) has fully developed a model for this line of thinking in his *Language as Work and Trade: A Semiotic Homology for Linguistics and Economics*.
3. "So you are saying that human agreement decided what is true and false? It is what human beings *say* that is true and false; and they agree in the language they use. That is not agreement in opinion but in form of life" (Wittgenstein, 1953, p. 241, original emphasis).
4. Frank Smith also takes the separation of language and thought as the starting point for rethinking literacy: "Our language is generated by our thought, but is itself not thought, of which it is arbitrarily and conventionally related"

(1982, p. 65). Those two elements once more set apart, Smith adds an interaction between them which allows for language to create and reflect upon thought. He would encourage teachers to engineer a thoughtful writing process in which the students "generate" language out of thought only to "reflect" on that thought once it is articulated before generating "more language" (p. 66).

5. For a critique of Foucault's attack on humanism as so total that it negates modern society and thus, in a sense, his own attack as a product of it, see Pader (1987). Pader argues for Habermas's (1983) position in which humanism's ideal of emancipation can still be achieved through improvement and correction in the social sciences analysis of the obscured forms of power. George Herbert Mead (1935) remains the standard work on how the self-concept is formed out of the voices of significant others, a theory which finds its fullest linguistic expression in Emile Benveniste's (1971) treatment of the use of personal pronouns as "I" declare myself in language by saying in effect that's "me."

6. For a more extensive introduction to the theory of the subject see Coward and Ellis (1977) and Belsey (1982).

7. The topic of subjectivity and self in *Hamlet,* that cornerstone of cultural literacy, is explored most sensitively by Francis Barker: "Pre-bourgeois subjection does not properly involve subjectivity at all, but a condition of dependent membership in which place and articulation are not defined at all, but a condition of dependent membership in which place and articulation are not defined by an interiorized self-recognition—complete or partial, percipient or unknowing, efficient or rebellious—(of none the less socially constituted subject positions), but by incorporation in the body politic which is the king's body in its social form" (1984, p. 31). The New Literacy works in earnest with "interiorized self-recognition," although it may still represent incorporation in the body politic in its social form.

8. Irigaray is building on the work of psychoanalyst Jacques Lacan (1968; 1977) who holds that the child finds a center of subjectivity and self through language. It is in Lacan's phrase, a *parle-être* and this being-in-speech introduces the child into the order of symbolic relations such as those at the root of gender as a division of the subject into masculine or feminine. Lacan ascribes this urge to meaning in language as a literal attempt to speak against the experience of loss the infant suffers in being separated from the mother as a source of satisfaction. Language, in turn, offers the child a form of control over objects; it can seem to bring the mother near again. Yet language also affirms the distance, or sense of alienation, between child and object. Language carries an implicit expression of desire that is never fully articulated which is often echoed in conversations between child and parent, and is perhaps never quite outgrown (Henriques et al., 1984). Language allows us to recognize the otherness of another which it seeks to overcome. This profound urge to expression becomes the unarticulated reason for building an educational program of connection and response around its realization.

9. I am thinking here of Althusser's theory of the subject "interpellated" by ideology as if living in a sea of understanding that is transparent to us even

as it makes us fish: "*all ideology has the function (which defines it) of 'constituting' concrete individuals as subjects*" (1971, p. 171, original emphasis). The New Literacy, I have been suggesting challenges his notion that schools are simply part of the state ideological apparatus as well as this concept of being constituted rather than actively participating in the making and seeking of meaning.

9
Critical Futures

It should be our delight to watch this turmoil, do battle with
the ideas and visions of our own time, to seize what we can
use, to kill what we consider worthless, and above all to be
generous to the people that are giving shape as best they can to
the ideas within them.
Virginia Woolf, *"Hours in a Library" ([1916] 1987, p. 59).*

After venturing into anthropology, history, literature, psychology,
and poststructuralism, it seems only fair to return to the front lines with
scenes from two classrooms "generous to the people that are giving
shape as best they can to the ideas within them." Neither of these
classrooms is typical New Literacy. These two idiosyncratic programs
contain elements that have been under-represented up to this point; they
are weighted toward *product* as the guiding light of the literacy process,
to reaching *out* rather than simply *within*. They are both rich in forms
of cultural participation and history, as if to meet in closing both the old
charges of anti-intellectualism inveighed against progressive education
and the more recent ones leveled by E. D. Hirsch (1987). These two
instances also serve to reiterate the promise and reveal the road still to
be shored up in places. The first example offers the missing scene of
success from the heart of the inner-city at the hands of a conceptual
artist/teacher, Tim Rollins, and the second from the small town in which
I finally offer an instance of my own practices with these programs.

Tim Rollins runs the Art and Knowledge Workshop in the South Bronx
of New York City (Glueck, 1988). His intermediate school students have
been engaging in a highly creative form of reader-response with such
works as Hawthorne's *The Scarlet Letter,* Defoe's *Journal of the Plague*

229

Year, Melville's *Moby Dick, The Autobiography of Malcolm X,* and Kafka's *Amerika.* The students' response to these books begins with a good deal of preliminary work with visual interpretations that capture the common ground between the book and the students' experience; this work is brought together by students and teacher in a single, collective mural that blends painting and collage. While Rollins's interdisciplinary method hardly exhausts the creative possibilities for reading literature with intermediate school students, he has been able to galvanize a literate and creative engagement from groups of students that have not otherwise been reached by the New Literacy.

To give an example of their work, the students' response to Daniel Defoe's description of the devastating black plague which swept through Europe three centuries ago, was to consider how AIDS had affected life in the South Bronx and beyond. Under Rollins's direction, they literally turned the pages of Defoe's *Journal* into a large canvas. They decided to work with the magical spell "ABRACADABRA" that was thought to ward off the plague in Defoe's day. They printed the spell over and over from top to bottom in the form of an inverted pyramid, decreasing the number of letters one row at a time as they moved down the canvas, to suggest the trailing off of the spell as the book progresses and the journal records the devastation and machinations of the plague. "Today's equivalent of such foolishness," Rollins explained to a *New York Times* reporter, "is the pretense that AIDS is not happening" (Glueck, 1988, p. 20Y).

The success of "Tim Rollins + K.O.S.," as this group is known in the art world, can be measured in the critical and financial recognition it has received from major galleries which has afforded the students visits to European museums. But the success is also found in the individual stories of the "survival" students. If some of these students still have trouble with reading, as Rollins admits, they have begun to see the literate enterprise from a new perspective and one in which they have a creative stake. Rollins describes his way of working with the students as going beyond the production of art: "My job is to promote structure and discipline in the kids' lives and give them the training to use their talents toward something positive and socially responsible."[1] In his own idiosyncratic way, Rollins is providing a responsible vehicle for a small number of students; the students' painting over the pages of literature can be read as New Literacy graffiti which began with Rollins's own initiative at Intermediate School 52 in the Bronx and now takes place in the nonprofit Art and Knowledge Workshop. What is also important to

Rollins, as well as to my case for the New Literacy, is how this work, this organization of the collaborative classroom in the inner city, forms a vehicle for the teacher's vision as well as for the student's, a fact that Rollins is more than a little candid about: " 'I couldn't do what I do without the kids; they couldn't do without me. It's kind of like a baseball team.' He smiles. 'Without this, I'd be another boring Conceptual artist' " (Glueck, 1988, p. 20Y).

The second scene of New Literacy rites takes place a long way from New York. It arises from my experiments with these programs while I was teaching in northern Ontario. I immodestly include it, not only to demonstrate the manner in which I have practiced what I preach, but to bring in a variation that focuses on the humanities in taking up an historical approach to expression. In a year like no other in my career, I traveled from school to school, taking over classes, from grades 4 to 8, for nine days at a time while the teacher enroled in a professional development program conducted by the school district.[2] Over the course of those nine days, I staunchly directed the students through 3,000 years of publishing; that is, they "published" their poetry in a half-dozen historical and contemporary techniques which writers have employed in their efforts to bring their words home to their readers. The program drew them into the historical culture of literacy, albeit from a Eurocentric viewpoint, even as it asked them to reach within to give their publications substance. It began with Homer and the oral tradition of publication; the students learned that the simple act of reciting a work is an important and sometimes lasting step in reaching others with a composition that is both fresh and familiar. Staying with the Greeks, we moved through the early days of drama when prop and action were subsumed to the word that told the story, and the classroom became their amphitheater. Within a few days we had entered the scriptorium of the medieval monk and nun, and the students created beautifully illuminated manuscripts with intricate borders framing the students' poetry. Their writing also drew on historical models as the program employed Kenneth Koch's method of "teaching great poetry to children" (1973).

We soon plunged into the Gutenberg galaxy of movable type and printing presses; students carved out their own printer's marks to designate their publications and produced poster-size broadsides, flooding the school with their poetry in imitation of this early public broadcasting system that first stirred and entertained Reformation Europe. Each day began with the short, illustrated history lesson in the ways of publishing which were very much entwined with the events of the day, from the monastic preservation of classical civilization to the broadsided proclamations of the Riel Rebellion in western Canada. Finally, after a visit to a local printing shop to see the state of current technology, we leaped ahead to desk-top publishing of our own "small magazine" modeled on such intrepid sources of literary innovation as the *Dial* and *Paris Review*. It was a harried program with every day given to another historical set of publishing practices, writing new works, and preparing them for publication and delivery to school and community. Writing, as a form of public expression, was seen as a production process that was not fully realized until the work was shared.

One strong and certain thread between Rollins's program and mine is the intended shift in the meaning of literacy and schooling for these students. Literacy offered a forum for students to explore their reach and engagement in a cultural enterprise; the classroom became more of a space for them to make their mark and less of an institution given to marking them, although there are still plenty of opportunities for evaluating the students' work and contribution.[3] Rollins's program has blurred the boundaries between school and art in its reach into the art world, following the New Literacy emulation of real-world practices. My work retained more of the trappings of a school project with a decided twist in the function of literacy for these students. The New Literacy program stands in marked contrast to the students' work with literacy in other classes and grades, a fact which is not lost on them. It operates, in effect, as a critique of literacy in schools. In fact, this critique strikes me as part of the untapped educational force in the New Literacy. It begins with the basic notion that there is no given form to literacy, to optimum manner of reading and writing. The way we work with literacy represents a decision about ourselves and about the lives of others in the classroom.

It would be an err to imply, as I may have at times, that the New Literacy is a *true* literacy compared to the artifice of the skills and drills approach promoted by other programs. The lesson throughout this book has been that literacy takes on the contours of its context. We are choosing *forms* of literacy which will teach students about the nature and purpose of reading and writing. This classroom work with literacy has the power alone to demonstrate the breadth of possibilities for this activity, from lyric poem to letter of complaint, and the depth of engagement it can elicit, from responding to a devastating health crisis to exploring the forms of pleasure which young adult romance novels elicit.

The urgency in this choice about the form of literacy lies in the

232

silencing that students experience in schools. In her sensitive work on this question, Michele Fine (1987) has uncovered the "terror of words, a fear of talk" which students acquire in their classes, along with the injustice that accrues from this state of quietude. Fine implicates the school in "what doesn't get talked about," as a "fear of naming" over such issues as quitting school; but she also finds silence imposed in classrooms, staff rooms and student councils, as the means of efficient management (pp. 159–70). Yet the most poignant statement of this silence is found in Fine's field notes on the frustrations of a student and a researcher:

> Patrice is a young black female, in eleventh grade. She says nothing all day in school. She sits perfectly mute. No need to coerce her into silence. She often wears her coat in class. Sometimes she lays her head on her desk. She never disrupts. Never disobeys. Never speaks. And is never identified as a problem. . . . Is she so filled with anger, she fears to speak? Or so filled with depression she knows not what to say? (1987, p. 172)

Patrice's silence is, in one sense, the simple target of the New Literacy. Not that she should be compelled to speak or write, but that she should find the classroom a safe enough place to take off her jacket, share a little conversation with her peers in the process of learning, and explore forms of expression, including the meaning of the different sorts of silence which Michele Fine found in the school. It can happen around a cultural theme, as with Rollins's or my work, or it can take on a more political orientation as it has at Hackney Downs School in London where John Hardcastle has found that his New Literacy approach lead to enormous amounts of literate interest and strength among the students over issues of race, class, and school. One student summed up the program rather directly in terms of empowerment: "If the type of English work which we have been discussing continues, then the possibility of taking control of our own lives, our own education, and becoming our own experts, is extremely exciting" (McLeod, 1986, p. 49).

This type of English work will continue and continue to develop, I believe, if New Literacy programs look for greater integration within reading, writing, and literature programs, and if they seek to expand their interests in literacy as a cultural, historical, political and economical phenomenon. The integration means a greater realization of the integrity of literacy activities. The reading is inspired by, and in turn inspires the writing, the speaking, the listening. Promising work in connecting reading and writing now points the way to that greater integration of literacy pleasures and activities (Mason, 1989; Noyce & Christie, 1989; Petersen, 1986). To site but one example from the research, Guy Pinnell (1989) reports on a successful program with "at-risk" children that demonstrates the ways in which children in Reading Recovery programs can be encouraged to make the connections between their reading and writing as a means of boosting their academic standing. The task is not simply a matter of rub-off or transfer between the two literacy activities, but immersion in the textual community of discourse, that is, to write with an eye on what you have read, speaking to it, in admiration of it, or simply in response to having read, and to read with an eye to how you have written and may learn to write better.

The second path ahead for the New Literacy is to elaborate its research program, specifically to provide greater support for teachers drawn to its work, to recall the argument of Chapter 6. The New Literacy can only do so by taking close stock of the current political climate for education. Pinnell's work (1989), for example, serves as a model in combining quantitative and qualitative methods that speaks to a large audience. In each case, the investigator needs to assess the current state of the field to determine what factors in literacy might most helpfully be examined, what populations need to be involved, what measures will be heard, what innovations can be advanced in both teaching and research methods.[4] The third and related future may seem, perhaps, unduly removed from the direct concerns of the classroom. Still, I feel the New Literacy needs to stay abreast of inquiries into the relationship between literacy and subjectivity—in the writing out of oneself—which post-structuralists in feminist, continental, and literary theory are conducting. The practical implications of this work for such topics as autobiography have been mentioned in Chapter 8, but I also recommend attending to and participating in this complex area of investigation for the larger questions it raises, the edge it brings us to, in understanding the subject we are teaching, the subject in that double sense, student and literacy.

Yet the primary classroom focus here and ahead remains the nature of literacy and the different manners in which language operates to define ourselves and the situation of schooling, family, friendship, and other invaluable institutions. The lessons we would teach about literacy, and here is where the critique must be made explicit, can also be drawn from those approaches to the subject we are attempting to avoid. This is to inquire after how literacy operates in different settings, from filling out late slips at the school office to completing standardized tests. But with this extra step, the New Literacy is obviously wading into the radical waters of educational critique. Yet the New Literacy treatment of students as meaning-makers distinguishes it programs from other radical postures in the very manner that Henry Giroux has been calling for: "Radical educators have failed to develop a language that engages schools as sites of possibility, that is, as places where students can be educated to take their places in society from a position of empowerment rather than from a position of ideological and economic subordination" (1986, p. 49). The New Literacy is above all a form of rhetoric about literacy "that engages schools as sites of possibility"; but one of its persistent and major weaknesses is its failure to bring explicitly into its new curriculum this inherent critique.

In a rare case of radical critic meeting liberal practitioner, Giroux has had occasion to address the work of Donald Graves. While Giroux speaks of Graves's program as a "critical literacy," his comments carry a veiled criticism: "I believe that Professor Graves' approach to literacy gains an important theoretical dimension when it incorporates a more critical understanding of how experience is named, produced, sustained, and rewarded in the schools" (1987, p. 177). The key clause is "*when* it incorporates a more critical understanding"; when indeed, we might ask. It is rarely a topic on the classroom agenda of the writing process movement. What Graves has actually introduced is acknowledged in Giroux's conclusion that these programs provide opportunities for "students to share their experiences, work in social relations that emphasize care and concern for others, and be introduced to forms of knowledge that provide them with the opportunity to take risks and fight for the quality of life by which all human beings benefit" (p. 181).

However, the critical understanding of meaning which Giroux refers forms at this point only a latent lesson in the New Literacy. Consider, for example, the ideology of subjectivity that infuses literature—to write is to be alone or from Sir Philip Sidney's sonnet sequence, *Aristophel and Stella* (1591): " 'Fool,' said my muse to me, 'Look in thy heart and write.' " New Literacy programs have the topic in hand by exploring the private and public aspects of writing and reading, and by experimenting with different forms of collaboration and shared meaning. These programs need only to raise these popular conceptions of writing as a question worth considering to add the critical element to the process. To pursue a range of topics, from autobiography to school policy, as discourse forms which constitute their subjects, whether self or school is to know this power of naming, producing, sustaining, rewarding. The New Literacy cannot shy away from questions that seem dangerously close to the discrete discourse of power, for there comfortably rests the ways in which literacy operates with great effectiveness.

In pursuing the ways in which literacy constitutes its subject, I am playing into the scholastic end of this critique, as if all that was at stake is a better understanding of literacy *in situ*. For Giroux, there is a good deal more; the question with which he would interrupt Donald Graves and his students busily engaged in the writing process is an emphatic, *"What is it this society has made of me that I no longer want to be?"* (1987, p. 178, original emphasis). This is the crucial query of critical pedagogy. It may well stop the class cold. But the question is too big to give the class more than a momentary pause. It calls for lessons in the possibilities of *being* and the powers of society, lessons which I am suggesting need a medium, a vehicle, such as the subject of literacy that examines its own processes in constituting meaning. The ultimate reflectiveness of a curriculum about curriculum, a literacy about literacy, is an ingredient of *empowerment* which the New Literacy could profit by adding to its repertoire. Roger Simon (1987) has been especially effective in making the empowerment of reflexivity the educational agenda of critical pedagogy: "Teaching and learning must be linked to the goal of educating students to take risks, to struggle with ongoing relations of power, to critically appropriate forms of knowledge that exist outside of their immediate experience, and to envisage versions of a world which is not 'not yet'—in order to be able to alter the grounds upon which life is lived" (p. 375). The key "form of knowledge" that is "critically appropriate" for the New Literacy is, in fact, a knowledge of process, of how ideas are worked into a polished piece that will reach and persuade, or a response to a text can form the basis of its undoing or celebration.

But equally so, New Literacy projects, such as Rollins's K.O.S. and my publishing project, need to find ways of dealing openly with the "ongoing relations of power" which are also part of the literacy process. These two programs bring students into the actual processes of production, in art and publishing, but they can do so less naively by turning the political economy of the process into an object lesson on the situation of language. This is to return to a theme that no one has presented more forcefully than Foucault. In this excerpt from the opening to his "Discourse on Language," he presses the mix of subjectivity and institution that arises within literacy, dramatizing the hidden voices of desire and reluctance in each of us, but also in a way that should recall Patrice's silence cited above:

> Inclination speaks out: "I don't want to have to enter this risky world of discourse; I want nothing to do with it insofar as it is decisive and final; I would like to feel it all around me, calm and transparent, profound, infinitely open, with others responding to my expectations, and truth emerging, one by one. All I want is to allow myself to be borne along within it, and by it, a happy wreck." Institutions reply: "But you have nothing to fear from launching out; we're here to show you discourse is within the established order of things, that we've waited a long time for its arrival, that a place has been set aside for it—a place which both honors and disarms it; and if it should happen to have great power, then it is we, and we alone, who give it that power." (1972, pp. 215–16)

The inclination to expression, against a resistance to discourse, is very much the call of the student, a happy wreck; the educational imperative of the New Literacy is to plunge into this honoring and disarming, this bequeathal of power in language as a topic of interest and an institutional bounty to be grasped by these young writers. Foucault brings to our attention the organizing principles of discourse which becomes the very lesson that New Literacy advocates often seem intent on escaping. The ways in which literacy is controlled and contested within the established order of things should not be eschewed as a topic for a program concerned with students learning the ways of language and literacy. Producing creative works for public distribution is learning how the market operates and regulates, how the production of discourse and silence is managed with great dexterity.

To return to my program where I was introducing to my students the history of publishing as an urge to expression, I had to let them see that it is as often met with suppression and insurrection in the struggle to regulate discourse. The power of writing is often taught to students as solely a literary artifact, one they must come to appreciate, if not actually feel or see felt by others. How easy it is to find instances of another vibrant, irrepressible literacy, as, for example, Robert Darnton has rendered it on the two-hundredth anniversary of the storming of the Bastille: "When the revolutionaries grasped the bar of the press and forced the platen down on type locked in its forms, they sent a new energy streaming through the body politic. France came to life again and humanity was amazed" (1989, p. xiv). Along with their struggle for literary meaning on the page, I had to begin to let students see such contested sites for literacy and language as the broadsides of time past and the billboard and subway cars of today where spray paint tackles commercial lithography in gaining the right to representation (Posner, 1982; Castleman, 1982). If this seems to unduly romanticize these uncivil writers and outlaw artists, and that is clearly a danger, their work still presents an easily grasped instance of this symbolic struggle for representation and meaning that is also part of the functioning of literacy in this society. What is at stake in representation is made readily apparent to students, for example, by Jill Posner's photograph of a London billboard advertisement for a Fiat car. The ad offers the caption, "If it were a lady, it would get its bottom pinched," to which was appended with a spray bomb, "If this lady was a car she'd run you down" (1982, p. 12).[5]

Perhaps a more legitimate unsettling of public expression is found in the conceptual art of Jenny Holzer (1986) who, rather than spray bombing New York, rents electronic signs in such prominent spots as Times Square, and flashes across the screen reflections along the lines of "Fathers often use too much force," "Money creates taste," or "Go where people sleep and see if they're safe." She also uses t-shirts, baseball hats, and bronze wall plaques to bring the "truisms" of this culture into a new, public light—"Abuse of power should come as no surprise." These bold statements about language and expression in public settings shatter the commonplaces of literacy, as one might look up from the street to catch a glimpse of a commercial sign bearing the message "Savor kindness because cruelty is always possible later." Art has a way of resetting the given, making it a question again, and with Holzer, it is text and truths, social issues and public places, that are shaken as part of her work within a contemporary movement dubbed "Unexpressionism" (posing an interesting exercise in naming; Celant, 1988). It encompasses Barbara Kruger's posters resembling old *Life* magazine covers—"I shop therefore I am"—and Joseph Kossuth's work with pictures opposed to their dictionary definitions, as well as, I would suppose, Tim Rollins + K.O.S. The connection with the New Literacy is in bringing a new context to literacy, shifting the common sources of authority and authorship. In this way the New Literacy also participates in this critique of culture and thus might call on these artistic acts to raise questions about the public nature of literacy, as message and medium.

The idea is to foster a new level of consciousness in the pervasiveness of language on the street, in the media, in the schools and the family, which forms these students' home in the world; the New Literacy can make the ways of this language more apparent, vital, and engaging. It challenges conventional distinctions about language, beginning with the great divide in anthropology which sets oral cultures apart from literate ones; it advances a new voice for literacy in the great educational debate between the phonics-first basal programs against those of the look-say persuasion. In terms of educational history, New Literacy programs side with the excitable forces of a popular literacy; with literary theory, it constitutes a field-test for reader-response criticism in its shift of authority from text to reader. The New Literacy offers far-reaching cultural connections, but it also challenges the personal and public distinctions in literacy. Like the gender distinctions of the last century, in which women were seen to exist happily in a "separate sphere" of activity, the New Literacy challenges the separation of powers in literacy. It acts like a zoom lens which can focus on the reader sitting alone with a book thinking about story or theme, characters or author; with a slight twist, the lens extends its focus to take in the organization of the library or school where the book was found; or it can broaden to include the writer, publisher, bookseller, and reviewer, until finally the depth of field brings into view the literary and social history of which this reader, not so alone with a book anymore, is unmistakably a part. If anything, I am advocating a little more of this wide-angle viewing than has previously been the case in our best visions of literacy at work. The social side of literacy has been underplayed both in rhetoric and practice.

In moving between the personal and public poles, New Literacy advocates, myself among them, have tended to speak of literacy principally in terms of its enhancement of personal growth. In now seems closer to the truth of the matter to assume that the personal side of literacy, as the private meeting of self and word, still partakes of the public sphere. Ian Hacking has captured the point well by pointing out that "there is nothing private about the use of acquired words and practical techniques," to which he adroitly adds, "the cunning of conscience and self-knowledge is to make it *feel* private (1986, p. 236). The other side of this coin is the extent to which the sociability of literacy entails *imagined* or projected responses on the part of readers and writers.

While writing, I pause to think of the ways in which the words will work on others, as I think while reading about the author at work on the piece or, at a less sophisticated level, at the characters living out the story being told; equally so, as a teacher in working with others in reading and writing I am constantly projecting and filling in their intentions, meanings, connotations, and direction.

The social estate of meaning needn't be gregarious or boisterous, and literacy isn't the only manner of communicating by any means. But literacy remains a powerful form of connection and, more importantly for this book, one that still offers the greatest possibility in making a difference in the work of teacher and student. As I have stressed, these personal and public elements of literacy entail a different manner for teachers spending their time with students, sharing their responses to texts, playing editor and agent for their writing. This reconception of teaching reading and writing has drawn me to the New Literacy. Its strikes me as possessing the sort of romance of literacy one finds in reading by rivers and writing in restaurants. It calls up images of the collective, backstage energy of a play's opening night or of dealing with the pressures of getting out a weekly magazine by going for a walk, only to return with new ideas for another issue. In finding the meaning of literacy for the classroom, we have no more certain source than the role that it plays and that we would have it play in our own lives.

I return to this question of the appeal of New Literacy programs, which is where this book began in the Preface, because it is a pressing one. This book has not dealt with the problems of implementation on a school-wide basis, for which I would recommend Mark Clarke's (1987) work with a Whole Language program in the Denver public schools. It has instead treated the New Literacy as a teacher's issue during a time when teachers are struggling to retain a hold on their work. Patrick Shannon (1989) has portrayed the degree to which teachers follow where the textbook guides and state-testing programs lead. While it would be a mistake to assume that *all* are unhappily guided with such a firm and well-organized hand, there are signs that a number of teachers are responding to what Michael Apple (1988) has termed a "new accord" in education that has formed around the recognition of minority and gender rights and interests. He offers the instances of the Boston Women's Teachers Group, Public Education Information Network, based in St. Louis, and Rethinking Education in Milwaukee, which are fighting to restore teachers' control of their work and supporting a larger but related concern with sustaining the cause of equality as the necessary goal of a liberal democracy, against the forms of "competitive individualism" which are further dividing the country (1988, p. 181). The New Literacy might well be seen as part of that new accord, as it speaks to the teacher's place in the educational system as well as, at least as I see it, to education's role in realizing a greater equality of rights and voice in the classroom.

Another encouraging sign for this new accord has been the formation of the English Coalition in 1987, a collaborative effort by school and university English teachers toward a program of common purpose in the teaching of language and literature (Lloyd-Jones & Lunsford, 1989). I take special comfort in their official slogan "Democracy through Language" as it offers a certain hope that the balance of Rosenblatt's original position between individual and society may have begun to find its time again, and that we might continue to "develop curriculums based on the vital role of literature in the lives of individual students and in the development of a democratic society" (Rosenblatt, 1969, p. 1,012).

This renewed curricular interest, girded by a sense of social conscience, might herald the way for Henry Giroux's vision of teachers as "transformative intellectuals" (1988b, pp. 121–28). For teachers drawn to this stance, the New Literacy offers new possibilities for intellectual action in the classroom, even as we are less certain about its ultimate impact as a transformer. New Literacy programs are full of opportunities to delve into the structure and history of literacy, to bring a wider range of literature and other texts into the classroom, while students turn these elements toward their own works of art and argument. But this intellectual interest also lies in educators stepping back from the classroom in order to see that literacy teaching is a struggle of ideas about which we are curious and uncertain, hopeful and probing, ideas that exist on a contested court. The first step in transforming the world is to begin to see it anew. This book has covered the range and promise of these programs in order to help educators find their own happy place in the world as teachers of literacy, new or otherwise. My concern has been to facilitate an understanding of literacy, not simply as a way of organizing a classroom period, minimizing the stress and maximizing the results, but as a source of pride and pleasure in the creative life of this culture.

A remaining difficulty for educators and the public in assessing the New Literacy is that we are still uncertain about precisely what long-term impact this program will have on students and what, at best, we would have of these programs. The questions left unanswered by these programs and this book form a large and intriguing part of the critical future of the New Literacy: Will a good number of these students go on to be writers? Distribute self-published, political pamphlets on the streets? Write vociferous letters to editors? Create immensely successful grant applications for innovative projects in impoverished communities? Or, to turn to reading, will they delve into books more often or more deeply? Will they mount head-turning critiques of key public documents? Will they spend their evenings chatting up books with friends and family, writing imitations and parodies? What is it we are modeling for these New Literates; what is it we hope for their literacy? Can we expect it to carry with the student into other years or even across the summer holidays? What is to come of all this reading and writing?

In addressing an earlier age when it was "frequently told that everyone can write," Virginia Woolf captures both the apprehension and hope of this proliferation of writing: "Yet we do not doubt that at the heart of this immense volubility, this flood and foam of language, this irreticence and vulgarity and triviality, there lies the heat of some great passion which only needs the accident of a brain more happily turned than the rest to issue in a shape which will last from age to age" (1987, p. 59). Yes, there may be that one work that rises out of all this writing, but the great passion of the New Literacy—encouraging the flood and foam of language, risking the vulgar and trivial—is for the *rest* of these writers in the heat of engagement and the potential of empowerment. The New Literacy unabashedly calls for the populist pleasures of literacy and the powers of text-making, amid the accidents that will still offer "a shape which will last." As Woolf suggests in the quotation which heads this chapter, observing this "turmoil" should be our "delight" and we should "above all be generous to the people that are giving shape as best they can to the ideas within them" (1987, p. 59). The truth is that we may need look no further than the scene of the New Literacy itself for what it can best do for students. For what is certain about the New Literacy is its immediate effect on the turmoil, delight, and generous work of teacher and student.

This book has been about those educational practices which share common assumptions about the nature of teaching and literacy. I have grouped them under the rubric of New Literacy to suggest how, taken together, they make a new work out of teaching reading and writing. These programs have grown out of progressive trends over the course of this century, with their deeper roots in popular literacy and Romanticism. They extend from emergent literacy programs in kindergarten to college

242

level composition classes in the writing process; they move from acting out versions of Maurice Sendak's books to elaborating responses to Margaret Atwood's novels; they lead to student-produced music videos and editorials on the rights of skateboarders. New Literacy programs redefine reading and writing in the schools as the active pursuit of the meaning; participation in this meaning is treated as the right of every student. Through the efforts of these programs, literacy finds a lively home in the engaging and critical community of the classroom. It reaches out from the students' page in many directions, allowing these students, as they look up from their work, to see beyond the classroom to the entirety of the world-in-progress, while finding a place for themselves in the breadth of this redefinition.

Notes

1. Rollins adds to this comment his displeasure with another creative outlet that students from this neighborhood have found for themselves: "I oppose the idea of the graffiti movement which is totally irresponsible" (Glueck, 1988, p. 20Y). I would not be as quick as Rollins to dismiss graffiti "writers," who are working from that same urge toward expression and use similar apprenticeship/workshop methods in the same urban setting; graffiti writers have also taken to the commercial and "responsible" world of galleries, even before their "writers' corners" in the subway yards of New York became consistently unworkable sites to carry on their trade (Lachman, 1988). Yet another outlaw form that both represents a similar urge and that can also find its place is rap; while some schools ban it from the schoolyard, with a little imagination Peg Griffin and Michael Cole (1987) have been able to turn it into a literate form of dialogue through electronic mail.
2. This program of mine is treated in more detail in Willinsky (1985).
3. I would be the first to admit that the evaluation question has not received adequate attention in this book, and thus I was especially grateful to obtain Kenneth Goodman, Yetta Goodman and Wendy Hood's new and comprehensive collection, *The Whole Language Evaluation Book* (1989), although it arrived too late for me to incorporate the work into my coverage of the New Literacy.
4. To work again from my own example and the lessons I have learned form this work, I have begun a project with Shannon Bradley Green that takes the desk-top publishing of a teen magazine as an alternative model for remedial education in the language arts; the research uses a combination of standardized measures and ethnographic data, as well as two control groups, to assess the viability and long-term impact of having students designated for remedial support engage in writing and electronically producing a magazine for their peers.

5. One of the women who added the line to the Fiat ad spoke to Posner about her motives: "The ad was opposite my place of work. I had to stare at it out of the window. . . . It was a way of taking over the poster. You have to have a lot of money to afford billboards like that. We wanted to reclaim the open spaces that have been colonized by advertisers. By writing angry but humorous graffiti, we were also making the point that ad agencies don't have the monopoly on wit. It feels great to see it reproduced everywhere. It's made the point that woman can do something instead of just seethe" (Posner, 1982, p. 12).

References

Abbs, P. 1982. *English within the arts: A radical alternative for English and the arts in the curriculum*. London: Hodder & Stoughton.

Abrams, M. H. 1953. *The mirror and the lamp: Romantic theory and the critical tradition*. New York: Oxford University Press.

Alberta Education. 1987. *Junior high language arts curriculum guide*. Edmonton, AB: Alberta Education.

Allen, T. D. 1982. *Writing to create ourselves: New approaches for teachers, students and writers*. Norman, OK: University of Oklahoma Press.

Allington, R. 1983. "The reading instruction provided readers of differing reading abilities." *Elementary School Journal* 83: 548–59.

Althusser, L. 1971. "Ideology and ideological state apparatus." *Lenin and philosophy and other essays,* translated by B. Brewster, pp. 127–87. New York: Monthy Review Press.

Anderson, C., & L. D. Travis. 1983. *Psychology and the liberal consensus*. Waterloo, ON: Wilfrid Laurier University Press.

Anderson, R, & P. D. Pearson. 1984. "A schema-theoretic view of basic processes in reading." In *Handbook of reading research,* edited by P. D. Pearson, pp. 255–93. New York: Longman.

Anderson, R. C., E. H. Heibert, J. A. Scott, & A. A. Wilkinson. 1985. *Becoming a nation of readers: The report of the Commission on Reading*. The National Academy of Education, The National Institute of Education, The Center for the Study of Reading. Washington DC: National Institute of Education.

Apple, M. W. 1981. "Reproduction, contestation, and curriculum: An essay is self-criticism." *Interchange* 12(2–3): 27–47.

———. 1982. *Education and power*. Boston: Routledge & Kegan Paul.

———. 1986. *Teachers and texts: A political economy of class and gender relations in education*. New York: Routledge & Keagan Paul.

———. 1988. "Redefining equality: Authoritarian populism and the conservative restoration." *Teachers College Record* 90(2): 167–84.

Applebee, A. N. 1981. *Writing in the secondary school: English and the content areas*. Urbana, IL: National Council of Teachers of English.

245

Applebee, A. N., & J. A. Langer. 1987. *How writing shapes thinking: A study of teaching and writing*. Urbana, IL: National Council of Teachers of English.

Applebee, A. N., J. A. Langer, & I. V. S. Mullis. 1986. *The writing report card: Achievement in American schools*. National Assessment of Educational Progress. Princeton, NJ: Educational Testing Service.

———. 1987. *Learning to be literate in America: Reading, writing, and reasoning*. The nation's report card. Princeton, NJ: Educational Testing Service.

———. 1988. *Who reads best: Factors related to the reading achievement in grades, 3, 7, and 11*. The nation's report card. Princeton, NJ: Educational Testing Service.

Arendt, H. 1959. *The human condition*. New York: Anchor Doubleday.

Arnold, M. 1908. *Reports on elementary schools, 1852–1882*. London: HMSO.

Aronowitz, S., & H. Giroux. 1985. *Education under siege: The conserative, liberal and radical debate over schooling*. South Hadley, MA: Bergin & Garvey.

Ashton, P. 1980. *Of mice & men*. With D. Denario, M. Simmons, & M. Raleigh. London: English Centre.

Ashton-Warner, S. 1965. *Teacher*. New York: Simon & Schuster.

Atwell, N. 1987. *In the middle: Writing, reading, and learning with adolescents*. Montclair, NJ: Boynton/Cook.

Babbit, I. [1919]. 1977. *Rousseau and Romanticism*. Austin: University of Texas.

Ball, S. J. 1988. "Relations, structures and conditions in curriculum change: A political history of English Teaching." In *International perspectives in curriculum history*, edited by I. Goodson, pp. 17–45. London: Routledge.

Barker, F. 1984. *The tremulous private body: Essays on subjection*. London: Methuen.

Barnes, D. 1975. *From communication to curriculum*. Harmondsworth, UK: Penguin.

Barnes, D., & D. Barnes. 1984. *Versions of English*. With S. Clark. London: Heinemann.

Baron, D. 1982. *Grammar and good taste: Reforming the American language*. New Haven, CN: Yale University Press.

Bartlett, E. C. 1932. *Remembering: A study in experimental and social psychology*. New York: Macmillan.

Bauman, J. F. 1988. "Direct instruction reconsidered." *Journal of Reading*, 31(8): 712–18.

Beck, I. L., & M. G. McKeown. 1984. "Applications of theories of reading to instruction." In *Literacy in American schools: Learning to read and write*, edited by N. L. Stein, pp. 63–83. Chicago: University of Chicago Press.

Belsey, C. 1980. *Critical practice*. London: Methuen.

Benjamin, W. 1969. "The work of art in the age of mechanical reproduction." In *Illuminations*, pp. 217–51. New York: Schocken.

Benveniste, E. 1971. *Problems in general linguistics*, translated by M. E. Meek. Coral Gable, FL: University of Miami Press.

Bereiter, C. 1984. "The limits of interpretation." *Curriculum Inquiry* 14: 211–16.

Bereiter, C., & M. Scardamalia. 1987. "An attainable version of high literacy: Approaches to teaching higher-order skills in reading and writing." *Curriculum Inquiry* 17: 9–30.

Bernal, M. 1987. *Black Athena: The Afroasiatic roots of Classical Civilization*. Vol. 1. *The fabrication of Ancient Greece, 1785–1985*. New Brunswick, NJ: Rutgers University Press.

Bernstein, B. 1971. *Class, codes and control: Theoretical studies toward a sociology of language*. Vol. 1. New York: Schocken Books.

Berthoff, A. E. 1981. *The making of meaning: Metaphors, models, and maxims for writing teachers*. Upper Montclair, NJ: Boynton/Cook.

———. 1983. The intelligent hand and the thinking eye. In *The writer's mind: Writing as a mode of thinking*, edited by J. Hays, P. A. Roth, J. R. Ramsey, & R. D. Foulke, pp. 191–96. Urbana, IL: National Council of Teachers of English.

Bleich, D. 1975. *Reading and feelings: An introduction to subjective criticism*. Urbana, IL: National Council of Teachers of English.

———. 1978. *Subjective criticism*. Baltimore: Johns Hopkins University Press.

———. 1985. "The identity of pedagogy and research in the study of response to literature." In *Researching response to literature and the teaching of literature: Points of departure*, edited by C. R. Cooper, pp. 253–72. Norwood, NJ: Ablex.

———. 1986. "Intersubjective reading." *New Literary History* 17(3): 401–21.

———. 1987. "Gender interests in reading and language." In *Gender and reading: Essays on readers, texts, and contexts*, edited by E. A. Flynn & P. P. Schweickart, pp. 234–66. Baltimore: Johns Hopkins University Press.

Bloom, A. 1987. *The closing of the American mind: How higher education has failed democracy and impoverished the soul of today's students*. New York: Simon & Schuster.

Bobie, A., & J. Willinsky, 1986. "When tests dare to be progressive: Contradictions in the classsroom." Paper presented at National Reading Conference, Austin, TX.

Bond, G. L., & R. Dykstra. 1967. "The co-operative research program in first-grade reading instruction." *Reading Research Quarterly* 2(4): entire issue.

Boomer, G. 1985. *Fair dinkum teaching and learning: Reflections on literacy and power*. Upper Montclair, NJ: Boynton/Cook.

Bourdieu, P. 1973. "Cultural reproduction and social reproduction." In *Knowledge, education, and cultural change*, edited by R. Brown, pp. 71–112. London: Tavistock.

————. 1977. *Outline toward a theory of practice.* Translated by R. Nice. Cambridge: Cambridge University Press.

Bourdieu, P., & Passeron, J. C. 1977. *Reproduction in education, society and culture.* Translated by R. Nice. London: Sage.

Boyer, E. 1983. *High school: A report on secondary education in America.* Princeton, NJ: Carnegie Foundation for the Advancement of Teaching.

Brand, A. G. 1980. "Creative writing in English education: An historical perspective." *Journal of Education* 62: 63–82.

Britton, J. 1971. "What's the use? A schematic account of language functions." *Educational Review* 23(3): 205–19.

————. 1972. *Language and learning.* Harmondsworth, UK: Penguin.

————. 1980. "Shaping at the point of utterance. In *Reinventing the rhetorical tradition,* edited by A. Freedman & I. Pringle, pp. 61–66. Conway, AK: L & S.

————. 1982a. "Reflections on the writing of the Bullock Report." In *Prospect and retrospect: The essays of James Britton,* edited by G. M. Pradl, pp. 185–90. Upper Montclair, NJ: Boynton/Cook.

————. 1982b. "How we got here." In *Prospect and retrospect: The essays of James Britton,* edited by G. M. Pradl, pp. 169–84. Upper Montclair, NJ: Boynton/Cook.

————. 1984. "Message and text in poetic utterance." In *Changing English: Essays for Harold Rosen,* edited by M. Meek & J. Miller, pp. 220–35. London: Heinemann.

————. 1985. "Teachers, learners and leaning." In *Teachers as learner,* edited by M. Chorny, pp. 1–7. Calgary, AB: Language in the Classroom Project, University of Calgary.

Britton, J., A. Burgess, N. Martin, A. McLeod, & H. Rosen. 1975. *The development of writing abilities, 11–18.* London: Macmillan.

Brookover, W. B., A. Thomas, & A. Patterson. 1964. "Self-concept of ability and school achievement." *Sociology of Education* 37: 271–78.

Bruner, J. 1960. *The process of education.* New York: Vintage.

————. 1986. *Actual minds, possible worlds.* Cambridge: Harvard University Press.

Bullock, A. 1975. *A language for life: Report of the Committee of Inquiry appointed by the Secretary of State for Education and Science.* London: HMSO.

Burgess, T. 1984. "Diverse melodies: A first year class in a secondary school." In *Eccentric propositions: Essays on literature and the curriculum,* edited by J. Miller, pp. 56–69. London: Routledge & Kegan Paul.

Burke, E. [1757]. 1968. *A philosophical enquiry into the origin of our ideas of the sublime and beautiful,* edited by J. T. Boulton. Nortre Dame, IN: University of Notre Dame Press.

Calkins, L. M. 1983. *Lessons from a child: On teaching and learning of writing.* Portsmouth, NH: Heinemann.

————. 1986. *The art of teaching writing*. Portsmouth, NH: Heinemann.

Callahan, R. E. 1962. *Education and the cult of efficiency*. Chicago: University of Chicago Press.

Calvino, I. 1988. *Six memos for the next millennium*. Translated by P. Creagh. Cambridge: Harvard University Press.

Campbell, B. P. 1965. *Self-concept and academic achievement in middle grade schoolchildren*. Unpublished doctoral dissertation, Wayne State University.

Castleman, C. 1982. *Getting up: Subway graffiti in New York*. Cambridge: MIT Press.

Cazden, C. B. 1985. "Social context of learning to read." In *Theoretical models and processes of reading,* edited by H. Singer & R. B. Ruddell, pp. 595–611. 3d ed. Newark, DE: International Reading Association.

Celant, G. 1988. *Unexpressionism: Art beyond the contemporary*. New York: Rizzioli.

Chall, J. S. 1983. *Learning to read: The great debate*. 2d ed. New York: McGraw-Hill.

Chall, J. S., & V. A. Jacobs. 1983. "Writing and reading in the elementary grades: Developmental trends among low SES children." *Language Arts* 60: 617–626.

Chandler, J. 1984. *Wordsworth's second nature: A study of poetry and politics*. Chicago: University of Chicago Press.

Chapman, L. J. 1987. *Reading: From 5–11 years*. Milton Keynes, UK: Open University Press.

Christensen, F. A. 1978. "Generative rhetoric of the sentence." In *Notes toward a new rhetoric: Nine essays for teachers,* edited by F. A. Christensen, pp. 23–44. New York: Harper & Row.

Church, S., & J. M. Newman. 1985. "Danny: A case history of an instructionally induced reading problem." In *Whole language: Theory in use,* edited by J. M. Newman, pp. 169–80. Portsmouth, NH: Heinemann.

Church, S., R. Gamberg, A. Manicom, & J. Rice. 1989. " 'Whole language' in Nova Scotia. Part 1: Benefits, difficulties and potential." *Our Schools/Our Selves* 1(2): 46–58.

Clark, K. 1973. *The romantic rebellion: Romantic versus classic art*. Don Mills, ON: Longman.

Clarke, M. A. 1987. "Don't blame the system: Constraints on 'Whole language' Reform." *Language Arts* 64(4): 384–97.

Clay, M. 1975. *What did I write?* London: Heinemann.

Cohen, D. K. 1988. "Teaching practice: Plus ça change . . . In *Contributing to educational change: Perspectives on research and practice,* edited by P. Jackson. Berkeley, CA: McCutchan.

Coleridge, S. T. [1817]. 1983. *Biographia literaria*. Edited by J. Engell & W. J. Bate. Princeton, NJ: Princeton University Press.

Cotes-Cardenas, M. 1980. "A new kind of reader: The Chicano feminist." *Reader* 8: 23–28.

Coward, R., & J. Ellis. 1977. *Language and materialism: Developments in semiology and the theory of the subject.* Boston: Routledge & Kegan Paul.

Cowley, M. 1957. *Writers at work: The Paris Review interviews.* New York: Viking.

Cox, C. B., & R. Boyson 1975. *The fight for education: Black paper, 1975.* London: Dent.

Crawford, M., & R. Chaffin. 1987. "The reader's construction of meaning: cognitive research on gender and comprehension." In *Gender and reading: Essays on readers, texts, and contexts,* edited by E. A. Flynn & P. P. Schweickart, pp. 3–30. Baltimore: Johns Hopkins University Press.

Cremin, L. 1961. *The transformation of the school: Progressivism in American education, 1876–1957.* New York: Vintage.

Cummins, J. 1986. "Empowering minority students: A framework for intervention." *Harvard Educational Review* 56: 18–36.

Daniels, H. 1983. *Famous last words: The American language crisis reconsidered.* Carbondale, IL: Southern Illinois University Press.

Daniels, H., & A. Zemelman. 1985. *A writing project: Training teachers of composition from kindergarten to college.* Portsmouth, NH: Heinemann.

Darnton, R. 1982. *The literary underground of the old regime.* Cambridge: Harvard University Press.

———. 1989. "Introduction." In *Revolution in print: The press in France, 1775–1800,* edited by R. Darnton & D. Rochem, pp. xiii-xv. Berkeley: University of California.

Davis, N. 1965. "Printing and the people." In *Society and culture in early modern France.* Stanford: Stanford University Press.

Davis, F. 1984. "In defense of grammar." *English Education* 16: 151–164.

Davis, F., & R. Parker. 1978. *Teaching for literacy: Reflections on the Bullock Report.* New York: Agathon Press.

de Lauretis, T. 1987. "The technology of gender." *Technologies of gender: Essays on theory, film, and fiction,* pp. 1–30. Bloomington, IN: Indiana University Press.

Defoe, D. [1702]. 1961. An essay on several projects. In *English examined: Two centuries of comment on the mother tongue,* edited by S. Tucker. Cambridge: Cambridge University Press.

Derrida, J. 1976. *Of grammatology.* Translated by G. Spivak. Baltimore: Johns Hopkins University Press.

Dewey, J. 1900. *The school and society.* Chicago: University of Chicago Press.

———. 1932. *Ethics.* 2d ed. New York: Holt, Rinehart & Winston.

———. 1938. *Experience and education.* London: Collier-Macmillan.

———. [1914]. 1944. *Democracy and education.* New York: Macmillan.

———. [1934]. 1986. *Art as experience.* New York: G. P. Putman.

———. [1897]. 1988. My pedagogic creed. In *Readings from Progressive Education: A movement and its professional journal,* edited by S. I. Brown

& M. E. Finn, pp. 169–70. Vol. I. Lanham, MD: University Press of America.

Dias, P. 1987. *Making sense of poetry: Patterns in process*. Ottawa: Canadian Council of Teacher of English.

Dixon, J. 1967. *Growth through English*. London: Oxford University Press.

Dixon, J. 1986. "Is it growth or social inculcation? Dartmouth revisited." Paper presented at Fourth International Conference on the Teaching of English, Ottawa, ON.

Donovan, T., & B. McClelland, eds. 1980. *Eight approaches to teaching composition*. Urbana, IL: National Council of Teachers of English.

Doughty, P. 1974. *Language, "English" and the curriculum*. London: Edward Arnold.

Doughty, P., G. Throton, & J. Pearce. 1971. *Language in use*. London: Edward Arnold.

Dykstra, R. 1984. "Foreward." In *Handbook of reading research*, edited by P. D. Pearson, pp. xix-xx. New York: Longman.

Eagleton, T. 1983. *Literary theory: An introduction*. Minneapolis: University of Minnesota Press.

———. 1985/86. "The subject of literature." *Cultural Critique* 2: 95–104.

Eco, U. 1979. *The role of the reader: Explorations in the semiotics of texts*. Bloomington: Indiana University Press.

Egan, K. In press. *Rationality, imagination, and Romantic understanding: Education during the middle school years*. New York: Routledge.

Ehri, L. C., & L. S. Wilce. 1987. "Does learning to spell help beginners learn to read words?" *Reading Research Quarterly* 22(1): 47–65.

Eisenstein, E. 1979. *The printing press as an agent of social change*. Cambridge: Cambridge University Press.

Elasser, N., & V. John-Steiner. 1987. "An interactionist approach to advancing literacy." In *Freire for the classroom: A sourcebook for liberatory teaching*, edited by I. Shor, pp. 45–63. Upper Montclair, NJ: Boynton/Cook.

Elbow, P. 1973. *Writing without teachers*. New York: Oxford University Press.

———. 1981. *Writing with power*. New York: Oxford University Press.

Emig, J. 1971. *The composing processes of twelfth graders*. Urbana, IL: National Council of Teachers of English.

Engell, J. 1981. *The creative imagination: Enlightenment to Romanticism*. Cambridge: Harvard University Press.

Epps, J. 1985. "Killing them softly: Why Willie can't write." In *Tapping potential: English and language arts for the black learner*, edited by C. Brooks, pp. 154–59. Urbana, IL: National Council of Teachers of English.

Estes, T. H., C. J. Gutman, & J. J. Estes. 1989. "Cultural literacy: Another view from the University of Virginia." *Curriculum Inquiry*, in press.

Evancheko, P., L. Ollila, J. Downing, & C. Braun. 1973. "An investigation of the reading resources domain." *Research in the Teaching of English* 7: 61–78.

Fader, D. N., & E. B. McNeil. 1968. *Hooked on books: Program and proof.* New York: Berkley.

Fadiman, C., & J. Howard. 1979. *Empty pages: A search for writing competence in school and soceity.* Belmont CA: Fearon Pitman.

Fetterley, J. 1978. *The resisting reader: A feminist approach to American fiction.* Bloomington: Indiana Unversity Press.

Fields, M. V. 1988. "Talking and writing: Explaining the whole language approach to parents." *The Reading Teacher* 41(9): 898–903.

Fine, M. 1987. "Silence in public schools." *Language Arts* 64(2): 157–74.

Fish, S. 1980. "Literature in the reader: An effective stylistics." In *Is there as text in this class? The authority of interpretive communities,* pp. 21–67. Cambridge: Harvard Univerity Press.

Flesch, R. 1981. *Why Johnny still can't read: A new look at the scandal of our schools.* New York: Harper & Row.

Flower, L., & J. R. Hayes. 1981. "A cognitive basis for problems in writing." *College English* 41: 19–37.

Flower, L., J. R. Hayes, L. Carey, K. Schriver, & J. Stratman. 1986. "Detection, diagnosis, and the strategies of revision." *College Composition and Communication* 37(1), 16–55.

Flynn, E. A. 1983. "Women as reader-response critics." *New Orleans Review* 10: 20–25.

———. 1987. "Gender and reading." In *Gender and reading: Essays on readers, texts, and contexts,* edited by E. A. Flynn & P. P. Schweickart, pp. 267–88. Baltimore: Johns Hopkins University Press.

Flynn, E. A., G. A. McCulley, & R. K. Gratz. 1986. "Writing in biology: Effects of peer critiquing and analysis of models on the quality of biology laboratory reports." In *Writing across the disciplines: Research into practice,* edited by A. Young & T. Fulwiler, pp. 160–75. Upper Montclair, NJ: Boynton/Cook.

Flynn, E. A., & P. P. Schweickart, eds. 1987. *Gender and reading: Essays on readers, texts, and contexts.* Baltimore: Johns Hopkins University

Foster, H. M. 1979. *The new literacy: The language of film and television.* Urbana, IL: National Council of Teachers of English.

Foucault, M. 1970. *The order of things: An archeology of the human sciences.* New York: Random House.

———. 1972. *The archeology of knowledge and the discourse on language.* Translated by A. M. S. Smith. New York: Harper & Row.

———. 1980. *Power/knowledge: Selected interviews and other writings, 1972–1977.* Edited by C. Gordon. New York: Pantheon.

———. 1988. "Technologies of the Self." In *Technologies of the self: A seminar with Michel Foucault,* edited by L. H. Martin, H. Gutman, & P. H. Hutton, pp. 16–49. London: Tavistock.

Fox, C. 1988. " 'Poppies will make them grant.' " In *Language and literacy in the primary school,* edited by M. Meek & C. Mills, pp. 53–68. East Sussex, UK: Falmer Press.

Fox, M. 1988. "Notes from the battlefield: Toward a theory of why people write." *Language Arts* 65(2), 112–125.

Freedman, S. W. 1987. *Response to student writing.* National Research Report No. 23. Urbana, IL: National Council of Teachers of English.

Freire, P. 1974. *Cultural action for freedom.* Harmondsworth, UK: Penguin.

———. 1987. "Letter to North-American teachers." In *Freire for the classroom: A sourcebook for liberatory teaching,* edited by I. Shor, pp. 211–15. Translated by C. Hunter. Upper Montclair, NJ: Boynton/Cook.

Freire, P., & M. Donaldo. 1987. *Literacy: Reading the word and the world.* South Haley, MA: Bergin & Garvey.

Friedenberg, E. Z. 1959. *The Vanishing Adolescent.* New York: Dell.

Frye, N. 1957. *Anatomy of criticism: Four essays.* Princeton NJ: Princeton University Press.

———. 1968. *A study of Romanticism.* Chicago: University of Chicago Press.

Fulwiler, T. 1986. "The argument for writing across the curriculum." In *Writing across the disciplines: Research into practice,* edited by E. A. Young & T. Fulwiler, pp. 21–32. Upper Montclair, NJ: Boynton/Cook.

Gender: Material for discussion. 1984. London: The English Centre, Sutherland Street, SW1.

Geoffrey of Vinsauf. [1200]. 1967. *Poetria nova.* Translated by M. Nims. Toronto: Pontifical Institute of Medieval Studies.

Giacobbe, M. E. 1984. "Helping children become more responsible for their writing." *Live Wire* (October).

Giroux, H. A. 1986. "Radical pedagogy and the politics of student voice." *Interchange* 17(1), 48–69.

———. 1987. "Critical literacy and student empowerment: Donald Graves' approach to literacy." *Language Arts* 64(2): 175–181.

———. 1988a. "Literacy and the pedagogy of voice and political empowerment." *Educational Theory* 38(1): 61–75.

———. 1988b. *Teachers as intellectuals: Toward a critical pedagogy of learning.* Granby, MA: Bergin & Garvey.

Glueck, G. 1988. "'Survival kids' transform classics to murals." *New York Times,* November 13, pp. 1Y, 20Y.

Goodlad, J. 1983. "Improving schooling in the 1980s: Toward the non-replication of non-events." *Educational Leadership* 41: 4–10.

———. 1984. *A place called school.* New York: McGraw-Hill.

Goodman, K. S. 1965. "A linguisitic study of cues and miscues in reading." *Elementary English* 42: 639–43.

———. 1982. "The reading process: Theory and practice." In *Language and literacy; The selected writings of Kenneth S. Goodman.* Vol. 1. *Process, Theory, Research.* Cambridge: Harvard University Press.

———. 1985. "Unity in reading." In *Theoretical models and processes of reading,* edited by H. Singer & R. B. Ruddell, pp. 813–840. 3d ed. Newark, DE: International Reading Association.

———. 1986a. *What's whole in Whole Language?* Richmond Hill, ON: Scholastic.

———. 1986b. "Basal readers: A call to action." *Language Arts* 63: 358–63.

Goodman, K. S., Y. M. Goodman, & W. J. Hood, eds. 1989. *The whole language evaluation book.* Portsmouth, NH: Heinemann.

Gordon, D. R. 1971. *The new literacy.* Toronto: University of Toronto Press.

Gorman, T. 1986. *The framework for the assessment of language.* Windsor, UK: NFER/Nelson.

Gough, P. B. 1972. "One second of reading." In *Language by ear and by eye,* edited by J. F. Kavanagh & I. G. Mattingly, pp. 331–58. Cambridge, MA: M.I.T. Press.

———. 1985. "One second of reading reconsidered." In *Theoretical models and processes of reading,* edited by H. Singer & R. B. Ruddell, pp. 687–688. 3d ed. Newark, DE: International Reading Association.

Graff, H. J. 1979. *The literacy myth: Literacy and social structure in the nineteenth century city.* New York: Academic Pres

———. 1981. *Literacy and social development in the West: A reader.* Cambridge: Cambridge University Press.

Graves, D. 1983. *Writing: Teachers and children at work.* Portsmouth, NH: Heinemann.

———. 1984. "Write with the children." In *A researcher learns to write: Selected articles and monographs,* pp. 134–140. Portsmouth, NH: Heinemann.

Green, B. 1988. "Literature as curriculum frame: A critical perspective." In *Shifting frames: English/literature/writing,* edited by K. Hart, pp. 46–71. Victoria, AU: Centre for Studies in Literary Education, Deakin University.

Gregory, G. 1984. "Community-publishing working class writing in context." In *Changing English: Essays for Harold Rosen,* edited by M. Meek & J. Miller, pp. 220–35. London: Heinemann.

Griffin, P., & M. Cole. 1987. "New technologies, basic skills, and the underside of education: What's to be done?" In *Language, literacy and culture: Issues of society and schooling,* edited by J. Langer, pp. 199–231. Norwood, NJ: Ablex.

Groff, P. 1980. "Research versus psycholinguistic approach to beginning reading." *Elementary School Journal* 81: 54–58.

Grumbacher, J. 1987. "How writing helps phsyics students become better problem solvers." In *The journal book,* edited by T. Fulwiler, pp. 323–29. Upper Montclair, NJ: Boynton/Cook.

Grumet, M. R. 1988. *Bitter milk: Women and teaching*. Amherst, MA: University of Massachusetts.

Gutteridge, D. 1988. *The dimension of delight: A study of children's verse, ages 11–13*. London, ON: Althouse.

Habermas, J. 1983. "Modernity—An incomplete project." In *The anti-aesthetic: Essay on postmodern culture*, edited by H. Foster, pp. 3–15. Port Townsend, WA: Bay Press.

Hacking, I. 1986. "Self-improvement." In *Foucault: A critical reader*, edited by D. C. Hoy, pp. 235–40. Oxford: Blackwell.

Haley-James, S., ed. 1981. *Perspectives on writing in grades 1–8*. Urbana, IL: National Council of Teachers of English.

Halliday, M. A. K. 1973. *Explorations in the functions of language*. London: Edward Arnold.

Hampton, C. 1984. *A radical reader: The struggle for change in England, 1381–1914*. Harmondsworth, UK: Penguin.

Hansen, J. 1987. *When writers read*. Portsmouth, NH: Heinemann.

Harris, R. W. 1969. *Romanticism and the social order, 1780–1830*. London: Blanford.

Harste, J. C., V. A. Woodward, & C. L. Burke. 1984. *Language stories and literacy lessons*. Portsmouth, NH: Heinemann.

Hartman. G. H., & S. Budick, eds. *Midrash and literature*. New Haven, CN: Yale University Press.

Havelock, R. 1977. *Origins of Western literacy*. Toronto: Ontario Institute of Studies in Education.

Hays, J., P. Roth, J. Ramsey, & R. Foulke, eds. 1983. *The writer's mind: Writing as a mode of thinking*. Urbana, IL: National Council of Teachers of English.

Heath, S. B. 1983. *Ways with words: Language, life, and work in communities and classrooms*. Cambridge: Cambridge University Press.

Hefferman, K. 1982. "Responding to children's writing." In *Whole language: Translating theory into practice* (Monographs on teaching and learning), edited by J. Newman. Halifax, NS: Department of Education, Dalhousie University.

Henriques, J., W. Holloway, C. Urwin, C. Venn, & V. Walkerdine. 1984. *Changing the subject: Psychology, social regulation and subjectivity*. London: Methuen.

Herman, E. S., & N. Chomsky. 1988. *Manufacturing consent: The political economy of the mass media*. New York: Pantheon.

Hillocks, G. Jr. 1986. *Research on written composition: New directions for teaching*. Urbana, IL: National Conference on Research in English, ERIC.

Hirsch, E. D. Jr. 1987. *Cultural Literacy: What every American needs to know*. Boston: Houghton Mifflin.

Hoffman, J. V., ed. 1986. *Effective teaching of reading: Research and practice*. Newark, DE: Interantional Reading Association.

Hofstadter, R. 1962. *Anti-intellectualism in American life*. New York: Vintage.

Hohendahl, P. U. 1982. *The institution of criticism*. Ithaca, NY: Cornell University Press.

Holbrook, D. 1986. "Creativity in the English programme." In *Creativity in English,* edited by G. Summerfiled, pp. 1–12. Urbana, IL: National Council of Teachers of English

Holdaway, D. 1979. *Foundations of literacy*. Sydney: Ashton Scholastic.

Holland, N. H. 1975. *The dynamics of literary response*. New York: W. W. Norton.

Holland, N. H., & L. F. Sherman. 1987. "Gothic possibilities." In *Gender and reading: Essays on readers, texts, and contexts,* edited by E. A. Flynn & P. P. Schweickart, pp. 215–33. Baltimore: Johns Hopkins University Press.

Hollis, P. 1970. *The pauper press: A study in working-class radicalism in the 1830s*. Oxford: Oxford University Press

Holzer, J. 1986. *Jenney Holzer: Signs*. Forward by Joan Simon. Des Moines: Des Moines Art Center.

Hourd, M. 1949. *The education of the poetic spirit*. London: Heinemann.

Houston, R. 1987. "The literacy campaign in Scotland, 1560–1803." In *National literacy campaigns: Historical and comparative perspectives,* edited by R. F. Arnove & H. J. Graff, pp. 65–98. New York: Plenum Press.

Hubbard, R. 1985. "Second graders answer the question 'Why publish?' " *The Reading Teacher* 38(7): 658–62.

Huey, E. B. [1908]. 1968. *The psychology and pedagogy of reading*. Cambridge, MA: M.I.T. Press.

Illich, I. 1970. *Deschooling Society*. New York: Harper & Row.

———. 1979. "Vernacular values and education." *Teachers College Record* 81(1): 31–76.

———. 1987. "A plea for research on lay literacy." *Interchange* 18(1/2): 147–163.

Inglis, F. 1985. *The management of ignorance: A politicial theory of the curriculum*. Oxford: Blackwell.

Innis, H. 1951. *The bias of communication*. Toronto: University of Toronto Press.

Irigaray, L. 1985. *This sex which is not one*. Translated by C. Porter. Ithaca, NY: Cornell University Press.

Jacobus, M. 1984. "The art of managing books: Romantic prose and the writing of the past." In *Romanticism and language,* edited by A. Reed, pp. 215–46. Ithaca, NY: Cornell University Press.

Jameson, F. 1972. *The prison-house of language: A critical account of structuralism and Russian formalism*. Princeton, NJ: Princeton University Press.

Javal L. E. 1879. "Essai sur la psychologie de lecture." *Annales d'Oculistique* 82: 243–53.

Jay, P. 1984. *Being in the text: Self-representation from Wordsworth to Roland Barthes.* Ithaca: Cornell University Press.

Jensen, A. 1980. *Bias in Mental Testing.* New York: Free Press.

Johansson, E. 1987. "Literacy campaigns in Sweden." In *National literacy campaigns: Historical and comparative perspectives,* edited by R. F. Arnove & H. J. Graff, pp. 65–98. New York: Plenum Press.

Johnson, R. 1976. "Notes on the schooling of the English working class, 1780–1850." In *Schooling and capitalism: A sociological reader,* edited by R. Dale, G. Esland, & M. MacDonald, pp. 44–53. London: Routledge & Kegan Paul.

Jones, R. F. 1953. *The triumph of the English language.* Stanford: Stanford University Press.

Kahane, H., & R. Kahane. 1979. "Decline and survival of Western prestige languages." *Language* 55(1), 183–99.

Kamil, M. L. 1984. "Current traditions of reading research." In *Handbook of reading research,* edited by P. D. Pearson, pp. 39–62. New York: Longman.

Kennard, J. E. 1986. "Ourselves behind ourselves: A theory for lesbian readers." In *Gender and reading: Essays on readers, texts, and contexts,* edited by E. A. Flynn & P. P. Schweickart, pp. 63–80. Baltimore: Johns Hopkins University Press.

Kingman, J. 1988. *Report of the Committee on inquiry into the teaching of English language.* London: HMSO.

Kirchhoff, H. J. 1989. "From daddy to Rushdie, it's all germane to Greer." *Globe and Mail,* August 5, p. C2.

Knoblauch, C. H., & L. Brannon. 1984. *Rhetorical traditions and the teaching of writing.* Upper Montclair, NJ: Boynton/Cook.

Koch, K. 1970. *Wishes, lies and dreams: Teaching children to write poetry.* New York: Random House.

Koch, K. 1973. *Rose, where did you get that red? Teaching great poetry to children.* New York: Vintage.

Kozol, J. 1985. *Illiterate America.* New York: Doubleday.

Kazemek, F. E. 1986. "Commentary: Whose reality and preparation for what kind of future?" *The Reading Teacher* 40(3): 260–62.

Kristeva, J. 1980. "From one identity to another." In *Desire in language: A semiotic approach to literature and art,* edited by L. S. Roudiez, pp. 124–47. Translated by T. Gora, A. Jardine, & L. S. Roudiez. New York: Columbia University Press.

———. 1984. *Revolution in poetic language.* Translated by M. Waller. Introduction by L. S. Roudiez. New York: Columbia University Press.

Kuhn, T. 1962. *The structure of scientific revolutions.* Chicago: University of Chicago Press.

Lablanca, D. A., & W. J. Reeves. 1985. "Writing across the curriculum: The science argument." *Journal of Chemical Education* 62: 400–62.

Labov, W. 1973. "The logic of nonstandard English." In *Tinker, tailor: The myth of cultural deprivation,* edited by N. Keddie, pp. 21–66. Harmondsworth, UK: Penguin.

Lacan, J. 1968. *Speech and language in pscyhoanalysis.* Translated by A. Wilden. Baltimore, MD: Johns Hopkins University Press.

———. 1977. *The four fundamental concepts of psycho-analysis.* Translated by J.-A. Miller. New York: Norton.

Lachman, R. 1988. "Graffiti as career and ideology." *American Journal of Sociology* 94: 229–250.

Langer, J. A. 1982. "The reading process." In *Secondary school reading: What research reveals for classroom practice,* edited by A. Berger & H. A. Robinson, pp. 39–51. Urbana, IL: National Conference on Research in English.

Lankshear, C. 1987. *Literacy, schooling and revolution.* East Sussex, UK: Falmer Press.

Laqueur, T. 1976. "The cultural origins of popular literacy in England 1500–1850." *Oxford Review of Education* 2: 255–275.

Le Guin, U. 1989. "The hand that rocks the cradle writes the book." *New York Times Book Review,* January 22, pp. 1, 35–37.

Leonard, S. [1929] 1962. *The doctrine of correctness in English usage: 1700–1800.* New York: Russell & Russell.

Livingston, M. C. 1984. *The child as poet: Myth or reality.* Boston: Horn.

Llosa, M. V. 1986. *The prepetual orgy: Flaubert and Madame Bovary.* Translated by H. Lane. New York: Farrar, Strauss, Giroux.

Lockridge, K. 1974. *Literacy in colonial New England: An inquiry into the social context of literacy in the early modern West.* New York: Norton.

Lowth, R. [1762]. 1979. *A short introduction to English grammar.* Nelmar, NY: Scholars' Facsimiles and Reprints.

Lloyd-Jones, R., & A. A. Lunsford. 1989. *The English Coalition conference: Democracy through language.* Urbana, IL: National Council of Teachers of English.

Lovejoy, A. O. 1960. "On the discrimination of romanticisms." In *English Romantic poets: Modern essays of criticism,* edited by M. H. Abrams, pp. 39–52. London: Oxford University Press.

Luke, A. 1988. *Literacy, textbooks and ideology.* East Sussex, UK: Falmer Press.

Luke, A., P. Gilbert, K. Rowe, R. Gilbert, G. Ward, & R. Baldauf, Jr. 1989. *An evaluation of literacy strategies in two Australian sites.* Canberra: Department of Employment, Education and Training.

Luke, C., S. de Castell, & A. Luke. 1983. "Beyond criticism: The authority of the school text." *Curriculum Inquiry* 13: 111–27.

Luria, A. R. 1976. *Cognitive development: Its cultural and social foundations.* Translated by M. Lopez-Morillas & L. Solotaroff. Cambridge: Harvard University Press.

Lyman, R. L. 1929. *Summary of investigations relating to grammar, language and composition.* Chicago: University of Chicago.

Maclean, R. 1988. "Two paradoxes of phonics." *The Reading Teacher* 41(6): 514–17.

Maeroff, G. I. 1988. *The empowerment of teachers: Overcoming the crisis of confidence.* New York: Teachers College Press.

Maguire, P., R. Mills, D. Morley, R. O'Rourke, S. Shrapnel, K. Worpole, & S. Yeo. 1982. *The republic of letters: Working class writing and local publishing.* London: Comedia.

Mare, R. D. 1981. "Change and stability in educational stratification." *American Sociological Review* 46(1): 72–87.

Marland, M., ed. 1977. *Language across the curriculum.* London: Heinemann.

Martin, N. 1983. "Language across the curriculum: A paradox and its potential for change." In *Mostly about writing: Selected essays,* pp. 100–11. Upper Montclair, NJ: Boynton/Cook.

Mashayekh, F. 1974. "Freire—the man, his ideas and their implications." *Literacy Discussion* (Spring): 1–62.

Mason, J. M. 1984. "Early reading from a developmental perspective." In *Handbook of reading research,* edited by P. D. Pearson, pp. 505–44. New York: Longman.

Mason, J. M., ed. 1989. *Reading and writing connections.* Boston: Allyn & Bacon.

Massaro, D. W. 1984. "Building and testing models of reading processes." In *Handbook of reading research,* edited by P. D. Pearson, pp. 111–46. New York: Longman.

Mathieson, M. 1975. *The preachers of culture: A study of English and its teachers.* London: Allen & Unwin.

McCracken, M., & R. McCracken. 1979. *Reading, writing and language: A practical guide for primary teachers.* Winnipeg: Peguis.

McDermott, R. P. 1976. *Kids make sense: An ethnographic account of the interactional management of success and failure in one first-grade.* Unpublished doctoral dissertation, Stanford University.

———. 1985. "Achieving school failure: An anthropological approach to illiteracy and social stratification." In *Theoretical models and processes of reading,* edited by H. Singer & R. B. Ruddell, pp. 558–94. 3d ed. Newark, DE: International Reading Association.

McGann, J. 1983. *The Romantic ideology: A critical investigation.* Chicago: University of Chicago Press.

McGee, L. M., R. G. Lomax, & M. H. Head. 1988. "Young children's written language knowledge: What environmental and functional print reading reveals." *Journal of Reading Behavior* 20(2): 99–118.

McLeod, A. 1986. "Critical literacy: Taking control of our own lives." *Language Arts* 63(1): 37–50.

Mead, G. H. 1934. "Self." In *On social psychology: Selected papers,* edited by A. Strauss, pp. 199–247. Chicago: University of Chicago Press.

Medway, P. 1980. *Finding a language: Autonomy and learning in school.* London: Writers & Readers.

Meek, M. 1988. *How texts teach what readers learn.* Avonset, UK: Thimble Press.

Merleau-Ponty, M. 1963. "Studies in the literary use of language." In *In praise of philosophy and other essays,* translated by J. Wilde, J. Edie & J. O'Neill. pp. 80–86. Evanston, IL: Northwestern University Press.

Metha, A., & M. A. Rothschild. 1985. "Women's studies and the high school English teacher." *English Journal* 74(3): 26–28.

Mills, C. 1988. "Making sense of reading: Key words or Grandma Swagg." In *Language and literacy in the primary school,* edited by M. Meek & C. Mills, pp. 27–52. East Sussex, UK: Falmer Press.

Moffet, J. 1981. "Integrity in the teaching of writing." In *Coming on center: English education in evolution.* Upper Montclair, NJ: Boynton/Cook.

Moffett, J., & L. Wagner. 1983. *A student-centered language arts curriculum, K–13.* 2d ed. Boston: Houghton Mifflin.

Mortimore, P., P. Sammons, L. Stoll, D. Lewis, & R. Ecob. 1988. *School matters.* Berkeley: University of California Press.

Murray, D. 1986. "Writing before writing." In *To compose: Teaching writing in the high school,* edited by T. Newkirk, pp. 37–46. Portsmouth, NH: Heinemann.

———. 1982. *Learning by teaching.* Upper Montclair, NJ: Boynton/Cook.

Murray, E. 1977. *Caught in the web of words: James M.H. Murray and the Oxford English Dictionary.* New Haven, CN: Yale University Press.

Myers, C. 1983. "Drawing as prewriting in preschool." In *Theory and practice in the teaching of composition: Processing, distancing, and modeling,* edited by M. Myers & J. Gray, pp. 75–85. Urbana, IL: National Council of Teachers of English.

Myers, M. 1983. "Approaches to the teaching of composition." In *Theory and practice in the teaching of composition: Processing, distancing, and modeling,* edited by M. Myers & J. Gray, pp. 3–43. Urbana, IL: National Council of Teachers of English.

National Commission on Excellence in Education. 1983. *A nation at risk: The imperative of educational reform.* Washington, DC: U.S. Dept. of Education.

Nell, V. 1988. "The psychology of reading for pleasure: Needs and gratifications." *Reading Research Quarterly* 23: 6–50.

Newman, J. 1985. "Insights from recent reading and writing research and their implications for developing whole language curriculum." *Whole language: Theory in use,* edited by J. Newman, pp. 7–36. Portsmouth, NH: Heinemann

Newsome, D. 1974. *Two classes of men: Platonism and English Romantic thought.* London: John Murray.

Nicholson, T., & D. Hill. 1985. "Good readers don't guess—Taking another look at the issue of whether children read words better in context or in isolation." *Reading Psychology: An International Quarterly* 6(3/4): 181–98.

North, S. 1987. *The making of knowledge in composition: Portrait of an emerging field.* Upper Montclair, NJ: Boynton/Cook.

Noyce, R. M., & J. F. Christie. 1989. *Integrating reading and writing instruction in grades K–8.* Boston: Allyn & Bacon.

Oakes, J. 1985. *Keeping track: How schools structure inequality.* New Haven, CN: Yale University Press.

Ohmann, R. 1976. *English in America: A radical view of the profession.* New York: Oxford University Press.

Ogbu, J. U. 1983. "Literacy and schooling in subordinate cultures: The case of black Americans." In *Literacy in historical perspective,* edited by D. P. Resnick, pp. 129–154. Washington: Library of Congress.

Olson, D. R. 1977. "From utterance to text: The bias of language in speech and writing." *Harvard Educational Review* 47(3): 257–281.

Ong, W. J. 1980. "Literacy and orality in our times." *Journal of Communication* 30: 197–204.

Ormond, J. E. 1986. "Learning to spell: Three studies at the university level." *Research in the Teaching of English* 20(2): 160–173.

Pader, R. 1987. "Post-structuralism and neo-romanticism or is MacIntrye a young conservative?" *Philosophy & Social Criticism* 3: 125–143.

Pappas, C. C., & E. Brown. 1987. "Learning to read by reading: Learning how to extend the functional potential of language." *Research in the Teaching of English* 21(2), 160–77.

Parker, J. 1982. *The writer's workshop.* Don Mills, ON: Addison Wesley.

Parker, J., & V. Goodkin. 1987. *The consequences of writing: Enhancing learning in the disciplines.* Upper Montclair, NJ: Boynton/Cook.

Pearson, P. D. 1985. "Changing the face of reading comprehension instruction." *The Reading Teacher* 37: 724–38.

Peckham, M. 1970. "Toward a theory of Romanticism." In *The triumph of Romanticism,* pp. 3–26. Columbia, SC: University of South Carolina Press.

Petersen, B. T. 1986. *Convergences: Transactions in reading and writing.* Urbana, IL: National Council of Teachers of English.

Pichet, J. W., & R. C. Anderson. 1977. "Taking a different perspective on a story." *Journal of Educational Psychology* 69: 309–15.

Pinnell, G. S. 1989. "Success of at-risk children in a program that combines writing and reading." In *Reading and writing connections,* edited by J. M. Mason, pp. 237–60. Boston: Allyn & Bacon.

Posner, J. 1982. *Spray it loud.* London: Routledge & Kegan Paul.

Powers, W. 1983. "Relationships between reader-response and the research of Kenneth and Yetta Goodman." *Reader* 10: 28–36.

Probst, R. E. 1988. *Response and analysis: Teaching literature in junior and senior high school.* Portsmouth, NH: Heinemann.

Radway, J. A. 1984. *Reading the romance: Women patriarchy and popular literature*. Chapel Hill, NC: University of North Carolina.

Resnick, D. P., ed. 1983. *Literacy in historical perspective*. Washington: Library of Congress.

Resnick, D. P., & L. B. Resnick. 1977. "The nature of literacy: An historical exploration." *Harvard Educational Review* 47(3): 370–85.

Rist, R. 1970. "Student social class and teacher expectations." *Harvard Educational Review* 40: 411–51.

Rohman, R. 1965. "Pre-writing: The stage of discovery in the writing process." *College Composition and Communication* 16: 106–12.

Romano, T. 1987. *Clearing the way: Working with teenage writers*. Portsmouth, NH: Heinemann.

Rosen, C., & H. Rosen. 1973. *The language of primary schoolchildren*. Harmondsworth, UK: Penguin.

Rosen, H. 1972. *Language and class: A critical look at the theories of Basil Bernstein*. Bristol, UK: Falling Water.

———. 1969. "Toward a language policy across the curriculum." In *Language, the learner and the school* by D. Barnes, J. Britton, H. Rosen and the L.A.T.E. pp. 117–168. Harmondsworth, UK: Penguin.

Rosenblatt, L. M. 1938. *Literature as exploration*. For the Commission of Human Relations. New York: Appleton-Century.

———. 1964. "Poem as event." *College English* 26(2): 123–29.

———. 1969. "Pattern and process—polemic." *English Journal* 58(7): 1005–12.

———. 1977. "A way of happening." In *Challenge and change in the teaching of English*, edited by A. Daigon & R. Carter, pp. 155–69. Boston: Allyn and Bacon.

———. 1978. *The reader, the text, the poem: The transactional theory of poetry*. Carbondale, IL: Southern Illinois University Press.

———. 1980. "What facts does this poem teach you." *Language Arts* 54(4): 386–94.

———. 1981a. "Interview with Louise Rosenblatt: The reader's contribution in the literary experience." *English Quarterly* 14: 3–12.

———. 1981b. "On the aesthetic as the basic model of the reading process." *Bucknell Review* 26(1): 17–32.

Rosenblaum, N. 1987. *Another liberalism: Romanticism and the reconstruction of liberal thought*. Cambridge: Harvard University Press.

Rossi-Landi, F. 1983. *Language as work and trade: A semiotic homology for linguistics and economics*. South Hadley, MA: Bergin & Garvey.

Rousseau, J.- J. 1979. *Emile or on education*. Translated by A. Bloom. New York: Basic.

Ruddell, R. B., & R. Speaker. 1985. "The interactive reading process: A model." In *Theoretical models and processes of reading*, edited by H. Singer

& R. B. Ruddell, pp. 751–93. 3rd ed. Newark, DE: International Reading Association.

Rumelhart, D. E. 1977. "Some problems with the notion of literal reading." In *Metaphor as a way of thought*, edited by A. Ortony, pp. 78–90. Cambridge: Cambridge University Press.

———. 1980. "Schemata: The building blocks of cognition." In *Theoretical issues in reading comprehension*, edited by R. J. Spiro, B. C. Bruce & W. F. Brewer, pp. 33–58. Hillsdale, NJ: Erlbaum.

———. 1985. "Toward am interactive model of reading." In *Theoretical models and processes of reading*, edited by H. Singer & R. B. Ruddell, pp. 722–50. 3d ed. Newark, DE: International Reading Association.

Rupley, W. H., & J. W. Logan. 1985. "Elementary teachers' beliefs about reading and knowledge of reading content: Relationships to decision about reading outcomes." *Reading Psychology: An International Quarterly* 6(3/4): 145–56.

Russell, J. 1989. "Getting high on moral indignation." *New York Times*, August 6, pp. H31, 33.

Salmans, S. 1988. "Go away, Dick and Jane." *Education Life, New York Times*, November 6, pp. EDUC67–69.

Samuels, S. J., & M. L. Kamil. 1984. "Models of reading process." In *Handbook of reading research*, edited by P. D. Pearson, pp. 185–224. New York: Longman.

Scardamalia, M. & C. Bereiter. 1985. "Development of dialectical processes in composition." In *Literacy, language, and learning*, edited by D. Olson, N. Torrance, & A. Hildyard, pp. 307–29. Cambridge: Cambridge University Press.

Schoolboys of Barbiana. 1970. *Letter to a teacher*. Translated by by N. Rossi & T. Cole. New York: Random House.

Schweinhart, L. J., & Weikart, D. P. 1988. "Education for young children living in poverty: Child-initiated learning or teacher-directed instruction." *The Elementary School Journal* 89: 213–25.

Scribner, S. & M. Cole. 1981. *The psychology of literacy*. Cambridge: Harvard University Press.

Searle, C., ed. 1977. *The world in a classroom*. London: Readers & Writers.

Segel, E. 1986. " 'As the twig is bent . . .' : Gender and childhood reading." In *Gender and reading: Essays on readers, texts, and contexts*, edited by E. A. Flynn & P. P. Schweickart, pp. 165–86. Baltimore: Johns Hopkins University Press.

Selfe, C. L., M. E. Gorman, & M. E. Gorman. 1986. "Watching our garden grow: Longitudinal changes in student writing apprehensions." In *Writing Across the disciplines: Research into practice*, edited by A. Young and T. Fulwiler, pp. 97–108. Upper Montclair, NJ: Boynton/Cook.

Selfe, C. L., Petersen, B. T., & Nahrgang, C. L. 1986. "Journal writing in mathematics." In *Writing across the disciplines: Research into practice*, edited by A. Young & T. Fulwiler, pp. 192–207. Upper Montclair, NJ: Boynton/Cook.

Shannon, P. 1989. *Broken promises: Reading instruction in twentieth-century America*. Granby, MA: Bergin & Garvey.

Sharp, R., & A. Green. 1975. *Education and social control: A study in progressive primary education*. London: Routledge & Kegan Paul.

Shelley, P. [1821]. 1965. "A defence of poetry." In *The complete works of Percy Bysshe Shelley*, edited by R. Ingpen & W. F. Peck, pp. 109–42. Vol. VII. New York: Gordian.

Shor, I. 1977. *Critical teaching in everyday life*. Montreal: Black Rose.

———. 1986. *Culture wars: Schools and society in the conservative restoration*. London: Routledge & Kegan Paul.

Sidney, P. [1595]. 1970. *An apology for poetry*. Edited by F. Robinson. New York: Bobs-Merrill.

Simon, R. I. 1987. "Empowerment as a pedagogy of possibility." *Language Arts* 64(4): 370–383.

Simon, R. I., & J. Willinsky. 1980. "Beyond a high school literacy policy: The surfacing of the hidden curriculum." *Journal of Education* 162(1): 111–21.

Singer, H. 1985. "A century of landmarks in reading." In *Theoretical models and processes of reading,* edited by H. Singer & R. B. Ruddell, pp. 8–20. Newark, DE: International Reading Association.

Singer, H., & R. B. Ruddell, eds. 1985. *Theoretical models and processes of reading*. Newark, DE: International Reading Association.

Sizer, T. J. 1984. *Horace's compromise: The dilemma of American education*. Boston: Houghton Mifflin.

Sledd, J. 1983. "In defense of the students' right." *College English* 45: 667–75.

Smith, A. 1968. "From 'The philosophy of poetry' 1835." In *Romantic criticism: 1800–1850,* edited by R. A. Foakes, pp. 174–91. London: Edward Arnold.

Smith, F. 1978. *Understanding reading: A psycholinguistic analysis of reading and learning to read*. 2d ed. New York: Holt, Rinehart & Winston.

———. 1982. *Writing and the writer*. New York: Holt, Rinehart & Winston.

———. 1985. "A metaphor for literacy: Creating worlds or shunting information." In *Literacy, language, and learning,* edited by D. Olson, N. Torrance, & A. Hildyard, pp. 195–213. Cambridge: Cambridge University Press.

———. 1988. "Misleading metaphors of education." In *Joining the literacy club: Further essays into education,* pp. 93–108. Portsmouth, NH: Heinemann.

Spencer, M. 1984. "The place of literature in literacy: 'Dip a finger into Fafnir.' " In *English teaching: An international exchange,* edited by J. Britton, pp. 195–213. London: Heinemann.

Spender, D., & E. Sarah, eds. 1980. *Learning to lose: Sexisim and education*. London: Women's Press.

Spender, L. 1983. *Intruders on the rights of men: Women's unpublished heritage*. London: Pandora.

Spiro, R. J., & A. Myers. 1984. "Individual differences and underlying cognitive processes." In *Handbook of reading research*, edited by P. D. Pearson, pp. 471–501. New York: Longman.

Spufford, M. 1981. *Small books and pleasant histories: Popular fiction and its readership in seventeenth-century England*. Cambridge: Cambridge University Press.

Stedman, L. C., & C. F. Kaestle. 1987. "Literacy and reading performance in the United States, from 1880 to the present." *Reading Research Quarterly* 22(1): 8–46.

Stallybass, P., & A. White. 1986. *The politics and poetics of transgression*. Ithaca, NY: Cornell University Press.

Stansky, P. 1985. *Redesigning the world: William Morris, the 1800s, and Arts and Crafts*. Princeton: Princeton University Press.

Stevens, W. 1954. *The collected poems of Wallace Stevens*. New York: Alfred A. Knopf.

Stock, B. 1983. *The implications of literacy: Written language and models of interpretation in the eleventh and twelfth centuires*. Princeton, NJ: Princeton University Press.

Stone, L. 1969. "Literacy and education in England, 1644–1640." *Past and Present* 42: 69–139.

Street, B. 1984. *Literacy in theory and practice*. Cambridge: Cambridge University Press.

"Students' right to their own language." 1974. *College Composition and Communication* 25: 1–32.

Suffinsky, F. 1938. "Self-expression—creative work." *Educational Method* 13: 76–91.

"Symposium on the year of the reports: Responses from the educational community." 1984. *Harvard Educational Review* 54(1): 1–32.

Tharp, R. G. 1982. "The effective instructive of comprehension: Results and description of the Kamehameha Early Education Program." *Reading Research Quarterly* 17(4): 503–527.

Thompson, E. P. 1963. *The making of the English working class*. Harmondsworth, UK: Penguin.

Thompson, P. 1967. *The work of William Morris*. New York: Viking.

Thorndyke, E. L., & R. Woodworth. 1901. "The influence of improvement in one mental function upon the efficiency of other functions." *Psychological Review* 8: 247–61, 384–95, 553–64.

Tomkinson, W. S. 1921. *The teaching of English: A new approach*. Oxford: Clarendon.

Tompkins, J. 1980. "An introduction to reader-response criticism." In *Reader-response criticism: From formalism to post-structuralism*, edited by J. Tompkins, pp. ix-xxvi. Baltimore: Johns Hopkins University Press.

Torrance, N., & Olson, D. 1985. "Oral and literate competencies in the early school years." In *Literacy, language, and learning,* edited by D. Olson, N. Torrance, & A. Hildyard, pp. 256–84. Cambridge: Cambridge University Press.

Trachtenburg, P., & Ferrugia, A. 1988. "Big books from little voices: Reaching high risk beginning readers." *The Reading Teacher* 41: 284–89.

Updike, J. 1989. "Here I am." *The New Yorker,* January 23, pp. 34–37.

Venezky, R. L. 1984. "The history of reading research." *Handbook of reading research,* edited by P. D. Pearson, pp. 3–38. New York: Longman.

Volosinov, V. N. 1973. *Marxism and the philosophy of language.* Translated by L. Matejka & I. R. Titunik. (Attributed to M. Bakhtin.) Cambridge: Harvard University Press.

Vygotsky, L. S. 1962. *Thought and language.* Translated by E. Hanfmann & G. Vakar. Cambridge: MIT Press.

———. 1978. *Mind in society: The developoment of higher psychological processes* Edited by M. Cole, V. John Steiner, S. Scibner, & E. Souberman. Cambridge: Harvard University Press.

Walker, C. P., & D. Elias. 1987. "Writing conference talk: Factors associated with high- and low-level writing conferences." *Research in the Teaching of English* 21(3): 266–285.

Walkerdine, V. 1986. "Progressive pedagogy and political struggle." *Screen* 13: 54–60.

Warren, R. P. 1975. *Democracy and poetry.* Cambridge: Harvard University Press.

Weaver, C. 1980. *Psycholinguistics and reading: From process to practice.* Boston: Little, Brown.

———. 1985. "Parallels between new paradigms in science and in reading and literary theories: An essay review." *Research in the Teaching of English* 19: 298–316.

Weiner, G. 1985. *Just a bunch of girls: Feminist approaches to schooling.* Milton Keynes, UK: Open University Press.

Weldon, F. 1984. *Letters to Alice: On first reading Jane Austen.* Kent, UK: Hodder & Stoughton.

Wells, C. G. 1981. *Learning through interaction: The study of language development.* Cambridge: Cambridge University Press.

———. 1986. "Styles of interaction and opportunities for learning." In *Literacy: Teaching and learning language skills,* edited by A. Cashdan, pp. 17–31. Oxford: Blackwell.

Wheeler, T. C. 1979. *The great American writing block: Causes and cures of the new illiteracy.* New York: Viking.

Whitehead, A. N. 1967. *The aims of education.* New York: Free Press.

Whitehead, F. 1966. *The disappearing dias.* London: Chatto and Windus.

Wilkinson, A. 1971. *The foundations of language: Talking and reading in young children.* London: Oxford University Press.

Williams, J. P. 1985. "The case for explicit decoding instruction." In *Reading education: Foundations for a literate America*, edited by J. Osborn, P. T. Wilson, & R. C. Anderson, pp. 205–13. Lexington, MA: D. C. Heath.

Williams, R. 1961. *The long revolution*. London: Chatto & Windus.

Willinsky, J. 1985. "To publish and publish and publish." *Language Arts* 62: 619–23.

———. 1987a. "The paradox of text in the culture of literacy." *Interchange* 18(2/3), 147–63.

———. 1987b. "Learning the language of difference: The dictionary in the high school." *English Education* 19(3): 146–58.

———. 1988a. *The well-tempered tongue: The politics of standard English in the high school*. New York: Teachers College Press.

———. 1988b. "Five lexicographers in search of the new." *American Speech* 63(1): 44–66.

———. 1989. "Lessons from the Wordsworth and the domestic scene of writing." In *The Educational Legacy of Romanticism*, edited by J. Willinsky, pp. 16–28. Waterloo, ON: Wilfrid Laurier University Press.

———. In press. "The construction of a crisis: Literacy in Canada." *Canadian Journal of Education*.

Willinsky, J. M., & J. O. Bedard. In press. *"The fearful passage" in the high school: Romeo and Juliet under the influence of feminist literary criticism*. Ottawa: Canadian Council of Teachers of English.

Willinsky, J., & R. M. Hunniford. 1986. "Reading the romance younger: The mirrors and fears of a preparatory literature." *Reading-Canada-Lecture* 4(1): 16–31.

Wimsatt, W. K., & M. C. Beardsley. 1954. *The verbal icon*. Lexington: University of Kentucky Press.

Wittgenstein, L. 1953. *Philosophical investigations*. Translated by G. E. M. Anscombe. 3d ed. New York: Macmillan.

Wolfe, T. 1980. "What if he is right?" In *Active Voice: An anthology of Canadian, American and Commonwealth prose*, edited by W. H. New & W. E. Messenger, pp. 386–408. Scarborough, ON: Prentice-Hall.

Woolf, V. 1987. "Hours in a library." In *The essays of Virginia Woolf, 1912–1918*, edited by A. McNeillie, pp. 55–61. Vol 2. San Diego: Harcourt Brace Jovanovich.

Wordsworth, W. 1968. "Preface to lyrical ballads 1800; revised 1802." In *Romantic criticism: 1800–1850*, edited by R. A. Foakes, pp. 60–70. London: Arnold.

———. [1805/1850]. 1971. *The prelude: A parallel text*. Edited by J. C. Maxwell. New Haven, CN: Yale University Press.

———. 1977. *The poems*. Edited by J. O. Hayden. 2 vols. New Haven, CN: Yale University Press.

References

Young, R. 1980. "Arts, crafts, gifts and knacks: Some disharmonies in the new rhetoric." In *Reinventing the rhetorical tradition,* edited by A. Freedman & I. Pringle, pp. 53–60. Conway, AK: L & S.

Young, A., & T. Fulwiler, eds. *Writing across the disciplines: Research into practice.* Upper Montclair, NJ: Boynton/Cook.

Index